100 SI

100 SHAKESPEARE FILMS

BFI SCREEN GUIDES

Daniel Rosenthal

FOREWORD BY JULIE TAYMOR

bfi

First published in 2007 by the
British Film Institute
21 Stephen Street, London W1T 1LN

The British Film Institute's purpose is to champion moving image culture in all its
richness and diversity across the UK, for the benefit of as wide an audience as
possible, and to create and encourage debate.

Series cover design: Paul Wright
Cover image: *William Shakespeare's Romeo + Juliet* (Baz Luhrmann, 1996,
    Twentieth-Century Fox Film Corporation)
Series design: Ketchup/couch
Set by Fakenham Photosetting, Fakenham, Norfolk
Printed in the UK by The Cromwell Press, Trowbridge, Wiltshire

British Library Cataloguing-in-Publication Data
A catalogue record for this book is available from the British Library

ISBN 978–1–84457–170–3 (pbk)
ISBN 978–1–84457–169–7 (hbk)

Contents

Acknowledgments

I wish to thank the extremely supportive and dedicated team at the BFI: Rebecca Barden, for commissioning the book, Sarah Watt, for seeing it through to publication, and Sophia Contento, for supervising picture research and production. Chantal Latchford provided meticulous copy editing.

I am indebted to Julie Taymor for her illuminating Foreword. Her fellow directors, Alexander Abela, Kenneth Branagh (*As You Like It*) and Leonardo Henriquez, generously enabled me to view films that could not otherwise have been included before the book's deadline.

I'm very grateful to my friend and colleague Peter Cowie, who in 1999 initiated my interest in writing about Shakespeare films, and to the following for their advice and assistance: Geoff Andrew, Vishal Bhardwaj, Jules Cazedessus, Rebecca C. Cape (Lilly Library, Indiana), Kathleen Dickson (BFI), Alfredo Friedlander, Catherine Killingsworth, Lynne Kirwin, Marianne Landin (Scandinature Films), Erik Martens, Luke McKernan, Søren Nisted (Danish Film Institute), Nick Manzi (Lionsgate Films), Professor Karen Newman, Yvonne Ng, Mark Padilla (Arclight Films), Jonny Pegg, Punam Sawhney, Antti Selkokari, Olwen Terris, Tamar Thomas and all of the University of California students who took my 'Shakespeare on Film' course at Pembroke College, Cambridge, in July 2006, and whose classroom and essay work has informed my research and writing.

A note on the text: a number of the play synopses and film essays incorporate revised portions of writing first published, in different form, in my book *Shakespeare on Screen* (2000).

Finally, I would like to dedicate *100 Shakespeare Films* to my parents, Ann and Tom.

Foreword

It is no wonder that Shakespeare is the most produced screenwriter in cinematic history. His plays, with their epic grandeur and complex psychological twists and turns, transcend time and culture to speak to the human condition at its most base and elevated levels. Whether tragedy or comedy, the plays operate on multiple levels of sophistication simultaneously, ensuring a wide and diverse audience. One can appreciate the poetry, philosophy or politics of a Shakespeare history or simply enjoy the interplay of romance, violence and clowning that surrounds the diverse cast of characters.

What is so alluring to a director is not only the quality of story but also the immense freedom in imagining the settings and the constant play between reality, fantasy and myth. His plays are not limited by the supposed constraints of the theatre. As a theatre director I had my first experience with Shakespeare on *The Tempest*. A shipwreck, spirits, monsters, illusions – one can perform the action on a bare stage, allowing the language to fulfil the image in the eyes of the audience or find a clever way of visually interpreting the descriptive verse with all the artistry the theatre has to offer. Very rarely does Shakespeare specify stage directions, thus allowing the director and the actors tremendous opportunity for personal interpretation.

In many ways, though, these uncensored plays seem more suitable to cinematic interpretation than to the theatre because many are set in castles, forests or on battlefields – natural or expansive landscapes that can be depicted literally on film. For many film directors it is essential to complement the dialogue scenes with purely visual, visceral ones. This not only gives the audience a breather from hanging on every word but allows for the scope and scale of the world to be delineated further. What becomes tricky for the film director is to balance cinematic reality with the poetry of the language and its metaphors. While directing *Titus* all the clues for the world we needed to create came from the text itself: 'Rome is but a wilderness of tigers.' It was crucial that the images derived from the language were not presented on screen at the same moment that the words were uttered. The images must act as musical motifs, reoccurring in various modes to reinforce such verbal metaphors. This is particularly true in an age where the visual image seems to play more powerfully than the spoken word.

In *Titus Andronicus*, Lavinia, Titus's daughter, is raped and mutilated by the sons of the enemy queen, Tamora. In my theatre production, Lavinia is left standing on a broken Greek column, like some twisted Butoh statue. Her hands were covered in black fabric with twigs bound to them. The words of Marcus, her uncle – asking 'what stern ungentle hands/Hath lopp'd and hew'd and made thy body bare/Of her two branches?' – were the inspiration for the setting and the depiction of the ravaged girl. In the theatrical production the lone, severed column with the girl trapped on top suggested a broken goddess on a pedestal. Indeed the character of Lavinia, till that moment, is treated much like a perfect specimen of a virginal purity. In adapting this scene to film, it wouldn't have worked simply to deliver the highly stylised, symbolic image. I needed to create a landscape that would carry the same symbolic weight but be a believable location where the event could have taken place. I chose a swamp filled with the charred remains of a forest fire. In other words, the literal landscape was the metaphor for the unseen rape itself. Lavinia was placed by her tormentors on a burnt-out stump, her hands removed via a blue screen effect and replaced with twigs. Thus the concept created for the theatre could be adapted to the strengths of the film medium. The scene felt 'real' without losing the poetry of the image.

The close-up in film is also a tremendous boon to the deliverance of a Shakespeare text. It is far easier to understand the language when one can see lips moving and nuanced facial expression. Many of the monologues or soliloquies also benefit from being voiceover, spoken in whispers or hushed tones, suggestive of thought rather than speech. One can choose to show the face caught in contemplation or fill the screen with action that moves the story to another place. The power of film editing allows for the juxtaposition of action, image and word in a way that frees the text from the obligatory entrances and exits of characters.

Many of the films talked about in this compendium are favourites of mine. In particular, Akira Kurosawa's Shakespeare adaptations, *Throne of Blood* (1957) and *Ran* (1985), Orson Welles's *Othello* (1952) and *Chimes at Midnight* (1966), Roman Polanski's *Macbeth* (1971) and Max Reinhardt and Willhelm Dieterle's *A Midsummer Night's Dream* (1935). I, like many, have experienced Shakespeare's works more on screen than in the theatre. There will never be too many versions of any of the Shakespeare plays because each artist brings his or her own vision to the script. The more you see these plays in all their varied forms, the deeper and richer they become. It's often not about the story at all, but all about how you tell it.

Julie Taymor, 2007.

Julie Taymor is the director of the films *Titus* (1999), *Frida* (2002), winner of two Academy Awards, and *Across the Universe* (2007). Her next feature film will be Shakespeare's *The Tempest*. On stage she has directed *The Tempest*, *Titus Andronicus*, *The Taming of the Shrew*, *Juan Darién: A Carnival Mass*, *The Green Bird* and the operas *Oedipus Rex*, *The Magic Flute*, *Salome*, *The Flying Dutchman* and *Grendel* and the musical *The Lion King*, for which she won Tony Awards for direction and costume design.

Introduction

'I really can't make a comparison between a movie-maker and Shakespeare. No movie that will ever be made is worthy of being discussed in the same breath.' **Orson Welles**

In January 2007, the Internet Movie Database identified William Shakespeare as writer of the screenplay or source play for 666 cinema and television productions. Its list of credits was by no means exhaustive. How, then, to select only 100 Shakespeare films?

The first goal was to reflect both the breadth of the Shakespearean canon and the diverse treatment of individual plays, in terms of the quantity, quality and style of screen adaptation. I have included one or more films based, to varying degrees, on twenty plays, including tragedies, histories, comedies and Roman plays.

Five tragedies provide more than half of my choices: *Hamlet* (fourteen entries), *Macbeth* (twelve), *Othello* (twelve), *Romeo and Juliet* (nine) and *King Lear* (six). Their predominance illustrates their position among the most popular Shakespeare works in theatre repertories and on examination set-text lists, and also how readily their stories have been reworked in alternative forms, which leads on to my second and most important selection objective: striking an appropriate balance between 'original-text' Shakespeare films and 'genre adaptations'.

By 'original-text', I mean films such as Laurence Olivier's *Henry V* (1944), Orson Welles's *Othello* (1952) and Grigori Kozintsev's Russian *King Lear* (1970), whose screenplays use Shakespeare's language, in English or in translation. By 'genre adaptations', I mean works that abandon

Shakespeare's pentameters and settings, then tailor his storylines and characters to the conventions of popular film genres: *Macbeth* becomes a gangster thriller set in 1950s' New York (*Joe Macbeth*, 1955) or twenty first-century Mumbai (*Maqbool*, 2003); *The Taming of the Shrew* becomes a Hollywood teen comedy (*10 Things I Hate About You*, 1999), and so on.

Historically, most original-text Shakespeare films have struggled at the box office, and all of them have taken a gamble, because the playwright's matchless poetry and prose, are, for film-makers, his greatest commercial liability. Miramax boss Harvey Weinstein wanted to change the title of *Shakespeare in Love* (1998) because he believed the Bard's name alone would be box-office poison, and the distributors of every original-text Shakespeare movie know that for every devotee delighted by the prospect of seeing (and hearing) *Othello* or *Much Ado about Nothing* on the big screen, many more will be indifferent or hostile, because Shakespeare means nothing to them, or because his language evokes compulsory attendance in the classroom, not a night out at the movies. Producers have continually tried to counter that resistance by casting major stars in original-text films (Mary Pickford and Douglas Fairbanks in *The Taming of the Shrew*, 1929; Marlon Brando in *Julius Caesar*, 1953; Mel Gibson in *Hamlet*, 1990); they cannot eradicate it.

Cinema's high costs compared to theatre, and consequent need to attract mass, ideally international audiences, while fighting in-built antipathy towards 'boring' Shakespeare, help to explain the production of so many genre adaptations. Although it may be true that in Hollywood 'nobody knows anything', producers all over the world know that by adapting Shakespeare in genre form without the original language, they can hang on to his compelling characters and storylines and market the end result to fans of the chosen genre, many of whom would not turn out for original-text Shakespeare. Wherever an original-text film is playing, more people scanning their local cinema listings will say 'Let's see that new gangster thriller' than 'Let's see the new *Hamlet*.' Millions of cinemagoers who might never attend an original-text Shakespeare film or stage production have enjoyed his work, whether in

1956, thanks to *Forbidden Planet* (adapted from *The Tempest*), or in 2006, thanks to *She's the Man* (*Twelfth Night*) – often without being aware of the playwright's involvement because Shakespeare's name is almost always kept off the trailers and posters for genre adaptations (and often, shamefully, the credits too), lest it scare away the target audience. This is the paradox: in the genre context, Shakespeare is often deemed unmentionable; whereas some original-text productions in the last decade have decided to exploit the name's 'brand value' as a prefix, emphasising their pedigree in the eyes of the playwright's admirers, by presenting *William Shakespeare's Romeo + Juliet* (1996), *William Shakespeare's A Midsummer Night's Dream* (1999) and *William Shakespeare's The Merchant of Venice* (2004).

Original-text sound films occupy fifty positions on my list, there are six silent films and sound films representing fifteen genres occupy forty-two positions, including five hybrids (part-original-text, part-genre): *A Double Life* (1947), *Chicken Rice War* (2000), *Kiss Me Kate* (1953), *The Lovers of Verona* (1949) and *Shakespeare in Love*. All five are fictional tales centred on the production of a Shakespeare play, film or musical (two rewarding works in similar vein, James Ivory's *Shakespeare Wallah*, 1965, and Douglas Hickox's *Theatre of Blood*, 1973, were regrettable omissions – not sufficiently dedicated to a single Shakespeare work to fit the book's play-by-play structure). In this original-text vs. genre context, three titles are sui generis: *Looking for Richard* (1996), *Otello* (1986) and *Rosencrantz & Guildenstern Are Dead* (1990).

Some genre adaptations edged out original-text films because I felt that the book would more accurately represent the breadth of screen Shakespeare if, to take one example, I looked at what happens to *Hamlet* as Chinese *wuxia* martial arts epic (*The Banquet*, 2006) instead of assessing a run-of-the-mill original-text production such as Campbell Scott's American TV *Hamlet* from 2000.

Indeed, genre adaptations produced in Britain, America and beyond are just as important to the history of Shakespeare on screen as the features in which we hear his poetry, because they reveal the playwright's profound influence on popular culture. That *Othello* works so well as the showbiz melodrama *All Night Long* (1961), that *The Tempest* inspires *Forbidden Planet*'s influential sci-fi story (both films are utterly accessible, at best middlebrow works) are as much proof of Shakespeare's timeless universality (dread phrase, but true) as the continued 'high-culture' production of his plays on stages all over the world.

Shakespeare himself was, of course, a great adapter. In borrowing from a huge range of historical and fictional sources, he wrote plays that Richard Eyre, former Director of Britain's National Theatre, terms 'the DNA' of all subsequent English stage drama. After watching well over 100 original-text and genre adaptations, I am inclined to extend Eyre's metaphor and view Shakespeare's plays as the genetic building blocks of much commercial cinema. Once you have seen the Scottish play transformed into several gangster pictures, it becomes impossible not to watch Al Pacino's demise in *Scarface* (1983), holed up in his Miami castle, screaming lone defiance against an overwhelming enemy assault, without thinking of Macbeth's last stand. The impact of *Henry V* on the structure and characterisation of World War II movies seems self-evident when you compare the intimate, eve-of-battle conversations in Kenneth Branagh's film of the play and in Steven Spielberg's *Saving Private Ryan* (1998). Cary Grant and Rosalind Russell in *His Girl Friday* (1940) wage a 'merry war' that echoes Beatrice and Benedick's sparring in *Much Ado about Nothing*. Every screen tale of 'star-crossed lovers' has a touch of *Romeo and Juliet*.

Shakespeare and world cinema

In original-text and genre form, screen production of the greatest English-language dramatist has, unsurprisingly, been dominated by English-language film industries, hence the inclusion of seventy-three productions using English dialogue or intertitles, the vast majority made in the US or Britain. From the silent era until today, the nature of Shakespearean cinema has always been a global phenomenon and I have included work with dialogue in thirteen languages other than English, by directors from fifteen countries outside America and the UK. I hoped in particular to draw attention to some of the most interesting and least well-known productions, several of which have had neither theatrical nor home video releases in the UK or US, among them *Bleeder* (2000), *Makibefo* (2000) and *Souli* (2004).

Regardless of nationality, two categories were eligible for inclusion: feature films intended for theatrical release, and TV movies with the production values of a feature film, of which I have picked seven (denoted as 'TVM' beside their running times), including *The Tempest* (1998), *Othello* (2000) and *King of Texas* (2002). All seven could (some more successfully than others) withstand scrutiny on a cinema screen, which cannot be said of *The BBC Shakespeare* (1978–85), extremely low-budget, almost wholly studio-bound original-text recordings of the Complete Works, which were therefore excluded from consideration, as were television records of stage Shakespeare, even though some of these, such as Trevor Nunn's RSC *Macbeth* and *Othello* and National Theatre *Merchant of Venice*, are widely acknowledged as among the finest productions ever staged; these belong in histories of Shakespeare on television and on stage.

I permitted two 'wild card' selections that meet neither criteria: one short, Percy Stow's *The Tempest* (1908), is included as a strong representative of the hundreds of silent Shakespeares that condensed the plays into one or two reels, and Celestino Coronado's experimental video *Hamlet* (1976) earns a place for its revelatory casting coups.

Each chapter begins with a play synopsis, partly, with space for each film at a premium, to enable shorthand reference in individual essays to, for example, 'the Mousetrap' or 'the fencing match' in *Hamlet*, without further explanation being necessary for readers who may not be familiar with the film's source play. With genre adaptations, readers who have not seen the film, but may wish to, should be aware that the essays always reveal the ending, which may not be the same as Shakespeare's.

The seven ages of screen Shakespeare

In balancing original-text and genre adaptations, English and foreign languages, my final goal was to trace a history that begins in 1899 with the first Shakespeare film, *King John* (an evocative glimpse of Sir Herbert Beerbohm Tree as the dying monarch), and continues to this day. My list takes us from Stow's *Tempest* to several films from 2006, and encompasses what I call the seven ages of screen Shakespeare.

The first is the silent era, when, in Britain, America and Europe, the nascent art form turned to Shakespeare as a source of popular, compelling stories, which might also lend theatre's upstart offspring some of its parent's cultural legitimacy – all without needing to pay the writer.

From the hundreds of films produced (many now lost), I have chosen five features and one short, a tiny selection that nonetheless illustrates how, even in the earliest days of the medium, Shakespeare was adapted in different ways. Stow's *Tempest* and James Keane's *The Life and Death of King Richard III* (1912) are closely based on the plays; the German *Merchant of Venice* (1923) and *Othello* (1922) make use of Shakespeare's texts and his sources; *Hamlet: The Drama of Vengeance* (1920) combines *Hamlet* and Shakespeare's sources with speculative academic theory; *Once Upon a Time* (1922) is genre adaptation, harnessing aspects of the *Shrew* and other Shakespeare plays to a Hans Christian Andersen fairytale.

The period from 1929 to 1936 belongs to Hollywood. Studios spent small fortunes on star-laden versions of *The Taming of the Shrew*, *A Midsummer Night's Dream* (1935) and *Romeo and Juliet* (1936), and achieved Oscar recognition and generally poor box-office results, prompting trade bible *Variety* to conclude in 1936 that 'the value of Shakespeare to the screen is more strictly in the creation of prestige for the individual production company than in the accumulation of receipts.' It would be seventeen years before Hollywood again turned to the playwright, with MGM's *Julius Caesar*, by which time Shakespeare cinema was in the midst of its third age: the Olivier/Welles era.

For original-text films, this was the most artistically rewarding age of all, accounting for twelve of my fifty original-text selections, and six of the finest Shakespeare movies ever made: Olivier's *Henry V* and *Hamlet* (1948) (the first original-text adaptations to win major awards *and* make serious money), Welles's *Othello* and *Chimes at Midnight* (1966), the

MGM *Caesar* and Kozintsev's magnificent *Hamlet*, which exposed the picture postcard shallowness of 1950s Soviet Shakespeares, including Sergei Yutkevich's *Othello* (1955) and Yakov Fried's *Twelfth Night* (1955) (Akira Kurosawa, meanwhile, adapted *Macbeth* into a Japanese masterpiece, *Throne of Blood*, 1957, p. 103).

The fourth age, from 1967 to 1972, was dominated by Franco Zeffirelli, who inherited his idol Olivier's mantle as cinema's greatest Shakespeare populist, when the box-office success of his *Taming of the Shrew* (1967) and *Romeo and Juliet* (1968) sparked a brief run of mostly very orthodox original-text features: Stuart Burge's *Julius Caesar* (1970), Roman Polanski's *Macbeth* (1971), Peter Brook's *King Lear* (1971; the one unconventional adaptation of the period) and Charlton Heston's *Antony and Cleopatra* (1972). None came close to emulating Zeffirelli's box-office success, and Heston's flop was followed by the wilderness years.

From 1973 to 1988, as Hollywood and the world surrendered to the Spielberg/Lucas blockbuster, and annual British feature production slipped to a low point of just twentyfour films in 1981, the odds of raising finance and distribution support for anything as rarefied as Shakespeare became longer and longer on both sides of the Atlantic. In those sixteen years, only one original-text film emerged from either country: Derek Jarman's low-budget *Tempest* (1979), leaving the BBC, with the Complete Works, and ITV, with a handful of productions (mostly RSC-originated), to fill the void.

The arrival of Kenneth Branagh as herald of the sixth age, in 1989, was entirely in keeping with what had gone before, proving that this unfashionable and largely unprofitable branch of film-making would always need champions whose enthusiasm and force of personality could overcome the in-built reluctance of the money men: first Olivier, then Welles and Zeffirelli, now Branagh.

The success of Branagh's *Henry V* (1989), swiftly followed by Zeffirelli's *Hamlet* (1990) made The Branagh Era, 1989–2000, the most prolific period for Shakespeare since the advent of sound, yielding fifteen of the fifty original-text films in this book. Its *annus mirabilis*, from

December 1995 to December 1996, witnessed American and British theatrical releases for Oliver Parker's *Othello* (1995), Richard Loncraine's *Richard III* (1995), Al Pacino's *Looking for Richard*, Trevor Nunn's *Twelfth Night* (1996), Baz Luhrmann's *William Shakespeare's Romeo + Juliet* and Branagh's *Hamlet* (all 1996).

Although the 1990s films were not all successful, and only Branagh's *Much Ado About Nothing* (1993) and Luhrmann's *Romeo + Juliet* were big hits, the general climate for Shakespeare films had never been more favourable, not least because the explosion of the home video and, later, DVD markets had made Shakespeare a more bankable proposition, appealing to discerning adult viewers outside the key sixteen–thirty age group so slavishly served by Hollywood, and to teachers and students wrestling with examination syllabuses that, in Britain, were increasingly open to candidates analysing filmed Shakespeare. By buying the films on tape or disc, Shakespeare enthusiasts and school and college librarians could be relied upon to deliver steady ancillary income for years after a film's theatrical release (these consumer and educational followings are largely responsible for so many films appearing in Appendix 2: Video and DVD Guide).

Home video success, however, is more likely on the back of at least moderate theatrical revenues (more people having seen the film and wanting to re-view it and/or recommend it to friends) and financiers want to start recouping as soon as possible after a film is premièred, and so, in the first six months of 2000, poor box-office figures caused the Shakespeare bubble to burst. Julie Taymor's *Titus* (1999), Michael Almereyda's *Hamlet* (2000) and Branagh's *Love's Labour's Lost* (2000) undeservedly grossed barely $4m between them in North America, and fared no better in the UK. Shakespeare films became much harder to finance, and after the 1990s' feast came famine: only one major English-language original-text film (Michael Radford's *Merchant of Venice*, 2004), reached UK or US cinemas between mid-2000 and February 2007, when this book went to press.

Audience, and perhaps also film-maker fatigue after the 1990s' glut may have played a part. So too, perhaps, the 'dumbed-down' twenty-first-century culture in which the BBC, once-proud progenitor of the largest original-text Shakespeare project in screen history, has become so ratings-conscious that it is no longer willing to fund anything as 'elitist' as original-text Shakespeare, and British and American school pupils turn to *No Fear Shakespeare* translations of their set texts, in which 'So Romeo would, were he not Romeo called,/Retain that dear perfection which he owes/Without that title' becomes 'Romeo would be just as perfect even if he wasn't called Romeo.' These are symptoms of the seventh age, the genre decade: Shakespeare's language has rarely been heard on screen, while no fewer than seventeen of the genre adaptations in this book were released or transmitted between 2000 and 2006, including *My Kingdom* (2001), *Scotland, PA* (2001), *Bleeder, Souli, The Banquet* and *Omkara* (2006).

Jaques's speech in *As You Like It* admits no future for us beyond our seventh age, but in early 2007 screen Shakespeare was far from 'mere oblivion', and there were signs that an eighth age might see original-text and genre streams converge and run on as one. Branagh's original-text *As You Like It* and Geoffrey Wright's *Macbeth* were awaiting UK and US release; another original-text *Macbeth*, entitled *Come Like Shadows*, to be directed by John Maybury, was in pre-production, and Taymor was preparing to follow *Titus* with *The Tempest*. On the genre front, American Scott Anderson had completed an LA gangster version of *Richard III*, featuring David Carradine as Buckingham, Universal Studios had hired Peter Morgan, writer of Stephen Frears's *The Queen*, to work on its long-gestating *American Caesar*, which moves the story of Caesar and Brutus to modern-day Washington, and Elton John and Tim Rice had begun contributing music and lyrics to Walt Disney's forthcoming animated feature, *Gnomeo and Juliet*.

From wooden 'O' to widescreen

In-depth discussion of what happens to Shakespeare's plays on their journey from stage to screen, from a metaphorical medium to a primarily literal one, is beyond the scope of this Introduction, so the following observations must suffice, touching on issues explored at far greater length by film-makers, actors, biographers and Shakespeare scholars in the volumes listed in Appendix 3: Further Reading.

Despite the undoubted power of his stage pictures – Romeo reaching up to Juliet; Lear cradling Cordelia; Macbeth confronted by Banquo's ghost – Shakespeare tells his stories through 'words, words, words', not images. The plays are supremely 'talky' and 'theatrical', adjectives that are almost invariably pejorative when applied in a film review, because, as Russell Jackson observes in his Introduction to *The Cambridge Companion to Shakespeare on Film* (2000), 'in writing for the mainstream cinema it is axiomatic that dialogue should be kept to a minimum.' Couple that axiom with the need to reduce works lasting three or four hours, if staged uncut, to running times of, ideally, between ninety and 150 minutes, and it is inevitable that original-text films cut Shakespeare to an extent that would make some theatre patrons demand a refund: 50% of *Hamlet* survives in the Olivier version, less than 40% in Zeffirelli; Welles's *Othello* lasts ninety minutes, Nunn's RSC *Othello* video lasts 205 minutes.

Branagh's four-hour *Hamlet* aside, filming Shakespeare necessitates great, and calculable, textual sacrifice; the loss of shared experience is harder to quantify. Film performances are fixed, theatre performances protean and ephemeral. The bond between cast and spectators formed in live theatre, particularly through soliloquies and asides, can never be replicated fully on celluloid, and this difference seems most acute when watching the comedies; Shakespeare is seldom, if ever, as funny on screen as on stage.

To take just one example, the eavesdropping in Act II, Scene v of *Twelfth Night* works so well on stage because the action proceeds in a 'wide shot', keeping all the characters in view while exploiting our delighted, disbelief-suspending acceptance that we can hear perfectly the 'whispered' running commentary from Maria, Fabian, Sir Toby Belch and Sir Andrew Aguecheek as Malvolio reads the forged letter from Olivia, while Malvolio appears stone deaf. Cinemagoers, however, are not 'in'

Olivia's garden with the characters, they watch it as a separate, closed space, so the stage-whisper/deafness convention does not apply; the film director feels obliged to cut between observers and observed; we lose the intimate complicity; the comic momentum is fragmented and falters.

More importantly, experienced theatre performers will always, to paraphrase Hamlet, suit the acting to the crowd, responding to and learning from the reactions of each unique combination of spectators, especially in comedy, so that jokes or bits of business that died at the first preview will, with luck, take off on opening night and soar by the end of the first week. Film actors play only to the camera, not knowing if a paying audience will laugh until the film has opened, by when it is too late (barring expensive re-shoots) to do anything about it. There is therefore an understandable tendency to over-compensate, in the hope of forcing laughter from the unseen audience. This might account for ill-judged turns like Michael Keaton's Dogberry in Branagh's *Much Ado*, or Mel Smith's Sir Toby in Nunn's *Twelfth Night*. The problem, as Michael Hattaway writes in the *Cambridge Companion*, is that 'energetic acting that can breed delight in the theatre can seem merely frenetic on screen: clowns turn into buffoons.'

Captured in close-up

There are, however, huge gains to offset the losses. As Julie Taymor notes in her Foreword, the film close-up and voice-over are perfectly suited to Shakespearean soliloquy. Spoken aloud and addressed to the camera, they give an approximation of the live, shared experience, or a hint of theatrical actor–audience complicity, never more so than with Olivier and Ian McKellen staring us down as Richard III. Voice-over can present soliloquy as unspoken interior monologue when a character is alone (Olivier's 'To be, or not to be'), or, if the speaker is placed in company, as counterpoint to the prevailing mood: in Geoffrey Wright's *Macbeth* , the voice-over of 'If it were done – when 'tis done' stresses Macbeth's anxiety while he circulates amongst his contented house guests.

The respective contributions made by the theatre audience and the camera lens define the differences between stage and film acting, as John Gielgud observed after playing Cassius in Hollywood, the 'gesticulation and shouting' that were 'necessary evils' for an actor trying to make every line of *Julius Caesar* reach the back of the Upper Circle could be reduced to a minimum when 'every look, every subtlety of phrasing, can be caught by the camera in a flash.' In theatre, only the front few rows may look into Cassius's resentful eyes; in the cinema, we all can.

In Joseph L. Mankiewicz, Gielgud had a director who trusted the text, and was more willing to keep his camera rolling on great actors delivering great dialogue for longer than many others in this book. At one extreme on this spectrum is Peter Hall, banishing all shots without dialogue from his *Dream* in 1969, at the other is Franco Zeffirelli, wont to banish all dialogue from his shots. For instance, in his *Hamlet* he turns Ophelia's Act II, Scene i account of the Prince's distracted behaviour into a wordless scene that might have come from a silent film: Hamlet and Ophelia together, covertly observed by Polonius. The original-text films in this book are filled with such moments, which adhere to an abbreviated version of the afore-mentioned film-making axiom: 'Show don't tell.' They depict off-stage events from the recent or distant past as prologues, flashbacks or cutaways from a particular scene as played on stage. We see a montage of the Moor's death-defying adventures in the opening sequence of Yutkevich's *Othello*; we see Duke Senior deposed at the start of Branagh's *As You Like It*. Both sequences, like the Zeffirelli *Hamlet* scene, are quite legitimately derived from the text. However, Zeffirelli removes dialogue that deepens our understanding of Ophelia and Polonius *and* the absent Hamlet, in order to give his star, Mel Gibson, yet more screen time. Yutkevich lends thrilling credibility to Othello's Senate recollections of 'battles, sieges, fortune' without cutting them (he shows before he tells); Branagh uses a few lines of exposition from Charles the wrestler in the play's first scene, to create an exciting, *cinematic* opening.

Crucially, Shakespeare could have written the Zeffirelli version of Act II, Scene i, if he had wanted to: Hamlet and Ophelia on the bare boards,

Polonius watching from the gallery, muttering an aside or two. Yutkevich and Branagh, on the other hand, both film action of a scale and complexity far beyond the scope of Shakespeare's stage, whose limitations he was determined so publicly to acknowledge at the start of *Henry V*, when he inadvertently bequeathed us a perfect summary of the difference between theatrical illusion and filmic verisimilitude:

> **Chorus:** can this cockpit hold
> The vasty fields of France? or may we cram
> Within this wooden O the very casques
> That did affright the air at Agincourt?
> O, pardon! since a crooked figure may
> Attest in little place a million;
> And let us, ciphers to this great accompt,
> On your imaginary forces work.

Whether at the original Globe in 1598 or at the reconstructed Shakespeare's Globe in 2007, if we do not let writer, director and actors work on our 'imaginary forces', theatre cannot function. We must picture the battle of Agincourt or Othello's heroic exploits in our mind's eye, or imagine ourselves to be the citizens packing the Forum in *Julius Caesar*. At the cinema we expect to see, not imagine, the toga-clad extras, the Moor's heroics and 'the very casques/That did affright the air at Agincourt', and in their *Henry V* films Olivier and Branagh duly oblige. Indeed, a simple stage direction, 'The field of battle. Alarum', has inspired some of the most memorable battles in all cinema, courtesy of Welles's *Chimes at Midnight* and Kurosawa's *Ran* (1985). Their graphic carnage is a devastating complement to Shakespeare's compassionate treatment of violence; one thinks of the soldier Michael Williams in *Henry V*, picturing 'all those legs and arms and heads, chopt off in battle'.

On film, restrictions are imposed not by the dimensions of the wooden O but by size of budget, length of schedule and the limits of technology. As a result, the use of landscape, architecture and detailed sets, for example in Kozintsev's *Lear* or Zeffirelli's *Romeo and Juliet*, can establish more successfully than any stage production ever could the sense of a real world in which Shakespeare's characters live and die.

What else can film bring to the plays? It can make *Dream* fairies disappear and fly without obvious theatre artifice. The same editing techniques that may dilute comedy can profitably alter the reflective mood of a scene or increase tension by stretching time, spreading continuous stage action across hours or days, as in Polanski's *Macbeth*, when confirmation of the first part of the witches' prophecy arrives the morning after it is made, not instantly. Post-production sound mixing allows film-makers to place sound effects and an original score under dialogue at just the right level, where theatre actors might be drowned out, or forced into histrionic yelling. In the Kozintsev *Lear*, Yuri Yarvet's king can be heard above the roar of the storm and the orchestra playing Shostakovich.

Film can attract to relatively minor roles actors of a calibre and fame who can spare a few days in the studio but would be extremely unlikely to commit to weeks of rehearsal and months of performance for the same part on stage. This is a huge boon with Paul Scofield as the Ghost in Zeffirelli's *Hamlet*, a disadvantage with Billy Crystal and Robin Williams's cameos in Branagh's *Hamlet*.

Beyond the individual films, original-text Shakespeares have unique collective value to anyone interested in the evolution of cinema, because they are all, essentially, remakes and thus a reliable barometer of changing performance styles, approaches to sex and violence, advances in sound and special effects. George Cukor and Baz Luhrmann's *Romeo and Juliet* films use the same language, and yet in acting (Leslie Howard vs. Leonardo DiCaprio), editing rhythm (stately vs. frantic) and music (Tchaikovsky vs. Radiohead), the six decades separating them feel more like light years.

The genre game

When you watch a number of genre adaptations, it is possible to see them fail and succeed for similar reasons. The failures – notably *Men of Respect* (1991), *A Thousand Acres* (1997), Paul Mazursky's *Tempest*

(1982), *She's the Man* and the BBC *Much Ado about Nothing* (2005) – all misguidedly ensure that there is an equivalent for almost every significant character in Shakespeare's dramatis personae, merely to satisfy some token character quota, even though these characters may only appear briefly and to little purpose.

The successful adaptations sensibly accept that it is impossible to pour everyone from a three-hour classical tragedy into a ninety-minute film – and in any case you are under no obligation to try. These writers discard subplots and characters, and time and again one sees two individuals conflated: in *Forbidden Planet*, Robby the Robot is mostly Ariel, but has one comic scene as Caliban; Iwabuchi in *The Bad Sleep Well* (1960) is Claudius *and* Polonius, and so on. Characters can be re-imagined to suit the new setting, and new characters can be added: Roderigo becomes a rookie cop with no romantic interest in Desdemona in Andrew Davies's *Othello* (2000); in *Ran*, we meet victims of the Lear figure who have no counterparts in Shakespeare.

The better film-makers make changes to ensure their adaptation works as genre film first, Shakespeare second, and the best make them hold a mirror to their society, just as the playwright reflected his. *The Bad Sleep Well* highlighted Japanese corporate corruption; *O* (2000) comments on US high-school massacres and contemporary attitudes to interracial sex.

Genre adaptation of the tragedies almost invariably reduces the scale of the original. The impact of seeing the decline and fall of Macbeth and Lear is greater in the plays, when the fortunes of a nation are also at stake, than when the hero rules a New York crime syndicate (*Joe Macbeth*) or Iowa farmland (*A Thousand Acres*). This gulf in heroic status can be exploited for bathetic humour (as in *Scotland, PA* and *Hamlet Goes Business*, 1987), as can the gap between Shakespeare's language and its modern translation (*Hamlet Goes Business* again). In genre adaptations with principally serious intent, however, if you know the original text well, the paraphrased dialogue has a tendency to sound like Shakespeare-lite. 'It scares me, all this feeling . . . I don't know if I could bear losing her,' says Andrew Davies's police chief Othello, singing his wife's praises in a line that might have dropped from the lips of a hundred soap opera husbands. At roughly the same point in *Othello*, the hero declares: 'Perdition catch my soul/But I do love thee! And when I love thee not,/Chaos is come again.'

Inspired by, or based on?

For a film to qualify as a genre adaptation in this book, Shakespeare had to have left a quantifiable and dominant imprint on the plot and characters. William Wellman's *Yellow Sky* (1948), the Western in which outlaws arrive in an abandoned mining town occupied only by an old man and his granddaughter, has been described as an adaptation of *The Tempest*, with the old-timer and the young woman as Prospero and Miranda, although the old man does not control the narrative like Prospero and it is a stretch to pin down the outlaws as counterparts for Ferdinand, Antonio, Gonzalo *et al.* Jack Bender's Civil War-set *The Tempest*, on the other hand, has character-for-character and scene-for-scene transpositions from the play. So, even though Wellman's is a much better Western than Bender's, the former is in my view Shakespearean, while the latter is a Shakespeare film. In close calls between rivals for a place in the same chapter, these 'degrees of separation' from the source play's action, characters and dialogue have always settled the issue.

Not every film in this book is good; some are lousy. The space allocated to each is partly my personal index of its artistic value (one page for *Tromeo and Juliet*, 1996, four pages for *Romeo + Juliet*), and the rewards it offers to anyone interested in comparing Shakespeare with his adaptations. That does not mean films criticised across one or two pages are not worthy of attention alongside great works like Welles's *Othello* or Kurosawa's *Throne of Blood*. One can appreciate the brilliance of Shakespeare's dramaturgy and poetry from seeing the original text abused in, say, Jeremy Freeston's *Macbeth* (1997), or idiotically adapted in Brian Percival's BBC *Much Ado About Nothing*, learning as much or more from their mistakes as from Welles's and Kurosawa's triumphs.

Whether masterpiece or disaster, original-text or paraphrase, every one of these 100 films makes me notice something new about the Shakespeare work concerned, and many lead me to re-read particular scenes, or the whole play. When that happens I recall a remark of Orson Welles, not overly modest about his own cinematic achievements, and yet happy to tell his friend and fellow director Peter Bogdanovich: 'I really can't make a comparison between a movie-maker and Shakespeare. No movie that will ever be made is worthy of being discussed in the same breath.'

Antony and Cleopatra (play synopsis)

Marc Antony, Octavius, nephew of Julius Caesar, and Lepidus have joint control of Rome. Their alliance faces two threats: the warlike intentions of young Pompey, whose father was Caesar's enemy, and Antony's love affair with Cleopatra, Queen of Egypt, which causes him to spend more and more time with her in Alexandria, where her capricious behaviour enflames and infuriates him.

When Octavius and Lepidus reprimand Antony for neglecting his responsibilities, he reluctantly agrees to shore up the triumvirate by marrying Octavius's sister Octavia (Antony's wife Fulvia having recently died). This angers Cleopatra and fails to heal the Roman leaders' widening rift. When they quarrel further, Antony forms an alliance with Pompey, and declares that he and Cleopatra are now commanders of the eastern part of the Roman empire.

The Roman fleet under Octavius fights Antony and Cleopatra's forces at Actium, but at a crucial moment the Queen turns her ships about and Antony is defeated. Enobarbus, Antony's loyal lieutenant, defects to Octavius and soon dies of a broken heart.

In a second battle, this time on land, Antony is again vanquished and blames Cleopatra because the Egyptian forces have once more fled the field. She takes refuge in her Monument and sends a false message to Antony indicating that she is dead. Overwhelmed by military defeat and apparent personal catastrophe, Antony falls on his sword. Dying, he is taken to the Monument, where he expires in the Queen's arms.

Knowing that if captured by Octavius she will face humiliation in Rome, Cleopatra commits suicide with her servants Charmian and Iras, allowing the poisonous asp smuggled into her Monument to bite her breast. Octavius enters the Monument and orders that Antony and Cleopatra be buried together.

Antony and Cleopatra
Spain/Switzerland/UK, 1972 – 160 mins
Charlton Heston

After playing Marc Antony in the 1950 and 1970 *Julius Caesar*s (pp. 70 and 76), Charlton Heston had become obsessed with adapting *Antony and Cleopatra*, which he considered Shakespeare's finest work, but which had never previously been filmed at feature length. His love affair with character and play reached a rocky conclusion in this overlong epic.

After writing a screenplay that removes several of Antony's and Octavius's friends and officers at negligible cost, he assumed directing duties only after being turned down by Orson Welles, who would surely not have allowed Shakespeare's inherently cinematic plot to crisscross between Alexandria, Rome, Syria and Athens as sluggishly as Heston; nor, one suspects, would Welles have introduced so much spurious background action, such as the gory bout between two gladiators, which distracts from what should be a riveting meeting between Antony and Octavius, from Act II, Scene ii.

The film's greatest handicap turns out to be its $1m budget, though these constraints are not immediately apparent as lushly photographed locations in southern Spain double for elegant Roman villas and the sea and sand of Egypt. The sets built for the queen's Alexandrian palace, though dwarfed by the splendour of *Cleopatra* (1963), serve well enough, and problems of scale only arise after Antony abandons his vapid new wife, Octavia (Carmen Sevilla).

For the battle of Actium, a naval clash Shakespeare could only allude to via 'noise of a sea-fight', Heston craved massive spectacle; he could only afford original footage of Antony's flagship ramming one of Octavius's galleys, embellished with outtakes from *Ben-Hur* (1959). The resulting close-ups of two vast, sturdy replicas, intercut with long shots of tiny, flimsy models are laughable, ruining the pivotal moment when Cleopatra betrays Antony. The later battle, at which Octavius's cavalry overwhelms Antony's infantry, is more effective, though Heston cannot resist over-indulging his own heroic image as Antony hacks his way through Roman horsemen with super-human strength.

As with all romantic epics, the challenge is not to let action-packed spectacle swamp the central love story – precisely what happens here because of fatally lop-sided casting. As we follow Antony's moving journey to self-knowledge and self-destruction, Heston is impressive, for once not over-reliant on his trademark steely gaze, clenched jaw and expansive laughter. With the ravishingly beautiful Hildegard Neil, however, Welles's warning that 'If you don't have a great Cleopatra, you can't do this play' proves all too prophetic. Neil's perfect cheekbones and lip gloss do not compensate for a nondescript personality and insensitive verse-speaking, particularly in the build-up to her suicide, when she is embarrassingly out-acted by her Charmian, the seductively moving Jane Lapotaire (a fine Cleopatra for the BBC in 1981). It is the experienced English actors who excel in a multinational supporting cast: Lapotaire, Freddie Jones's grizzled, boozy Pompey, Julian Glover's dignified Proculeius and Eric Porter's memorably cynical Enobarbus. Only John Castle's priggish, oddly disinterested Octavius disappoints.

Lousy reviews scuppered the movie's chances of wide distribution in America, and, in his autobiography, Heston lamented that 'the film I cared more about than any I've ever made was a failure.'

Dir/Scr: Charlton Heston; **Prod:** Peter Snell; **DOP:** Rafael Pacheco; **Editor:** Eric Boyd-Perkins; **Score:** John Scott, Augusto Alegueró; **Main Cast:** Charlton Heston (Antony), Hildegard Neil (Cleopatra), Eric Porter (Enobarbus), John Castle (Octavius), Jane Lapotaire (Charmian), Freddie Jones (Pompey), Fernando Rey (Lepidus), Julian Glover (Proculeius).

As You Like It (play synopsis)

Duke Senior, deposed and banished by his brother, Duke Frederick, lives happily in the Forest of Arden with the melancholy Jaques and other lords. At court, Oliver, a malicious nobleman, wants to kill his younger brother, Orlando, so that he can inherit all of their late father's property. Oliver asks Charles, a professional wrestler, to break Orlando's neck in their bout, but Orlando wins. When he is congratulated by Rosalind, Senior's daughter, they fall in love.

Fearful of public affection for Rosalind, Frederick banishes her. She disguises herself as a boy, 'Ganymede', and goes to seek her father, accompanied by her devoted cousin, Celia, Frederick's daughter, who is disguised as 'Aliena', and Touchstone, a clown.

Old Adam, a faithful servant, warns Orlando that Oliver is planning to set fire to his lodging, and the pair head for the forest, where they are welcomed by Senior and his fellows, who feed the exhausted Adam.

Corin, an elderly shepherd, shelters Rosalind and Celia. Touchstone falls in love with Audrey, a goatherd, and asks a vicar, Sir Oliver Martext, to marry them. 'Ganymede' persuades Orlando to woo her as Rosalind. Phebe, a shepherdess adored by Silvius, a young shepherd, falls for 'Ganymede'.

Sent by Duke Frederick to find Orlando, Oliver arrives in the forest. While sleeping, he is saved from being savaged by a lioness by Orlando, an act of mercy that instantly converts Oliver to goodness. He and Celia fall in love.

Rosalind and Celia reveal their true identities to Orlando and Senior, and the goddess Hymen marries all four couples: Rosalind and Orlando, Celia and Oliver, Phebe and Silvius, Touchstone and Audrey. Oliver and Orlando's brother arrives to announce that Frederick, who was preparing to murder Senior, has miraculously renounced the dukedom and decided to retire to a monastery, where he will be joined by Jaques. Senior and his companions prepare to return to court.

As You Like It
UK, 1936 – 95 mins (B&W)
Paul Czinner

Entrusted with a vast $1m budget to make Britain's first feature-length Shakespeare talkie, Hungarian-born Paul Czinner treated *As You Like It* as a fairytale showcase for his film star wife Elisabeth Bergner (a Polish-born Jew who had fled Nazi Germany with Czinner in 1933). Omitting most of Jaques's melancholy musings and Touchstone's cynical humour, Czinner ensured that no shadows marred Bergner's sunny performance, and did the play grave disservice.

Bergner and Sophie Stewart's radiantly cheerful Celia start off like rivals for the title role in *Sleeping Beauty*. Dressed in matching white satin, they walk dreamily through Duke Senior's palace – a studio-built marvel of high arches and reflective floors. Prince Charming arrives in the athletic form of Laurence Olivier (then a leading matinée idol), who defeats a bare-chested Charles in an exciting wrestling match.

Once Rosalind has fallen in love with Orlando, even banishment with Celia and Touchstone (the loose-limbed Mackenzie Ward, in full jester's outfit) is a jolly adventure, rather than a test of character. With Bergner in doublet and hose as 'Ganymede' one detects the influence of J. M. Barrie, whose treatment was the basis for R. J. Cullen's screenplay. Bergner is more Tinkerbell than Peter Pan, without the faintest masculine touch to her voice or gait, which denies us any of the delectable comic moments when other actresses show Rosalind's guard slipping to reveal the woman beneath, and may explain why Olivier makes Orlando appear slightly deranged; he would have to be to believe in 'Ganymede'. At least his verse-speaking is lively and varied; Bergner's incongruous German accent and bouncy enthusiasm (at one point she turns a somersault) give Rosalind's poetry a monotonous and eventually tiresome jollity, which, along with the perfunctory treatment of Leon Quartermaine's pompous Jaques, prompted Graham Greene to note in the *Spectator*: 'The streak of poison which runs through the comedy has been squeezed carefully out between hygienic fingertips.'

Czinner cares more for livestock than philosophy. Fawns and rabbits share the studio forest with Corin's flock of twenty or more sheep; Audrey milks a cow, surrounded by hens and goats; Rosalind and Celia's thatched cottage has a duck pond. 'How the ubiquitous livestock weary us before the end,' complained Greene.

The ending should provide a magical reunion, as Rosalind's 'transformation' leaves her father and fiancé joyously wondering 'if there be truth in sight'. Apparently chary of such a theatrical moment – perversely so, given the heightened suspension of disbelief required to accept Bergner's undisguised femininity – Czinner omits this revelation, cutting from Rosalind's last speech as 'Ganymede' to her and Celia's reappearance in matching wedding dresses. More understandably, he swaps Hymen's contribution for a less alien, if equally over-the-top, production number: dozens of flute-playing shepherds and skipping milkmaids singing a celebratory 'La-la' chorus.

Apart from the scale of the palace sets and the sheer weight of numbers (human and animal), there is little in Czinner's vision that one could not have found in a 1930s' theatre, and several of the performances, notably Quartermaine's, belong there, rather than on screen. As the *New York Herald Tribune* observed, this 'remains more a photographed version of a stringently cut stage presentation than a comic classic shaped to the cinema', though it holds landmark interest today as the youthful first stop in Olivier's remarkable screen journey through Shakespeare's works, which would end forty-six years later with his television King Lear.

Dir/Prod: Paul Czinner; **Scr:** R. J. Cullen; **DOP:** Hal Rosson; **Editor:** David Lean; **Score:** William Walton; **Main Cast:** Laurence Olivier (Orlando), Elisabeth Bergner (Rosalind), Sophie Stewart (Celia), John Laurie (Oliver), Mackenzie Ward (Touchstone), Leon Quartermaine (Jaques), Henry Ainley (Duke Senior), Felix Aylmer (Duke Frederick), Dorice Fordred (Audrey), J. Fisher White (Adam).

(*Opposite page*) 'You might take occasion to kiss.': as 'Ganymede', Rosalind (Elisabeth Bergner) encourages Orlando (Laurence Olivier) to woo her in Paul Czinner's *As You Like It*

As You Like It
UK, 1992 – 114 mins
Christine Edzard

It is hard to believe that Christine Edzard could follow the moving, Oscar-nominated *Little Dorrit* (UK, 1987) with this box-office disaster (UK takings of less than $30,000 on a $1.5m budget), a doomed marriage of original text and modernised setting.

Edzard presents Frederick's court as a 1990s' business empire, Oliver as a smug yuppy and Orlando a surly, donkey-jacketed scrounger. The Forest of Arden becomes a concrete jungle; Senior and his fellows live like tramps in cardboard boxes and polythene tents. This switch from idealised pastoral to realistic cityscape blends with *As You Like It* like oil with water.

All the court scenes unfold on a single set (columns, chess-board floor and multiple, mirrored doors), which serves as the lobby of Frederick's business HQ, Oliver's office, Old Adam's workshop and Rosalind's bedroom – a compact, economical approach for theatre, deeply unconvincing on film. We must accept Frederick holding a wrestling tournament in the lobby, and during the Charles/Orlando tussle we see only onlookers' tame reaction shots, not the bout itself, ruining the play's one action set piece and diminishing Rosalind's prime motive for falling in love.

In Shakespeare, Celia and Rosalind are of an age, inseparable since early childhood. Yet Frederick's daughter is played by Celia Bannerman, who looks old enough to be mother to Emma Croft's Rosalind. Elsewhere, Edzard opts for theatrical doubling: the two Dukes are played by husky-voiced Don Henderson, and Orlando and Oliver by the slightly creepy Andrew Tiernan. This trick works well with Henderson, since his slightly fey Frederick need never appear alongside his phlegmatic Senior. Orlando and Oliver, however, must face each other first in deadly enmity, then deep fraternal love, yet because Edzard cannot afford split-screen effects, she can never show both Tiernans in the same shot, and the play's most confrontational relationship falls flat.

Edzard's lifeless direction allows every scene to proceed at the same, gentle pace and as she has not rewritten Shakespeare to match poetry to setting in the 'forest' segment (shot in London's docklands), clashes between words and images abound. Corin and Silvius tend their one sheep on fields of concrete. Rosalind refers to her doublet and hose while wearing jeans and a hooded top. Oliver talks about being menaced by a lioness when threatened by a mugger.

City-of-London settings like this have been brilliantly employed by theatre directors staging *The Merchant of Venice* and *Timon of Athens* (plays addressing the corrupting effects of commerce) and Michael Almereyda had ample grounds in *Hamlet* (2000, p. 47) for creating a corporate Elsinore in present-day Manhattan. Not a word of *As You Like It*'s celebration of country life justifies transforming court into conglomerate or forest into wasteland.

Some of the cast give equally inappropriate performances, notably Griff Rhys Jones, whose Touchstone is a refugee from 1950s' Ealing comedy, gabbling in strangulated cockney. James Fox takes Jaques's melancholy to exhaustingly dull lengths. Only Croft, as an attractive, spirited and, when necessary, convincingly boyish Rosalind, emerges with credit.

Dir: Christine Edzard; **Prod:** George Reinhart, Olivier Stockman; **DOP:** Robin Vidgeon; **Editor:** Olivier Stockman; **Score:** Michel Sanvoisin; **Main Cast:** Andrew Tiernan (Orlando/Oliver), Emma Croft (Rosalind), Celia Bannerman (Celia), Griff Rhys Jones (Touchstone), James Fox (Jaques), Don Henderson (Duke Senior/Duke Frederick), Miriam Margolyes (Audrey), Cyril Cusack (Adam).

As You Like It
US/UK, 2006 – 127 mins
Kenneth Branagh

First announced by Branagh's Shakespeare Film Company early in 1999, his fifth original-text Shakespeare feature was finally shot in April 2005, opened in Italy and Greece in autumn 2006 and, as this book went to press, was scheduled for UK release in spring 2007. The prolonged wait was worthwhile: Branagh delivered the first truly cinematic *As You Like It* and his finest Shakespeare since *Henry V* (1989, p. 64).

After a caption explaining how in the late nineteenth century Western 'merchant adventurers' settled in Japan and built up empires akin to dukedoms, Branagh begins exactly as Michael Powell planned to open his abortive screen adaptation of *The Tempest*, with a prologue dramatising the brotherly coup that deposes a benevolent Duke.

In a waterside Japanese villa (bare wooden floors, sliding partitions, paper lanterns), Senior, Rosalind, Celia and Touchstone are listening to a kabuki singer when Frederick and his samurai warriors launch a stealth attack and drive Senior into exile with Japanese and European male retainers, followed separately by Janet McTeer's toweringly buxom Audrey (re-imagined as a household servant, and already lusted after by Touchstone). Orlando and Oliver trade kung-fu blows in a thunderstorm and Orlando (David Oyelowo) defeats Charles (Yee Tsou) in a convincing sumo bout before samurai raze his stable.

Though overbearingly scored by Patrick Doyle's Japanese-inflected themes (koto to the fore), the opening half-hour is so dark and violent that our first glimpse of daylight in the forest provides literal and figurative fresh air, superbly realising the play's contrast between court and Arden.

Branagh and Roger Lanser's fondness for shooting bright comedy in warm, natural light is in evidence here as in *Much Ado about Nothing* (1993, p. 155) and theirs is an Arden of gentle breezes, sunshine, bluebells and birdsong, where forest paths and the long footbridge leading over a reed-filled pond to Corin's ramshackle sheepcote lend themselves to lengthy 'walk-and-talk' shots.

Apart from glimpses of Senior's companions and Touchstone practising t'ai chi, there's little to suggest we are still in Japan and not, as is the case, verdant southern England (Wakehurst Place, West Sussex, and Virginia Water, Windsor) and the substitution of sumo for occidental wrestling is the only piece of cultural translation that feels organic to the play. Otherwise, the Japanese concept is largely cosmetic, but given that the apolitical plot does not depend on a specific location, this is a minor gripe.

Branagh knows that however good the ensemble, *As You Like It* stands or falls by its central romance, and sensibly lets Rosalind and Orlando's sparkling love 'duets' play almost uncut. He is rewarded with marvellous performances from Oyelowo, who convinces as macho hero and love-struck youth, and rising American star Bryce Dallas Howard, very fetching in brown cap, jacket and leather boots, and wholly at ease with the verse and her English accent .

The radiant Romola Garai proves herself a deft verbal and physical comedienne as Celia, and Adrian Lester makes Oliver's conversion remarkably credible. In contrast to his insufferable Bottom in *A Midsummer Night's Dream* (p. 146), Kevin Kline's grey-bearded, quietly spoken Jaques is an acute portrait of a manic depressive and Alfred Molina's Touchstone, tailcoat matching a black, top-hat hairdo, is nicely underplayed.

Members of Branagh's Shakespeare rep company ably fill other roles, including Brian Blessed, who growls in black armour as Frederick and purrs in grey as Senior, and the ever-genial, bearded Jimmy Yuill, whose tipsy Corin is the one significantly altered character. Now a vicar-turned-shepherd, he returns to his former role to stand in for the absent Sir Oliver Martext and Hymen, and marries all four couples, who rush back to court, accompanied by Doyle's choral arrangement of 'A Lover and His Lass'.

Branagh steers with such energetic, enchanting finesse that two hours fly by without any of the directorial inconsistencies or misjudged performances that mar all his other Shakespeares bar *Henry V*, and he echoes that film's illusion-breaking Chorus in a beautifully judged coda: Howard delivers the Epilogue while strolling through the trees, past crew members, co-stars and equipment vans, and disappears into her trailer on 'bid me farewell'.

Dir/Scr: Kenneth Branagh; **Prods:** Kenneth Branagh, Judy Hofflund, Simon Moseley; **DOP:** Roger Lanser; **Editor:** Neil Farrell; **Score:** Patrick Doyle; **Main Cast:** David Oyelowo (Orlando), Bryce Dallas Howard (Rosalind), Romola Garai (Celia), Adrian Lester (Oliver), Alfred Molina (Touchstone), Kevin Kline (Jaques), Brian Blessed (Duke Senior/Duke Frederick), Janet McTeer (Audrey), Richard Briers (Adam), Yee Tsou (Charles), Jimmy Yuill (Corin).

The Comedy of Errors (play synopsis)

In Ephesus, Aegeon a merchant of Syracuse has been arrested under a law stating that any Syracusan caught in Ephesus shall be executed unless he can raise a ransom. He tells the Duke, Solinus, that many years ago he lost his wife, one of their twin sons (both named Antipholus) and one of their twin servants (both named Dromio) in a shipwreck, and that ever since he has gone from town to town looking for them. Aegeon has no idea that Antipholus and Dromio of Syracuse have also arrived in Ephesus. All three are unaware that their long-lost twins, Antipholus and Dromio of Ephesus, are prosperous local residents.

The two visitors, both unmarried, are promptly mistaken for the Ephesus twins by various characters, including Antipholus's wife, Adriana. They believe the confusion relates to the town's reputation as home to magicians and ghosts. At his brother's house, Antipholus of Syracuse falls in love with Adriana's sister, Luciana, which, understandably, alarms both women. Dromio of Syracuse is baffled to be claimed as husband by a kitchen maid, Drowsabel. Antipholus and Dromio of Ephesus are locked out of their home, and Antipholus rages when a goldsmith, Angelo, refuses to hand over an expensive chain because he has already given it to 'him'; and Antipholus refuses to pay. Both masters beat their confused and protesting servants for failing to carry out instructions actually given to their twin.

Angelo has Antipholus of Syracuse arrested and treated as a madman (by the quack doctor, Pinch), but he flees into an abbey, where Aegeon, whose execution looms, has also sought sanctuary. Both recognise each other and realise that the abbess is Aegeon's wife. The two sets of twins are reunited, Aegeon is pardoned by the Duke and Antipholus of Syracuse promises to marry Luciana.

The Boys from Syracuse
US, 1940 – 73 mins (B&W)
A. Edward Sutherland

The Boys from Syracuse lies at several removes from its source, or as the end credits have it: 'This Picture is after "A Comedy of Errors" by William Shakespeare (long, long after).' Rodgers and Hart's 1938 Broadway musical-comedy is transformed from a witty satire into a burlesque scarcely of feature length.

The vainglorious Antipholus (Allan Jones) is now a general who has led Ephesus to victory over Syracuse and, ironically, introduced a law damning enemy visitors to execution. Adriana (Irene Hervey) retains her haughty, demanding nature from the play. Their servant Dromio (Joe Penner) is married to Adriana's 'clumsy slave girl', Luce (Martha Raye), who has a much bigger role than in Shakespeare. Luce and Dromio were once entertainers who did 'an act for Achilles/That gave him the willies', according to Raye's raucous rendition of 'The Greeks Had No Word for It', one of two new numbers introduced alongside four retained from the Broadway version. Jones croons the romantic ballad 'Who Are You?', while Adriana's sister, Phyllis (the bland Rosemary Lane), responds to Antipholus of Syracuse's marriage proposal with 'This Can't Be Love'.

Jones and the gurning Penner play both sets of twins, and although their crisscrossing entrances and exits create some enjoyable, deftly edited confusion, the mistaken identity comedy lasts barely thirty minutes and, apart from the risqué implication that Luce has unwittingly had sex with her brother-in-law while her husband was locked out, it never hints at the existential crises that envelop Shakespeare's characters.

Angelo and Pinch become camp English tailors (Motto: 'If U come CLEAN with us we'll DYE for you'), whom the chronically idle Duke threatens with execution unless they can force the miserly Antipholus to pay his bills and thereby clear the pair's back taxes. The Ephesus pair are jailed for treason, while Phyllis helps the Syracuse boys to free Aegeon; the Antipholuses are motherless, so there is no abbess.

After a Western-style chariot chase, the fugitives are recaptured and A. Edward Sutherland finally plays his trump card: both sets of brothers appear in the same shot, earning the film a Special Effects Oscar Nomination. Our heroes win over Ephesus's people's jury by launching into a reprise medley, leaving the Duke to faint at news that his wife has just given birth – to twins.

The film has less in common with Shakespeare than with other stage and screen comedies and musicals. Dromio's wisecracking disobedience anticipates Pseudolus in *A Funny Thing Happened on the Way to the Forum*, and script and production design are full of the anachronistic verbal and visual gags that would pepper the films of Mel Brooks and the *Carry On* . . . team. There are checkered chariot taxis and a street vendor sells stone tablet tabloids announcing 'Ephesus Blitzes Syracuse'. Hollywood in-jokes include a glimpse of a 'Los Angeles City Limits' sign and Dromio calling for help not from the *Comedy*'s servants, 'Maud, Bridget, Marian, Cicely, Gillian, Ginn!', but screen goddesses 'Carole, Lana, Greta, Hedy!' Charles Butterworth's droll Duke, burdened with a lame running gag involving the trumpeters who fanfare his every entrance, fires off one-liners like Groucho Marx: 'Get yourself a good hangover,' he tells Aegeon, 'and you'll actually enjoy getting your head cut off.'

Dir: A. Edward Sutherland; Prod: Universal Pictures; Scr: Leonard Spigelgass, Charles Grayson, Paul Gerard Smith, based on George Abbott's play; DOP: Joseph Valentine; Editor: Milton Carruth; Music: Richard Rodgers; Lyrics: Lorenz Hart; Main Cast: Allan Jones (Antipholus of Ephesus/Antipholus of Syracuse), Joe Penner (Dromio of Ephesus/Dromio of Syracuse), Martha Raye (Luce), Irene Hervey (Adriana), Rosemary Lane (Phyllis), Charles Butterworth (Duke of Ephesus), Eric Blore (Pinch), Alan Mowbray (Angelo), Samuel S. Hinds (Aegeon).

Hamlet (play synopsis)

Elsinore, Denmark. Following the death of old King Hamlet, his brother, Claudius, reigns and has married Gertrude, old Hamlet's widow. Hamlet, the dead King's grieving son, is appalled by his mother's remarriage. Old Hamlet's ghost appears and tells his son that he was murdered by Claudius; Hamlet swears revenge. Concerned at Hamlet's distracted behaviour, Claudius and Gertrude have summoned his friends, Rosencrantz and Guildenstern, to sound him out. Polonius, Claudius's Lord Chamberlain, suggests that Hamlet's madness is caused by love for his daughter, Ophelia.

Travelling players arrive at court and, on Hamlet's orders, stage a play mirroring the circumstances of old Hamlet's murder. Observed by Hamlet's university friend, Horatio, Claudius storms out of this performance, confirming his guilt in Hamlet's eyes. The Prince confronts Gertrude in her bedroom and stabs the concealed Polonius, mistaking him for Claudius.

The King orders Hamlet to sail to England with Rosencrantz and Guildenstern, who are carrying Claudius's letter ordering the English king to execute the Prince. Laertes, Polonius's son, returns from France demanding revenge for his father's murder. Ophelia, driven mad by Hamlet's scorn and Polonius's death, drowns herself.

Hamlet has returned to Denmark on a pirate ship, having forged a letter condemning Rosencrantz and Guildenstern to death on their arrival in England. He encounters Ophelia's funeral procession and violently confronts Laertes.

Claudius and Laertes devise a plot to kill Hamlet in a fencing bout. Using an untipped foil with a poisoned point, Laertes wounds Hamlet but they exchange swords and Hamlet injures his opponent. Gertrude dies after accidentally drinking from the cup that Claudius has filled with poisoned wine intended for Hamlet. Laertes dies denouncing Claudius's treachery and Hamlet kills the King, moments before succumbing to the poison. Fortinbras, Prince of Norway, arrives to lay claim to the Danish throne.

Hamlet: The Drama of Vengeance
Germany, 1920 – 124 mins (B&W)
Sven Gade, Heinz Schall

Danish-born Asta Nielsen (1881–1972), one of the greatest stars of European silent cinema, made more than seventy films and launched her own production company with this astonishing melodrama. It adapts Shakespeare, Saxo-Grammaticus's twelfth-century Danish Hamlet saga and American scholar Edward P. Vining's 1881 book *The Mystery of Hamlet*, which argued that the Prince was a woman.

At Elsinore, Queen Gertrude gives birth to a daughter, just before hearing that the King has been 'mortally' wounded in the epic victory that claims the enemy King of Norway's life, giving Denmark power over its neighbour. To avoid a dangerous vacancy on the throne, Gertrude has it proclaimed that the baby is a male heir, only for the King to recover. To conceal the deception, the couple must raise their princess as a prince and, with a *Winter's Tale*-like leap, the infant becomes Nielsen, her slim, boyish figure clad in black to match her side-parted hair and huge, expressive eyes, which sometimes make her resemble Buster Keaton.

At Wittenberg, she shares digs with the boorish Laertes, befriends Horatio and meets Fortinbras, both princes pledging friendship despite their fathers' enmity. After Claudius kills old Hamlet (off screen) with a poisonous snake, Nielsen returns to Elsinore, disrupting her uncle and mother's wedding feast with a diva-like entrance down a grand staircase. Her father's disembodied voice spurs her to revenge and, after finding Claudius's dagger in the castle snake-pit, her feigned madness showcases Nielsen's comic gifts; she can provoke laughter with a shrug of her shoulders or sideways glance, especially when Hamlet mocks Polonius (played as a tonsured Uriah Heep).

Yet she also conveys disgust at Gertrude's remarriage, and suicidal self-loathing; the 'rogue and peasant slave' and 'To be, or not to be' soliloquies are reduced to a despairing intertitle: 'Too weak to kill and

too weak to kill myself!' Her casting redefines *Hamlet*'s revenge plot (a woman assumes the traditionally violent male role) and adds a story of unrequited love: Hamlet adores the virile Horatio much as the disguised Viola adores Orsino in *Twelfth Night*. When Horatio falls for Ophelia (a fairytale maiden with blonde pigtails), Hamlet fakes affection 'to lead her away from my beloved', lending terrible irony to her accidental killing of Polonius, because Ophelia's consequent suicide eradicates the Prince's love rival. All this drives Hamlet into existential crisis, though it is articulated in ten words where Shakespeare uses hundreds; clutching her breasts, she cries at Gertrude: 'I am no man and may not be a woman!'

Eduard von Winterstein's brutish, demonic-looking Claudius attempts to have Hamlet killed in Norway by Fortinbras, his vassal, but Hamlet's rewriting of the King's letter condemns to execution the two nameless attendants who bore it. She returns to Elsinore, leaves her Norwegian ally and his soldiers poised to seize the throne on her behalf, and kills Claudius by burning the chamber where he lies in a drunken stupor. There is further tweaking of Shakespearean gender roles: Gertrude, complicit in King Hamlet's death, becomes a vengeful widow. She applies venom to Laertes's foil and poisons the wine that she then accidentally drinks during the fencing match after a servant rearranges the cups. Wounded by Laertes (who survives), Hamlet dies in Horatio's arms as his right hand recoils from a revelatory touch of her left breast. 'Death uncovers your tragic secret – your golden heart was a woman's!', Horatio exclaims, a line that is immediately hilarious and, on reflection, heartbreaking, because once crowned, Hamlet might have reigned as Queen not King, and, unlike Shakespeare's hero, dies tantalisingly close to romantic fulfilment.

Nielsen brought to Hamlet her trademark, often androgynous eroticism (in 1916's *The ABCs of Love* she cross-dressed to 'bring out the man' in a drippy boyfriend) and built on the tradition of stage actresses

(*Opposite page*) The Princess who became a Prince: Asta Nielsen as the heroine of Sven Gade and Heinz Schall's *Hamlet: The Drama of Vengeance*

playing the Dane, which stretches from the late eighteenth century. She also helped pave the way for the gender-challenging, suit-wearing characters played by Katharine Hepburn and Greta Garbo, who said of her co-star in 1925's *The Joyless Street*: 'She taught me everything I know.'

Dir: Sven Gade, Heinz Schall; **Prod:** Art-Film; **Scr:** Erwin Gepard, based on Edward P. Vining's book; **DOPs:** Curt Courant, Axel Graatkjaer; **Editor:** not known; **Score:** Giuseppe Becce; **Main Cast:** Asta Nielsen (Hamlet), Mathilde Brandt (Gertrude), Eduard von Winterstein (Claudius), Lilly Jacboson (Ophelia), Hans Junkermann (Polonius), Anton de Verdier (Laertes), Heinz Stieda (Horatio), Paul Conradi (King Hamlet).

Strange Illusion
US, 1945 – 87 mins (B&W)
Edgar G. Ulmer

Watching Edgar G. Ulmer, king of 'poverty row' B-movies, turn
Hamlet into over-ripe psycho-melodrama is a guilty pleasure. Hamlet
has 'bad dreams' and has dropped out of Wittenberg; Paul
Cartwright, *Strange Illusion*'s clean-cut hero, has ghostly nightmares
about the mysterious accident that killed his beloved father, former
Lieutenant Governor of California, two years earlier, and has broken
off from his law degree. Paul has two pals, middle-aged psychiatrist Dr
Vincent (Horatio) and young George Hanover (Laertes), and an on-off
relationship with George's Ophelia-lite sister, Lydia. His regal, beautiful
mother, Virginia, is about to marry Brett Curtis (Warren William), a shady
cad whom Paul suspects, rightly, may be a serial killer who once married
and drowned another wealthy widow.

Brett's Polonius-like accomplice is Professor Muhlbach (Charles Arnt),
warden of Restview Manor, and once Paul gets himself into this asylum
as a voluntary patient by semi-feigning madness, Muhlbach's
unbelievably stupid failure to dispose of incriminating evidence from
Paul's father's murder makes it a cinch for our Hamlet to team up with
the Doc and the DA and foil the dastardly plot. Muhlbach is arrested and
Brett gunned down by a cop as he's about to kill Paul.

Strange Illusion wants to be taken seriously, but that is impossible
with atrocious dialogue, lumbering direction and a third-rate cast
(William and Arnt come across like the dime-store Clark Gable and
Claude Rains), whose performances all suffer from the peculiar B-
movie malaise that gives actors the stiff posture and stiffer vocal
patterns of a public information film. The best pseudo-Shakespearean
moment is Muhlbach's diagnosis of Paul: 'I believe it is your emotional
aversion to your mother's remarriage which produces these neurotic
symptoms.' If only Polonius could have read Freud . . .

Dir: Edgar G. Ulmer; **Prod:** Leon Fromkess; **Scr:** Adele Comandini; **DOPs:** Philip Tannura, Eugene Schufftan; **Supervising Editor:** Carl Pierson; **Score:** Leo Erdody; **Main Cast:** Jimmy Lydan (Paul Cartwright), Sally Eillers (Virginia Cartwright), Warren William (Brett Curtis), Regis Toomey (Dr Martin Vincent), Jimmy Clark (George Hanover), Mary McLeod (Lydia Hanover), Charles Arnt (Professor Muhlbach).

Hamlet
UK, 1948 – 153 mins
Laurence Olivier

Laurence Olivier's *Hamlet* is both grim fairytale and psychological case study. The colourful pageant of *Henry V* (1944, p. 60) gives way to a monochrome engraving: sombre, disturbing and, as box-office success on both sides of the Atlantic proved, accessible. 'A movie for everybody,' declared the *Washington Post*, 'Be you nine or ninety, a PhD or just plain Joe.' Its $3m US gross was exceptional for any non-Hollywood picture and it became the only Shakespeare feature to win the Best Picture Academy Award (it also took the BAFTA for Best Film), while Olivier's remains the only original-text Shakespeare performance to have won Best Actor.

His decision to ignore the play's politics and make accessibility his watchword brought controversy as well as acclaim. Again using Alan Dent as Text Editor, Olivier removed about 50% of the text. Out went Reynaldo (Polonius's servant), Rosencrantz and Guildenstern, the second grave-digger and Fortinbras, and two soliloquies ('What a piece of work' and 'How all occasions'). Supposedly arcane words were changed; for example, 'maimed rites' became 'meagre rites'. All this prompted a *Times* leading article ('Alas, Poor Hamlet!') and furious letters, despite Olivier's attempt to forestall such hostility by writing in *The Film Hamlet: A Record of Its Production* that he had directed 'an "Essay in *Hamlet*", and not a film version of a necessarily abridged classic.' All this goes to show the extent to which Shakespeare's texts were viewed as sacrosanct.

Olivier's 'essay' took six months to make, cost £500,000 and begins with his famously simplified declaration: 'This is the tragedy of a man who could not make up his mind.' Swirling mist clears, and four soldiers on a platform carry the dead Hamlet, as Olivier reveals the fatal consequences of indecision (perhaps inspiring the funereal prologue in Orson Welles's 1952 *Othello*, see p. 165), before dissolving to the beginning of the play, inside the castle designed to Oscar-winning effect by Roger Furse and Carmen Dillon at Denham Studios.

Olivier requested 'significant austerity' and they gave him a clifftop Elsinore of cold grey stone, long, arched passageways and steep, winding staircases – credible yet not wholly realistic, clearly medieval yet somehow out of time. Aristocratic English accents resound in rooms largely devoid of furniture, and the strangely intense mood is heightened by William Walton's marvellously varied score (confined largely to interludes between spoken passages) and Desmond Dickinson's deep-focus photography, which keeps figures sharply defined, even when thirty metres from the lens.

Dickinson's numerous crane shots could be a Ghost's eye view. His camera pulls back from Jean Simmons's captivating Ophelia, weeping prostrate on a staircase, then rises to the battlements, zooms in and 'disappears' through Hamlet's skull as he begins 'To be, or not to be', delivered, like most of the soliloquies, in voiceover, by a man staring suicidally into the waves below, then holding up his dagger. While this is undoubtedly cinematic, as an actor Olivier still had one foot on the stage, and his contemplative poses and lyrical verse-speaking have worn less well than the film's psychology.

At times, Olivier appears so courageous that the 'indecisive' label seems inappropriate. He boldly confronts the Ghost (voiced through buzzing distortion by Olivier himself) and swings, Errol Flynn-style, onto the pirate ship in one of several 'Show and Tell' moments (we also see glimpses of old Hamlet's murder and the drowned Ophelia). He is admired by Norman Wooland's upstanding, handsome Horatio, the Player King (Harcourt Williams), the sentries and the grave-digger (Stanley Holloway). Even Terence Morgan's Laertes seems not to hate the man who killed his father, and Rosencrantz and Guildenstern's absence eliminates tricky questions about Hamlet condemning them to execution.

In male company, then, Hamlet is admirable; with women he is a disaster. Because of his warped relationship with Eileen Herlie's ravishing

(*Opposite page*) 'The play's the thing…': Ophelia (Jean Simmons) and Hamlet (Laurence Olivier) prepare to watch the dumb-show in Olivier's *Hamlet*

Gertrude he cannot respond normally to Ophelia, who glides through the film like *Hamlet*'s second ghost, accompanied by haunted oboe. Herlie looks young enough to be Hamlet's wife (at twenty-seven, she was thirteen years Olivier's junior) and their Oedipal chemistry dates back to Olivier's stage Hamlet in 1937, when a paper by Ernest Jones, biographer of Sigmund Freud, convinced him that repressed sexual desire for Gertrude and jealousy of Claudius largely explained 'what is wrong with the Prince'. Hamlet's yearning peaks after the murder of Polonius, when mother and son's brief, passionate kiss would shock even without the corpse beside them.

Herlie outshines Basil Sydney, whose Claudius lacks menace, and the Freudian interpretation affords her an unforgettable death scene. Gertrude *knows* the wine is poisoned and drinks willingly, killing herself to save her son. The thrilling fencing match in Elsinore's great hall ends with Olivier leaping onto Claudius from high above the throne. After Horatio has spoken Fortinbras's closing lines, the camera (as in *Henry V*) reverses its opening journey, passing Hamlet's empty chair, the chapel where Claudius prayed and Gertrude's bed, and settles on the Prince's body.

Dir/Prod: Laurence Olivier; **Text Editor:** Alan Dent; **DOP:** Desmond Dickinson; **Editor:** Helga Cranston; **Score:** William Walton; **Main Cast:** Laurence Olivier (Hamlet), Eileen Herlie (Gertrude), Basil Sydney (Claudius), Jean Simmons (Ophelia), Felix Aylmer (Polonius), Terence Morgan (Laertes), Norman Wooland (Horatio).

The Bad Sleep Well (Warui yatsu hodo yoku nemuru)
Japan, 1960 – 151 mins (B&W)
Akira Kurosawa

Akira Kurosawa's police thriller *Stray Dog* (1949) and yellow-press drama *Scandal* (1950) were *shakai-mono* (social problem films) commenting on his country's post-war woes, and he continued in similar vein with *The Bad Sleep Well*, using *Hamlet* to condemn public-sector corruption, which he considered 'one of the worst crimes' contributing to the rotten state of Japan.

A more radical reworking of Shakespeare than *Throne of Blood* (1957, p. 103) or *Ran* (1985, p. 84), its magnificently theatrical twenty-minute opening sequence uses a Greek chorus of newspaper reporters to identify the characters and explain their backstories. At a luxury Tokyo hotel, upstanding, bespectacled secretary Koichi Nishi (played with steely restraint by Toshiro Mifune) is marrying the lame, fragile Kieko, daughter of his fearsome boss, Iwabuchi, Vice-President of the Public Corporation for Land Development, which has taken a massive kickback from a construction firm. Detectives arrest Public Corp. official Wada, whose superiors, Shirai, Moriyama and Iwabuchi, were implicated in another corrupt deal five years earlier, which led a colleague, Furuya, to throw himself from the seventh floor of a government building. As the newlyweds cut their cake, a waiter wheels in another gateau shaped like the ministry building, a red rose protruding from its seventh floor. Shirai and Moriyama blanch; Iwabuchi is unmoved. An hour later we will realise this was the film's 'Mousetrap'.

As Nishi attempts to bring the executives to justice, his manipulation of suspects, dry humour and distinctive character tic (whistling a jaunty tune), plus the jazz elements of Masaru Sato's score, make him resemble a noir private eye. He stops Wada from throwing himself into a volcano (a tremendous, smoky scene), saves Shirai from the hitman Iwabuchi dispatches to stop him spilling the beans, then reveals to Shirai and Wada that he sent the giant cake: 'I'm Furuya's illegitimate son . . . [living] only to revenge my father's death.' Nishi is Hamlet, cloaking vengeful intent not with simulated madness but a fake persona; he has swapped identities with his friend and accomplice Itakura (Horatio), who is the real Nishi. The widowed Iwabuchi is Claudius *and* Polonius, responsible for the hero's father's death, and father to the woman he loves, Kieko (Ophelia), and her hotheaded brother, Tatsuo (Laertes).

Though killing Shirai would expose Iwabuchi, Nishi cannot bring himself to do it, just as Hamlet cannot murder Claudius at prayer. Lack of killer instinct helps seal both men's doom, though the script reduces Hamlet's soul-searching to the cumbersome moralising of Nishi's conversations with Wada, Itakura and Kieko – in tune with the film's morality tale title, perhaps, but still disappointingly explicit.

After an excessively drawn-out fourth Act, Iwabuchi, who has learned Nishi's true identity, tricks Kieko into revealing that he is hiding at a bombed-out munitions factory, where he and Itakura have starved Moriyama into proving Iwabuchi's guilt. Iwabuchi has Nishi murdered, making it look like suicide ('self-slaughter' is a more prevalent theme than in *Hamlet*, with repeated attacks on the bureaucratic cult that expects 'brainwashed' salarymen to kill themselves rather than implicate a superior). Iwabuchi seems not to care when Tatsuo says he will never again see him or Kieko (pushed by grief into Ophelia-like dementia). He ends secure on his corporate throne, and there's the rub: an individual cannot defeat institutionalised corruption, despite using tactics more questionable than Hamlet's. Nishi cynically exploits Kieko to get close to Iwabuchi (only for true love to help blunt his purpose), torments Wada by using him as the story's Ghost, drives Shirai insane, tortures Moriyama and, most ironically, has financed his plans with kickback money bequeathed by his father.

Dir/Editor: Akira Kurosawa; **Prods:** Tomoyuki Tanaka, Akira Kurosawa; **Scr:** Shinobu Hashimoto, Hideo Oguni, Ryuzo Kikushima, Eijiro Hisaita, Akira Kurosawa; **DOP:** Yuzuru Aizawa; **Score:** Masaru Sato; **Main Cast:** Toshiro Mifune (Koichi Nishi), Masayuki Mori (Iwabuchi), Kyoko Kagawa (Kieko), Tatsuya Mihashi (Tatsuo), Takeshi Kato (Itakura), Akira Nishimura (Shirai), Takashi Shimura (Moriyama), Kamatari Fujiwara (Wada), Natsuko Kahara (Mrs Furuya).

Ophélia
France, 1963 – 105 mins (B&W)
Claude Chabrol

A psychological-comical-satirical tale of a neurotic young man who convinces himself he is Hamlet, *Ophélia* opens with a dazzling visual translation of the Prince's 'the funeral baked meats/Did coldly furnish forth the marriage tables.' Yvan Lesurf (André Jocelyn), blond hair set off by the black suit he wears throughout, stares into the open coffin containing a middle-aged man and cries 'Father!' Bells usher the mourners into church and after haunting xylophone plays over the opening credits, the doors release the mourners – now joyful guests celebrating the wedding of Yvan's mother, Claudia (Alida Valli), and industrialist uncle, Adrien (Claude Cerval). Funeral and wedding have become one and the same.

Dazed by this double shock, Yvan cuts a lonely figure, drinking in a village café, wandering the countryside and shunning the love of the placid Lucie (Ophelia), whose elderly, widowed father André (Polonius) works for Adrien and worries that Yvan will deflower his daughter. Adrien's determination to break a factory strike has prompted death threats and at the Lesurf manor armed guards patrol the wooded grounds while tuxedoed waiters serve at three family dinners disrupted by Yvan's Hamlet-like provocation of the 'royal' couple. *Hamlet*'s political framework is replaced by broad satire on ruthless capitalism and the *haut-bourgeois* values also dissected in several of Chabrol's other films.

The Shakespearean parallels take a post-modern turn when the 'ghost' that prompts the Hamlet surrogate into action is another film. Yvan stares at publicity stills from Olivier's *Hamlet* as it begins screening in the Ernelés village hall and we hear lines from the French-dubbed soundtrack (Hamlet: 'Seems . . . I know not "seems"'). At home, he writes Ernelés in condensation on his bedroom window and, beneath it, Elseneur, and the uncanny coincidence of his family situation, the Olivier and the place names convinces him that Claudia and Adrien murdered his father; he tells Lucie that he *is* Hamlet and she *is* Ophelia. Chabrol's treatment of the play, with mannered performances and arch dialogue, veers between earnest psychology (Yvan's disquieting auto-suggestion) and parody, as when Yvan's tender stroking of the dead rodent in a mousetrap carried by sultry barmaid Ginette is his cue for the 'Mousetrap'. He enlists his only friend, the dim François (Horatio), Ginette and a jovially drunken grave-digger to appear in a silent film accorded a black-tie première party at the Lesurfs. Yvan provides piano and running commentary for this three-minute tale of a 1900s grocer poisoned by his wife and her lover. When it ends, Chabrol's post-modern maze becomes even more disorienting: Claudia and Adrien leave the salon and retire to bed in dazed silence. Are they moved because (like Claudius) genuinely guilty, or have they convinced themselves of Yvan's interpretation of events, just as he responded to Olivier's interpretation of Shakespeare?

Adrien sets André to spy on Yvan and while tailing him and François, André suffers a fatal heart attack; Lucie grieves, without going mad. Then Chabrol reverses Hamlet's abortive attempt to kill the praying Claudius: Adrien enters Yvan's bedroom armed, only to leave without shooting him. Off camera, he swallows poison and dies with Yvan at his side, murmuring 'My son.' Is he really Yvan's father, adding another twist to *Hamlet*? Is he raving, or wishing they could have been closer? As with every other teasing question, Chabrol declines to provide answers, only a tentatively optimistic final scene with Lucie reassuring the hero ('You are Yvan and I am Lucie. I love you'), and the inscrutability of all the characters makes *Ophélia* a peculiar viewing experience; you laugh at them, and suffer with them.

Dir: Claude Chabrol; **Prod:** Lux Compagne Cinématographique de France/Boreal Pictures; **Scr:** Claude Chabrol, Paul Gegauff, Martial Matthieu; **DOPs:** Jacques Rabier, Jean Rabier; **Editor:** Jacques Gaillard; **Score:** Pierre Jansen; **Main Cast:** Claude Cerval (Adrien Lesurf), Alida Valli (Claudia Lesurf), André Jocelyn (Yvan Lesurf), Juliette Mayniel (Lucie), Robert Burnier (André Lagrange), Serge Bento (François), Sacha Briquet (grave-digger).

Hamlet (*Gamlet*)
USSR, 1964 – 140 mins (B&W)
Grigori Kozintsev

To mark the tercentenary of Shakespeare's birth, Kozintsev used a
budget equivalent to more than $60m today to make an epic, moving
adaptation, dominated by Hamlet's belief that 'Denmark's a prison'.
When Innokenti Smoktunovsky's Prince enters a vast Elsinore (built on
Estonia's Baltic coast), its portcullis clanks ominously shut behind him.
Inside, Claudius's 'Big Brother' regime ensures that as the Prince walks
through wide stone halls he is deep in solitude but seldom alone, spied
on by Claudius, Polonius, Rosencrantz and Guildenstern, and by dozens
of armoured guards and courtiers in exquisite sixteenth-century

Gertrude (Elsa Radzin) pleads with the Prince (Innokenti Smoktunovsky) in Grigori
Kozintsev's *Hamlet*

costumes. When he reveals the whereabouts of Polonius's corpse, a scribe notes down his testimony, as though in a show trial.

'Hamlet is tormented by what is happening in the prison-state around him,' noted Kozintsev, who retained several actors from his Leningrad *Hamlet*, staged in 1954, only a year after Stalin's death. The film's ending can be viewed as allegory: the tyrannical Claudius/Stalin is replaced by the more liberal Fortinbras/Khrushchev, whose 'thaw' partially cleanses rotten Denmark/Russia. How ironic, therefore, that this version was released in the year that Leonid Brezhnev's harsher regime took hold.

Director and lead actor neatly balance the politics with a mixture of internalised and externalised emotions; some soliloquies are delivered quietly in voiceover, others out loud with unrestrained passion. Smoktunovsky starts distracted, moves through dazed disbelief after the Ghost's revelations and on to self-knowledge as he embraces the role of avenger, accompanied by engaging reminders of his mislaid mirth. More than any other screen Hamlet, Smoktunovsky is a completely changed man after his pirate adventure, so that his conversation with a plump, bald grave-digger becomes remarkably life-affirming.

The rhythms of Hamlet's thoughts are matched by wonderfully fluid camera movement, particularly in his frequent walks on clifftop fortifications, although Kozintsev over-uses fluttering banners, scudding clouds and crashing waves to symbolise the mental turmoil expressed by the verse (Pasternak's translation is subtitled with Shakespeare's English) and by supple music from Shostakovich, who had scored Kozintsev's *Hamlet* and *King Lear* in the theatre. The orchestra plays full tilt to accompany the Ghost, and panting woodwind drives an exhilarating stampede of courtiers after Claudius flees the outdoor 'Mousetrap', a night-time scene lit with the same moody precision as the interiors. Shostakovich devises a string lament for the madness of eighteen-year-old Anastasia Vertinskaya's fragile, blonde Ophelia, who aches with love for Hamlet and is Elsinore's second prisoner, attended by wizened old women, more like jailers than maids, especially at the unforgettable moment when they lock her into a black iron corset after Polonius's murder.

Hamlet overflows with these inspired touches, and the last transforms our connection to Elsa Radzin's elegant, oddly inscrutable Gertrude. Textual cuts make her a peripheral figure who comes tantalisingly close to surviving. She is enjoying a stroll when the cannon blast that opens the fencing match arouses her curiosity and sends her back indoors. It is suddenly clear that Claudius, true to his secretive nature, has not even told his wife of the bout, and her 'casual slaughter' becomes even more ironic than in the play.

Dir: Grigori Kozintsev; **Prod:** Lenfilm; **Scr:** Grigori Kozintsev, based on Boris Pasternak's *Hamlet* translation; **DOP:** Jonas Gritzius; **Editor:** E. Makhankova; **Score:** Dmitri Shostakovich; **Main Cast:** Innokenti Smoktunovsky (Hamlet), Elsa Radzin (Gertrude), Mikhail Nazvanov (Claudius), Anastasia Vertinskaya (Ophelia), Yuri Tolubeyev (Polonius), Stepan Oleksenko (Laertes), Vladimir Erenberg (Horatio).

Johnny Hamlet (*Quella sporca storia nel west*)

Italy, 1968 – 91 mins

Enzo G. Castellari

Johnny Hamlet opens as handsome Johnny Hamilton (Andrea Giordana), a Confederate soldier returning from the Civil War, dreams of his father and awakes near an actor reciting 'To be, or not to be' on a beach. Johnny rides to a cavernous cemetery, where a bibulous grave-digger shows him the grave of his murdered father, Chester. Johnny is threatened by Ross and Guild, henchmen for his uncle, Claude (creepy, blond Horst Frank), and rescued by his middle-aged guardian angel, Horaz (suave, moustachioed Gilbert Roland).

Johnny returns home to Ranch Elseñor (a lovely Tex-Mex-Shakespearean pun), sees his mother, Gertie, romping with Claude, and demands to know why she remarried without 'letting father's bed cool down'. He is reunited with his pre-war girlfriend, Emily, daughter of the corrupt local sheriff, Polomo.

Within half an hour, Castellari has merged *Hamlet* counterparts with spaghetti Western ingredients patented by Sergio Leone: whip-crack gunshots and deafening punches, thick tan make-up and saturated colours, extreme eye-line close-ups and crude, poorly dubbed acting; sadly, Leone's energetic pacing, wit and visual flair are absent. There is one stab at *Hamlet*-esque philosophy (Horaz's 'No one gets to choose death, but the life . . . that's what you choose'); the rest is violence.

Johnny's one-night stand with a travelling actress leads him to Santana, the Mexican bandit supposedly murdered by Claude for killing Chester, and he learns that Claude killed Johnny's father for $300,000 in gold that he was transporting to the Texan Confederate army. Claude kills Emily and frames Johnny for the murder. Santana's men attack Elseñor, where Claude kills the bandit and fatally wounds Gertie. Horaz, having saved Johnny from certain death five times, shoots dead the sheriff and Guild. Johnny kills Ross and, finally, Claude. This 'Dirty Story of the West' (the Italian title) ends as the grave-digger, like Fortinbras, surveys the Elseñor carnage and invites our departing heroes to contact him 'if you clean up another place'.

Dir: Enzo G. Castellari; **Prods:** Ugo Guerra, Elio Scardamaglia; **Scr:** Tito Carpi, Francesco Scardamaglia, Enzo G. Castellari; **DOP:** Angelo Filippini; **Editor:** Tatiana Casini Morigi; **Score:** Alessandro Alessandroni, Francesco De Masi, Audrey Nohra; **Main Cast:** Andrea Giordana (Johnny Hamilton), Françoise Prévost (Gertie Hamilton), Horst Frank (Claude Hamilton), Gabriela Grimaldi (Emily), Giorgio Sammartino (Sheriff Polomo), Gilbert Roland (Horaz).

Hamlet
Spain/UK, 1976 – 67 mins
Celestino Coronado

Royal College of Art student Celestino Coronado's $5,000 experimental video, shot almost entirely in close-ups, with the blacked-out backgrounds and minimal props of a studio theatre production, is one of the most memorable screen *Hamlet*s, entirely thanks to its casting.

Coronado presents Hamlet's divided personality in the shape of blue-eyed, identical twins David and Anthony Meyer, sinewy, frequently naked figures. Anthony is bathed in demonic red light as he torments the pallid, sleeping David: 'I am thy father's spirit.' The haunting thus becomes a nightmare, accompanied by the unsettling synthesizer chords of Carlos Miranda's score. In soliloquy and dialogue, Hamlet literally talks to himself, as when the 'sweet' Prince tells Ophelia 'I did love you once' only for his 'evil' twin to leap onto his back and yell: 'I loved you not!' He appears to fight himself rather than Laertes at Ophelia's graveside and at the climax.

Duality also inspires the second casting coup: Helen Mirren plays a coquettish Ophelia and, with bouffant curly hair, thick rouge and a lower pitch to her voice, a vampish Gertrude. As Hamlet lies in Mirren's lap during the ten-minute 'Mousetrap', we accept, without elaborate editing or trick photography, that both characters co-exist in the same shot. The impression that disgust and desire for Gertrude have so infected Hamlet's feelings for Ophelia that he cannot distinguish between the two women is overwhelming.

Only two other principals are glimpsed: Barry Stanton's bald, corpulent Claudius, clad in gold lamé like a camp circus ringmaster, and Quentin Crisp, in trademark hat and cravat, as Polonius. They, like Gertrude, survive until the final shot of David Meyer on the bare divan where we first saw him, moments after Hamlet says 'To tell my story'.

Coronado returned to Shakespeare with a more expansive, wildly camp ballet film of the Lindsay Kemp Company's *A Midsummer Night's Dream* (1984), featuring David Meyer as Lysander.

Dir/Prod/Scr: Celestino Coronado; **DOPs:** Dick Perrin, Robina Rose; **Editors:** Richard Melling, Derek Wallbank; **Score:** Carlos Miranda; **Main Cast:** David and Anthony Meyer (Hamlet/Ghost/Laertes), Helen Mirren (Gertrude/Ophelia), Barry Stanton (Claudius), Quentin Crisp (Polonius), Vladek Sheybal (Player Queen/Lucianus/1st Player).

Hamlet Goes Business
(*Hamlet liikemaailmassa*)
Finland, 1987 – 86 mins (B&W)
Aki Kaurismäki

Possibly influenced by Chabrol's *Ophélia* (p. 29), Finnish writer-director
Aki Kaurismäki's eccentric adaptation satirises capitalism and spoofs
Hamlet. Old Hamlet, president of a Helsinki timber, mining and shipping
empire, is poisoned by his managing director, Klaus, so that he and
Gertrud, already lovers, can marry.

The sweet prince as solipsistic glutton: Pirka-Pekka Petelius in Aki Kaurismäki's *Hamlet Goes Business*

When Hamlet, a horny, gluttonous layabout is ordered to avenge the murder by his father's ghost, he first attempts to block Klaus's plan to sell the business to a Norwegian tycoon in return for control of Swedish Rubber Ducks (board members pass one of the toys around like gold bullion).

Klaus's thugs, Rosencrantz and Guildenstern, escort Hamlet to execution in London, but he kills them before their ferry leaves dock, then accidentally shoots dead Polonius in his mother's bedroom. Ofelia kills herself, Gertrud accidentally eats the poisoned roast chicken that Klaus and Polonius's son, Lauri, send to Hamlet. Hamlet kills Lauri and Klaus, then tells his chauffeur, Simo (Horatio), that he knew Klaus was poisoning his father and upped the dose because he wanted the old man to hurry up and die. Lauri, a spy for the dockers' union, poisons Hamlet to stop him closing the family shipyard, proving that socialists can be just as lethal as industrialists like Klaus.

Kaurismäki complements multiple murders and final-reel, flashback revelation with equally noir-ish black-and-white cinematography; the grey costumes, production design and dialogue mean this should probably be dubbed *film gris*. Elsinore is a vast, faceless office block; every interior is drably furnished; every exterior scene takes place in murky night. Epic extracts from Tchaikovsky and Shostakovich symphonies accompany the hero's clumsy actions, and the greatest amusement comes from an equally bathetic gulf between Shakespeare's language and Kaurismäki's paraphrase. Hamlet's 'I have of late . . . lost all my mirth' becomes 'I feel like spewing all the time'; Polonius's advice to Lauri turns 'Neither borrower nor lender be' into 'Don't repay loans too quickly. If the lender dies, you're in pocket.' The acting is wonderfully deadpan, characters unaware their words and actions might seem amusing, and popular Finnish comedian Pirka-Pekka Petelius never varies Hamlet's voice or expression, whether confronted by the ghost or worrying about his weight.

All the men are portly, sick with self-love, utterly unappealing, and yet the women generate great sympathy. Gertrud fell into adultery after enduring years in which old Hamlet displayed 'no more passion than he would to a set of winter tyres'. Ofelia is pimped by her avaricious father and insulted by Hamlet, who lusts after her, whereas she adores him. Her suicide, drowning in the bath after swallowing sleeping pills, is shocking. Outinen plays a supermarket checkout girl in Kaurismäki's *Shadows in Paradise* (1986) and a rejected daughter stuck in a dead-end job in *The Match Factory Girl* (1990), so Ofelia's fate, like Hamlet's doomed plotting, aligns both characters with the director's peculiar cinematic world of loser heroes and mistreated, passive heroines.

Dir/Prod/Scr: Aki Kaurismäki; **DOP:** Timo Salminen; **Editor:** Raija Talvio; **Score:** Elmore James, Dmitri Shostakovich, Pyotr Ilyich Tchaikovsky; **Main Cast:** Pirka-Pekka Petelius (Hamlet), Elina Salo (Gertrud), Esko Salminen (Klaus), Kati Outinen (Ofelia), Esko Nikkari (Polonius), Kari Väänänen (Lauri), Puntti Valtonen (Simo).

Hamlet
US, 1990 – 135 mins
Franco Zeffirelli

Rumours that Mel Gibson was to play Hamlet – Mad Max as the 'mad' Prince – were initially dismissed by *The Independent* as 'no more than a spicy practical joke'. Franco Zeffirelli knew better. Watching Gibson contemplate suicide as a disturbed cop in *Lethal Weapon* (1987) had convinced him that the star could play the Dane, and he knew this would create another opportunity to bring Shakespeare to a mass audience. Gibson, like James Cagney (p. 139) and Marlon Brando (p. 73) before him, sensed that Shakespeare might bring the kudos never accorded to his mainstream tough-guy roles. The pair's handsome $15m movie vindicated Zeffirelli's populist instincts with a $20m US gross. It offers compelling moments while barely scratching the surface of the play.

To keep to 135 minutes, more than 60% of the text was ditched ('Frankly, Franco, this ain't cutting; it's axplay,' cried *Vogue*), with the opening scene and the Fortinbras subplot among the casualties. The script, closely modelled on Olivier's *Hamlet* (1948, p. 23), which Zeffirelli adored, ensures that Gibson dominates virtually every scene (even appearing at points where Shakespeare kept Hamlet off stage), and leaves him only a handful of the most demanding speeches. With no cars or armed crooks to pursue, Gibson chases words. Few soliloquies or conversations pass without the bearded, nimble Prince running up or down stairs, or along the Elsinore battlements (Dunnottar and Blackness Castles in Scotland, and Dover Castle, Kent). He almost stabs Rosencrantz (Michael Maloney) with a barbecue skewer, half-throttles him with a recorder and demonstrates jokey prowess with three different swords in the fencing match. Contemplation be damned; a performer with Gibson's relish for athletic screen violence was never going to 'lose the name of action'.

He handles the verse competently, in a semi-convincing English accent. His dazzling blue eyes dart expressively and he is overwhelmed with grief and disgust when he confronts Gertrude in her bedroom, some simulated bump'n'grind pushing Olivier's Oedipal interpretation to a more explicit extreme than was permissible in 1948. Otherwise, this Hamlet never stands still or speaks long enough, and with sufficient meaning, for us to see inside his head or heart – or care when he dies.

The Prince's melancholy is slightly at odds with the sunshine, seagulls and windswept heather of the coastal exteriors (a stark contrast with Olivier's misty monochrome). As always with Zeffirelli, the production design looks faultlessly authentic, and the medieval outfits and décor brought Oscar nominations for costume design and the art direction by the great Dante Ferretti (later to design *Titus*, p. 265). Yet you would happily sacrifice 'colour' for more complex portrayals from the other actors, to whom one imagines Zeffirelli having said: 'You're allowed one personality trait each.' Glenn Close's Gertrude, with haughty English accent, remains simply a lusty widow, unable to keep her hands off Claudius. Denied the King's great confessional soliloquy, Alan Bates makes him a raucous, Henry VIII caricature. Helena Bonham Carter's distracted, fidgety Ophelia seems half-gone from the outset, lessening our shock when she really loses her mind, and Ian Holm's Polonius is an absurdly gnomic chatterbox. Only Paul Scofield's despairing Ghost retains enough of his lines to make an affecting impression.

If this were your first encounter with a play often acclaimed as the greatest ever written, and you were unaware how much had been discarded, you would probably come away wondering what all the fuss was about. Even Gibson's voice coach, Julia Wilson-Dickson, admitted: 'It is, slightly, the comic-book version.'

Dir: Franco Zeffirelli; **Prod:** Dyson Lovell; **Scr:** Christopher De Vore, Franco Zeffirelli; **DOP:** David Watkin; **Editor:** Richard Marden; **Score:** Ennio Morricone; **Main Cast:** Mel Gibson (Hamlet), Glenn Close (Gertrude), Alan Bates (Claudius), Helena Bonham Carter (Ophelia), Ian Holm (Polonius), Nathaniel Parker (Laertes), Stephen Dillane (Horatio), Michael Maloney (Rosencrantz).

Rosencrantz & Guildenstern Are Dead
UK, 1990 – 118 mins
Tom Stoppard

Tom Stoppard originally sold the screen rights to *Rosencrantz and Guildenstern Are Dead*, the stage comedy which made his name, soon after its 1967 premières in the West End and on Broadway. He wrote a screenplay for MGM, then saw the project languish for twenty years until the rights were bought back and he rewrote the script and filmed it in what was then still Yugoslavia.

Film and play view the events of *Hamlet* entirely from the point of view of the Prince's doomed friends as they travel to Elsinore, kick their heels 'off stage', and sail to England. Tim Roth's irritable, sarcastic Guildenstern, who's not as clever as he thinks he is, and Gary Oldman's garrulous, goofy Rosencrantz, who's not as dumb as he appears, muse on why they have been summoned and how to plumb the madness of Iain Glen's mild-mannered, romantic Hamlet. Rosencrantz considers mortality in a rambling, banal equivalent of 'To be, or not to be', and keeps asking who he is, because Stoppard's most persistent running joke – spun from the moment in *Hamlet* when Gertrude reverses Claudius's 'Thanks, Rosencrantz and gentle Guildenstern' – is that neither they, nor anybody else at court knows which is which.

Stoppard likened this shabby, oddly likeable pair to 'a Shakespearean Laurel and Hardy or Abbott and Costello', although their clipped, question-and-answer routines are more like the idle chatter of Vladimir and Estragon in Samuel Beckett's *Waiting for Godot*: beautifully timed, inconsequential and better suited to stage than screen.

Conscious that theatrical duologues might not captivate a cinema audience, Stoppard introduces and over-indulges a new gag in which Rosencrantz casually makes 'scientific' discoveries, including steam power, gravity and the hamburger. Yet no matter how often he sends the pair clattering up and down flights of wooden stairs in a suspiciously deserted castle, his methods, as the *Independent on Sunday* noted, 'still reek of the stage'.

About 250 lines of Shakespeare are retained, to show the duo quizzing the Prince and to add a new layer of covert observation to *Hamlet*'s copious eavesdropping. Our heroes listen in on Hamlet, Donald Sumpter's brusque Claudius and Joanna Roth's doll-like Ophelia, and inadvertently cause the death of Ian Richardson's twittering Polonius.

The better you know *Hamlet*, the more enjoyable such moments are, and the same applies when the rather mysterious players whom Rosencrantz and Guildenstern first meet en route to Elsinore arrive there and précis *Hamlet*'s opening and closing sections in the middle of the film, with deft mime and puppetry from French and Eastern European actors. A bearded, English-accented Richard Dreyfuss (a late replacement for Sean Connery) plays their flamboyant, all-knowing leader with gusto and delivers a droll running commentary on the rules of Shakespearean tragedy.

Stoppard places the players on the ship bound for England, to introduce one final, bizarre twist. Rosencrantz reads aloud the letter ordering Hamlet's execution, the Prince overhears and replaces it with the order to kill his friends. After the pirate attack (the film's most cinematic sequence), Dreyfuss reads Hamlet's letter and on reaching England Rosencrantz and Guildenstern, still baffled by their fate, are strung up not by the king, but by the players.

Dir/Scr: Tom Stoppard; **Prods:** Michael Brandman, Emanuel Azenberg; **DOP:** Peter Biziou; Editor: Nicholas Gaster; **Score:** Stanley Myers; **Main Cast:** Gary Oldman (Rosencrantz), Tim Roth (Guildenstern), Richard Dreyfuss (The Player), Iain Glen (Hamlet), Joanna Miles (Gertrude), Donald Sumpter (Claudius), Joanna Roth (Ophelia), Ian Richardson (Polonius), Vili Matula (Horatio).

Hamlet
US/UK, 1996 – 243 mins
Kenneth Branagh

Armed with $15m and every line of the play, Kenneth Branagh made the longest Shakespeare movie in history. Here, at last, a director did justice to the domestic and political plots, and to the full depth of Hamlet *and* the supporting characters; the portrayals of Claudius, Ophelia and Polonius alone vindicate Branagh's faith in the uncut text used when he starred in a Royal Shakespeare Company *Hamlet* directed by Adrian Noble in 1992–3.

He moves the action to the late nineteenth century and Alex Byrne's costumes evoke Ruritania. For the snowy exteriors, Elsinore is represented by Blenheim Palace, and Alex Thomson's 70mm photography brings out every shimmering detail of Tim Harvey's opulent sets, dominated by a grand hall symbolising luxury and secrecy: chessboard floor lined with mirrored doors opening onto small rooms connected by concealed entrances. The long balconies serve Branagh well in the many 'walk and talk' scenes needed to keep his movie moving, as his restless Hamlet converses with Horatio, Polonius, Rosencrantz and Guildenstern.

The Prince seems remarkably sane, tearfully dedicated to his father's memory while displaying the requisite mean streak, and Branagh's verse-speaking is crisp and fluent, though given to theatrical roaring in soliloquies, ludicrously so when he leads into the Intermission (eighty minutes to go): against a superimposed backdrop of Fortinbras's army marching across an icy plain, he must virtually scream 'How all occasions do inform against me' above Patrick Doyle's Elgar-like and over-used score.

He establishes a strong rapport with Julie Christie's Gertrude, although hers seem an under-written part compared to Claudius, the greatest beneficiary of the unexpurgated text. Derek Jacobi is chillingly composed and the speeches omitted by most other directors help him fashion a disturbingly complex villain.

The screenplay keeps Kate Winslet's Ophelia in view when Shakespeare has forgotten her. A flashback showing her and Hamlet making love introduces shame at having lost her virginity as another strand to her suffering. Her decline from rosy-cheeked happiness to straitjacketed lunacy in a padded cell is devastating. Richard Briers rescues Polonius from the doddery caricature of the Olivier and Zeffirelli films; instead we see a ruthless apparatchik and flawed father, with a taste for young whores. Add a sensitive Laertes from Michael Maloney and Branagh succeeds where briefer adaptations fail, by stressing that *Hamlet* involves the destruction of two families.

If only these engrossing performances did not have to fight against star cameos. 'Oh, look!' you think, here's Jack Lemmon as Marcellus, and Gérard Depardieu as Polonius's spy, Reynaldo, and Charlton Heston as the Player King and Billy Crystal as a Brooklyn-accented grave-digger and Robin Williams as a cartoonish Osric. None lingers long enough to make you forget their stardom and accept their character.

Hamlet is equally hampered by hit-and-miss direction. A thoroughly unnerving 'Get thee to a nunnery' scene and a riveting 'Mousetrap', with the hall converted into a vertiginously raked auditorium, are superb. Yet we must endure a sub-Hammer Horror encounter with the Ghost (Brian Blessed), complete with laughable mini-earthquake, and Branagh cross-cuts awkwardly between the fencing match and an SAS-style assault by Fortinbras's army that is the definition of action for action's sake. Across four hours, then, *Hamlet* grips and infuriates, sometimes from one scene to the next.

Though it won five Academy Award nominations, grosses of $4.7m in America and about $1m in Britain suggested audiences were deterred by mixed reviews and, especially, the running time, which so worried Branagh's backers, Castle Rock Entertainment, that his contract obliged him to deliver a two-and-a-half-hour edit, which was released in several territories.

Dir/Scr: Kenneth Branagh; **Prod:** David Barron; **DOP:** Alex Thomson; **Editor:** Neil Farrell; **Score:** Patrick Doyle; **Main Cast:** Kenneth Branagh (Hamlet), Julie Christie (Gertrude), Derek Jacobi (Claudius), Kate Winslet (Ophelia), Richard Briers (Polonius), Michael Maloney (Laertes), Nicholas Farrell (Horatio).

Hamlet
US, 2000 – 111 mins
Michael Almereyda

After *Romeo + Juliet* (1996) established a precedent for original-text Shakespeare in contemporary America, Michael Almereyda moved *Hamlet* to present-day Manhattan, the setting for his low-budget features *Another Girl, Another Planet* (1992) and *Nadja* (1994).

Denmark becomes the Denmark Corporation, a vaguely defined multinational, headquartered in the high-rise Elsinore Hotel, Times Square, and as Kyle MacLachlan's power-suited Claudius succeeds his

'To be, or not to be . . .': Ethan Hawke's Blockbuster Video soliloquy in Michael Almereyda's *Hamlet*

murdered older brother as CEO and uses public relations to conceal corruption, ruthless commercial values sustain Almereyda's United States of Denmark. 'Global corporate power,' wrote Almereyda in his Preface to the published screenplay, 'is as smoothly treacherous and absolute as anything going on in a well-oiled feudal kingdom.'

His setting was inspired by *The Bad Sleep Well* (p. 27) and *Hamlet Goes Business* (p. 38) and Hamlet's meeting in a bar with Rosencrantz and Guildenstern and the shooting of Polonius are closely modelled on the equivalent scenes in the latter. Where Aki Kaurismäki mocked the play with banal dialogue and drab *mise en scène*, Almereyda retains Shakespeare's verse (heavily and skilfully edited), and finds visual poetry in chrome and glass skyscrapers, or the sleek interiors of Gideon Ponte's production design, dominated by shades of blue, red and green.

With Carter Burwell supplying moody electronic and orchestral themes, Almereyda roams effectively around the city, using a supermarket, a laundromat, JFK Airport and the coiled walkways of the Guggenheim Museum. He sacrifices the sense of imprisonment created in other screen *Hamlet*s (notably Olivier's and Kozintsev's), demonstrating instead how an individual, regardless of class and wealth, might feel as trapped by a metropolis as by castle walls. Such loneliness and alienation were stock-in-trade qualities for Ethan Hawke, whose self-pitying 'slacker' in *Reality Bites* (1994) and introspective student in *Before Sunrise* (1995) both share some of Hamlet's traits.

Aged twenty-nine, and convinced, he wrote, that 'Hamlet was always much more Kurt Cobain than Sir Laurence Olivier', Hawke is the 'grunge' prince: a poor little rich kid wearing a goatee and a wool hat, using his trust fund to make experimental digital films (including the 'Mousetrap' as a hilarious short privately screened for Claudius and Gertrude). He is slightly obnoxious, fatally missing the character's great wit and mumbling infuriatingly, even during 'To be, or not to be', ironically delivered in the 'Action' aisle of a Blockbuster Video store.

As well as introducing so many film-making references that some academics have interpreted this adaptation in part as autobiographical metaphor (Hamlet/Almereyda the indie film-maker bravely takes on the all-powerful Denmark/Hollywood system), Almereyda uses *Hamlet*'s eavesdropping and covert missives to comment on twenty-first-century media saturation, placing gadgetry in virtually every scene: fax machines, phones, answerphones, TV screens. Hamlet delivers one speech via his laptop; CCTV provides our first glimpse of the Ghost (a stern Sam Shepard as a tactile spirit in the mould of 1990's *Truly, Madly, Deeply* (1990) mould); Ophelia wears a wire-tap for the 'Get thee to a nunnery' scene and the film ends, like *Romeo + Juliet*, on a TV newscaster, who introduces Fortinbras as Denmark Corp.'s new boss.

All these transpositions are effective, and around Hawke's dull centre revolve strong performances from Diane Venora, evoking her Lady Capulet in *Romeo + Juliet* as a sensual, disarmingly contented Gertrude (as in Olivier, she knowingly drinks the poison), Liev Schreiber, a commanding Laertes, and Bill Murray, whose middle-aged Polonius is part buffoon, part concerned father. Completing her Shakespearean hat-trick, as Ophelia Julia Stiles is more mannered than in *10 Things I Hate about You* (p. 241) or *O* (p. 180).

Yet all too often one is distracted by glaring incongruity in the language or action. 'Watching the movie requires a certain suspension of disbelief,' the director acknowledged, hoping we would 'forgive words that don't seem right', yet that is impossible when, for example, Hamlet's pals Marcella and Bernardo address him as 'My Lord', not in ironic frat-boy endearment, but in earnest. When we are asked to accept that Hamlet and Laertes are both accomplished fencers for the climactic rooftop confrontation, much of the story's hard-won credibility evaporates.

Almereyda recalled how language problems contributed to his film earning the second-worst test preview scores in Miramax history (it eventually limped to a US gross of $1.5m, and took $130,000 in Britain) and concludes his Preface by calling this 'a collage, a patchwork of intuitions, images and ideas'. Judged against his own metaphor, some components blend to give the impression of a coherent whole, others come disastrously unstuck.

Dir/Scr: Michael Almereyda; **Prods:** Andrew Fierberg, Amy Hobby; **DOP:** John De Borman; **Editor:** Kristina Boden; **Score:** Carter Burwell; **Main Cast:** Ethan Hawke (Hamlet), Diane Venora (Gertrude), Kyle MacLachlan (Claudius), Julia Stiles (Ophelia), Bill Murray (Polonius), Liev Schreiber (Laertes), Karl Geary (Horatio).

The Banquet (Ye Yan)
China/Hong Kong, 2006 – 129 mins
Feng Xiaogang

The Banquet clothes the skeleton of *Hamlet* with the intrigues, doomed romance and gravity-defying *wuxia* action of Zhang Yimou's *Hero* (2002) and *House of Flying Daggers* (2004). In a nameless Chinese kingdom in AD 904, Crown Prince Wu Luan (solemnly played by Daniel Wu) loves Wan (Zhang Ziyi), but heads south when his father claims her as Empress, losing himself in music and dance (equivalent to Hamlet's studies at Wittenberg). Three years later, his uncle, Li, murders the Emperor and usurps the throne. His black-masked warriors massacre Wu Luan's fellow singer–dancers at a woodland bamboo theatre; forewarned by Wan, the Prince escapes and returns to the palace. Silent communion with his father's helmet motivates revenge frustrated less by Hamlet-esque hesitation than the sexual and political desires of others; in this ensemble-oriented adaptation, all six *Hamlet*-derived characters make life-or-death decisions.

Li craves Wan's 'rare beauty' more than empire. She agrees to marry him partly because Li is a greater lover than his brother and to protect Wu Luan, whom she still loves. The Prince mistrusts her remarriage ('Did I come back to grieve for my father or to congratulate my stepmother?', he asks, in one of the few lines paraphrased from *Hamlet*) and now loves and is adored by Qing (Ophelia), a demure palace attendant whose brother is General Yin Sun (Laertes). Their father is the bearded, sagacious Minister Yin (Polonius), although the Emperor relies more heavily on astrological counsel from his Lord Chamberlain (Zhou Zhonghe).

At the Empress's coronation, Wu Luan leads a mimed re-enactment of his father's murder, his performance skills neatly obviating *Hamlet*'s travelling players. After applauding ironically, Li sends the Prince on a diplomatic mission that is really a death-trap, from which Yin Sun saves him. He returns for a banquet that becomes a Jacobean bloodbath.

Forced to become Wan's accomplices to save Qing from her murderous jealousy, Yin and Yin Sun watch Wan hand Li a drink they know is poisoned. He innocently offers it to Qing for performing Wu Luan's favourite love song. She drinks, and perishes in the Prince's arms. He tries to stab the Emperor, who drinks the poison, overwhelmed by fratricidal guilt and Wan's treachery. Wu Luan cuts his hand stopping Yin Sun's poisoned blade inches from Wan's neck; she kills Yin Sun. Revenged, Wu Luan succumbs, whispering 'It is good to be able to die.' After exiling Yin, Wan's reign is cut short by an unseen killer, the blade perhaps hurled by Wu Luan's spirit.

With Tan Dun providing grand themes reminiscent of his Oscar-winning score for *Crouching Tiger, Hidden Dragon*, Feng Xiaogang tracks the characters through sumptuous, candle-lit halls lined with servants and guards and dominated by deep reds – especially Wan's lipstick, wardrobe, bath and bed. The colour matches the blood spilled in several of the wire-assisted, martial-arts 'ballets' choreographed by *Crouching Tiger*'s action director, Yuen Wo-ping. However, only the theatre massacre, Yin Sun's snowbound rescue of Wu Luan and the climax advance the plot, and even if you find the quasi-fantasy nature of *wuxia* fights captivating and not (as I do) risible, the superhuman swordplay repeatedly undermines realistic chamber drama, filled with tense duologues between Li and Wan, Wan and Wu Luan, Wu Luan and Qing, Qing and Yin, Yin and Yin Sun (Wu Luan has no soliloquies).

Zhang's ice-cool Wan is the most comprehensively re-imagined Shakespearean figure. Because she is the Prince's stepmother, four years his junior, *Hamlet*'s Oedipal strain disappears, and Gertrude becomes a childless, scheming femme fatale, reminiscent of Beatrice-Joanna, villainess of Middleton and Rowley's *The Changeling* (1622).

Dir: Feng Xiaogang; **Prods**: Wang Zhongjun, John Chong; Scr: Shen Heyu, Qiu Gangjian; DOP: Zhang Li; **Editor**: Liu Miaomiao; **Score**: Tan Dun; **Main Cast**: Daniel Wu (Prince Wu Luan), Zhang Ziyi (Empress Wan), Ge You (Emperor Li), Zhou Xun (Qing Nu), Ma Jingwu (Minister Yin), Huang Xiaoming (Yin Sun), Zhou Zhonghe (Lord Chamberlain).

Henry IV (play synopsis)

Part 1: The rebel Earl of Bolingbroke has become King Henry IV. Noblemen loyal to the murdered King Richard II, led by the Earl of Worcester, the Earl of Northumberland and his impetuous son, Harry 'Hotspur', set out to depose Henry and place Hotspur's brother-in-law, Edmund Mortimer, on the throne.

Meanwhile, Henry's elder son and heir, Prince Hal, devotes himself to wine, women and song with his friend Poins, the fat, cowardly Sir John Falstaff, and other wastrels at Mistress Quickly's tavern, the Boar's Head, in Eastcheap, London. Falstaff and co. rob some Canterbury-bound pilgrims, but are ambushed by Hal and Poins. Hal then saves Falstaff from arrest for the robbery.

Hal and Falstaff are called to arms as civil war looms. At the Battle of Shrewsbury, Hal saves his father's life and kills Hotspur. Falstaff, who has played dead, claims he killed Hotspur. Henry's army is victorious.

Part 2: Henry faces another rebellion, led by the Archbishop of York and supported by Northumberland. Hal continues in his 'loose behaviour' but is changing. Falstaff travels to Gloucestershire to recruit soldiers and spends time reminiscing with an old friend, Justice Shallow. Renewed civil war is avoided when Prince John tricks the rebels into dispersing their armies, then has them arrested. Just before the King's death Hal promises his father that he will mend his ways. Falstaff attends Hal's coronation as King Henry V at Westminster Abbey, confident of preferment. Hal contemptuously rejects him.

Chimes at Midnight
Spain/Switzerland, 1966 – 119 mins (B&W)
Orson Welles

Winner of the Grand Prix at Cannes, *Chimes at Midnight* has a cast of hundreds but is essentially about three men. Orson Welles's masterful screenplay, developed from his 1960 Belfast stage production, tailors the *Henry IV* plays to his vision of a tragicomic, triangular love story involving 'the prince, his king-father and Falstaff, who's a kind of foster father.' Evoking Hal's journeys back and forth between Eastcheap and court in richly contrasted monochrome, Welles tells his story with such compassionate verve that you readily forgive the atrocious, disjointed soundtrack (virtually all of the dialogue was post-synched) and accept the improbable landscapes, as the arid plains of southern Spain double for damp Olde England.

Welles's Falstaff, looking every inch Shakespeare's 'huge hill of flesh', with the beard and mottled nose of a boozy Santa, is at home amid the heavy timbers and giggling blonde whores of the Boar's Head. He drawls self-mocking jokes, refuses to pay Margaret Rutherford's long-suffering, jittery Mistress Quickly, and is waited on by a cute page (Beatrice Welles, the director's then nine-year-old daughter). Thanks to a warm cameo from Jeanne Moreau, you are instantly convinced that Doll Tearsheet loves this dissolute coward 'with a most constant heart', and there is an appropriately pathetic undertone to his devotion to Keith Baxter's calculating Hal, so that the comic set pieces of *Part 1* – the robbery of the pilgrims, wondrously filmed in a wintry, sunlit wood, and the mock-trial of Falstaff – are suitably heavy with foreboding.

Reprising his role from the stage *Chimes*, Baxter scarcely disguises Hal's contempt for Falstaff, each whispered soliloquy paving the way towards betrayal and ascension to the throne, which seems the coldest, loneliest place on earth, as the wide, low angles of the Boar's Head are set against the forbidding height of Henry's court (Spain's Soria Cathedral). The majestic, careworn John Gielgud, breath condensing in

'Do not thou when thou art king hang a thief.': Falstaff (Orson Welles), right, appeals to Hal (Keith Baxter) in Welles's *Chimes at Midnight*

the chilly air, is overcome with Henry's paternal regret and guilt at his role in Richard II's death.

Characters from the two worlds finally collide (midway through) in the astonishing Battle of Shrewsbury, shot in a Madrid park. For ten minutes, knights and soldiers hack and batter with lances, swords and clubs. Close-ups of writhing, muddy deaths alternate with shots of Falstaff encased in armour, frantically waddling between hiding places; somehow, his absurd cowardice enhances rather than diminishes the battlefield horrors.

Two great scenes round out Hal's symmetrical travels between 'king-father' and 'foster father': first, reconciliation with the dying Henry, then the shattering rejection of Falstaff at his coronation. Shakespeare ends *Part 2* here, but Welles has Rutherford deliver Quickly's account of Falstaff's final hours from *Henry V*, and the unforgettable last shot is of 'plump Jack' in his coffin, pulled away from the Boar's Head by Pistol and Bardolph.

Welles's filleting of Shakespeare is a miraculous feat of adaptation. He lifts comic scenes featuring Alan Webb's rickety Shallow from *Part 2* and fits them seamlessly into *Chimes* while it is still depicting events from *Part 1*. He discards most of the rebels from *Part 1*, and ignores the Archbishop's revolt, so, sadly, we miss out on *Part 2*'s compelling scenes of political opportunism, and only two of Henry's opponents leave an imprint: Fernando Rey's sinister Mortimer, and Norman Rodway's raucous Hotspur. Historical omissions are glossed over by Ralph Richardson's voiceover extracts from Shakespeare's main source, Holinshed's *Chronicles*.

Welles's magpie approach ensures that *Chimes* should never be recommended to anyone seeking a comprehensive version of the *Henry IV* plays. One doubts that anyone will ever capture their essence with greater or more affecting economy.

Dir/Scr: Orson Welles; **Prods:** Emiliano Piedra, Angel Escolano; **DOP:** Edmond Richard; **Editors:** Elena Jaumandreu, Fritz Muller, Peter Parasheles; **Score:** Francesco Lavagnio; **Main Cast:** Orson Welles (Sir John Falstaff), Keith Baxter (Prince Hal), John Gielgud (King Henry IV), Tony Beckley (Poins), Jeanne Moreau (Doll Tearsheet), Margaret Rutherford (Mistress Quickly), Norman Rodway (Hotspur), Fernando Rey (Mortimer), Alan Webb (Justice Shallow).

My Own Private Idaho
US, 1991 – 104 mins
Gus van Sant

In the 1980s, Gus van Sant was already writing a screenplay about gay hustlers in Portland, Oregon, when he saw Welles's *Chimes at Midnight* and was inspired to make *My Own Private Idaho* double as a partial, modern-day adaptation of *Henry IV*.

We first encounter gay hustler Mike (River Phoenix) turning tricks in Seattle, struggling with narcolepsy and haunted by home-movie memories of his mother, Sharon. He returns home to Portland with best friend Scott (Keanu Reeves), who is straight but has gay sex for money. A cod-medieval theme announces the Falstaffian Bob Pigeon (writer–director and occasional actor William Richert), a middle-aged, obese vagrant in a navy blue bathrobe, and young Budd (a rough substitute for Falstaff's page), as they arrive at the hustlers' squat, the abandoned Sovereign Hotel, 'managed' by elderly, frail Jane Lightwork (the Mistress Quickly figure).

Characters begin paraphrasing or quoting *Henry IV, Part 1*, and, though poorly spoken (Reeves and Phoenix both mumble) and wildly incongruous amid the predominant colloquialism, the language does at least clarify Scott's Prince Hal status and Mike's much looser association with Poins. Scott is the son of Portland's ailing, wheelchair-bound Mayor, Jack, who laments his son's wasteful association with 'street denizens'. On his twenty-first birthday in a week's time Scott will inherit a fortune and stun his parents by reforming after three years as a 'fuck-up'.

Bob leads the boys in a night-time mugging of small-time rock promoters (the film's Gads Hill robbery), then Scott and Mike ambush them and expose Bob's cowardice. The Mayor sends the police to the Sovereign (echoing the Lord Chief Justice's raid on the Boar's Head).

After twenty-five minutes of scene-for-scene adaptation, the Shakespeare is abandoned as abruptly as it was introduced. Mike and Scott visit Mike's drunken older brother, have sex with Hans (Udo Kier), a

German travelling salesman, and fly to Rome, believing Sharon is living there. In fact, she has returned to the US, but Scott falls in love with a beautiful Italian girl, Carmella, brings her back to Portland and, after claiming his dead father's fortune, rejects Bob in a restaurant version of the *Henry IV* coronation scene. Bob dies of a broken heart, mourned by Lightwork (paraphrasing Quickly's speech from *Henry V*). Mike hits the road again.

None of the transpositions work. Hal's conversion, burdened by royal heredity, is all too convincing; Scott seems more likely to squander his dad's cash than use it to preserve the family empire (van Sant even has him describe his transformation as 'incredible'). The Hal–Falstaff–Henry relationship, so painstakingly constructed by Shakespeare, is reduced to Scott's unambiguous declaration: 'Bob was fucking in love with me. I love Bob more than my mother and my father.' Henry IV is haunted for years by Richard II's death; the Mayor alludes vaguely to 'God trying to get back at me for something I've done.'

While editing the film, which eventually took $6.4m in the US and $1.7m in the UK, van Sant deleted a seven-minute version of Falstaff's mock-trial (now featured on the Region 1 DVD), because, he said, the *Henry IV* scenes 'were becoming like a movie within the movie', yet they remain exactly that. Surely baffling to anyone unfamiliar with its source, the Shakespearean content could be removed to create a perfectly coherent, though not especially engaging seventy-minute feature: part love story (Mike's unrequited passion for Scott; Scott's love for Carmella), part road movie (Mike's cross-country quest).

Dir/Scr: Gus van Sant; **Prod:** Laurie Parker; **DOPs:** Eric Alan Edwards, John Campbell; **Editor:** Curtiss Clayton; **Score:** Bill Stafford; **Main Cast:** River Phoenix (Mike Waters), Keanu Reeves (Scott Favor), William Richert (Bob Pigeon), Chiara Caselli (Carmella), Flea (Budd), Tom Troupe (Jack Favor), Sally Curtice (Jane Lightwork), Udo Kier (Hans).

Henry V (play synopsis)

The Chorus appeals to the audience to make up for the limitations of stagecraft by imagining the epic actions described by the actors. King Henry V is convinced by the Archbishop of Canterbury that ancient laws allow him to claim the French throne. France's King Charles refuses to yield to the demands made by Henry's uncle, Exeter, and Henry prepares an invading army. Before his fleet sails from Southampton, he orders the execution of three noblemen who have conspired to murder him.

Landlady Mistress Quickly and Henry's former drinking mates, Bardolph, Pistol and Nym, mourn the death of their beloved friend, Sir John Falstaff, at the Boar's Head Tavern. The three men and a boy, Robin, join the army and in France are caught up in the siege of Harfleur, where the brave Welsh captain, Fluellen, condemns their cowardice. Henry urges his men 'once more unto the breach' and Harfleur's governor surrenders to his threats of bloody destruction.

Anticipating marriage to Henry, Charles's daughter, Princess Katharine, learns basic English from her maid, Alice. Urged on by his arrogant son, the Dauphin, Charles sends a vast army to confront Henry's exhausted soldiers as they retreat to Calais.

Henry rejects the French invitation to ransom himself to avoid battle. Bardolph is executed for robbing a church. That night, Henry wanders, disguised, among common soldiers whose fears make him question his kingly responsibilities. One, Michael Williams, challenges the king to a duel.

Next day, Henry's rousing speech inspires his army – outnumbered five to one – to an astonishing victory in the Battle of Agincourt. Though English casualties are minimal, the French have killed Robin and the other baggage boys, in revenge for which Henry orders the execution of enemy prisoners.

The King quietly settles his argument with Williams. Fluellen humiliates Pistol for being rude about Wales. At the French court, Henry woos Katharine and Charles consents to their marriage, sealing peace between the countries.

Henry V
UK, 1944 – 137 mins
Laurence Olivier

Laurence Olivier's *Henry V* is Shakespeare as propaganda. In 1943, the government believed a film of this most patriotic play would boost morale as British troops fought Hitler. While fulfilling non-operational duties as a Fleet Air Arm pilot, Sub-Lieutenant Olivier was summoned by Jack Beddington, showbusiness propaganda chief at the Ministry of Information. Beddington wanted Olivier to play a Russian engineer in Anthony Asquith's *Demi-Paradise* (1943), a contemporary drama designed to shed sympathetic light on Britain's Soviet allies, and then turn his attentions to *Henry V*.

Olivier and *News Chronicle* theatre critic Alan Dent reduced the play from 3,000 to 1,500 lines. William Wyler, Terence Young and Carol Reed all declined Olivier's invitation to direct before he decided to take charge himself, with experienced editor Reginald Beck as his assistant on what was a vast project for any director, let alone a débutant. *Henry V* cost the Rank Organisation £475,000, the most yet spent on a British feature, and when it opened in November 1944 it had reviews to match ('Easily the most important film ever made,' *Sunday Pictorial*) and was a major hit, its success boosted by local councils paying for school parties; in America in 1946 it grossed $1m and Olivier received a Special Oscar. It was the first Shakespeare sound feature to achieve such critical *and* commercial success.

The most engaging segment is the first half-hour's vivid depiction of a Globe performance of *Henry V* in 1600, which surely influenced the theatre scenes in *Shakespeare in Love* (1998, p. 227). Raucous groundlings jeer the players; a nervous boy actor dresses up as Princess Katharine. On stage, Felix Aylmer's elderly Archbishop and Robert

(*Opposite page*) 'Cheerly to sea.': The King (Laurence Olivier) sets sail for France in Olivier's *Henry V*

Helpmann's bizarre-looking Ely stumble through the laws of succession and Olivier's nonchalant Henry tosses the crown onto the back of his throne. You anticipate two hours of filmed theatre; until Leslie Banks's Chorus announces 'Unto Southampton do we shift our scene', a curtain dissolves to reveal Henry's flagship at anchor on what is obviously a soundstage, and we soon enter the illusion of Paul Sheriff's out-of-scale depictions of French court and castles, built at Denham Studios and inspired by *Les très riches heures du Jean, duc de Berri*, a fourteenth-century illustrated calendar. They look 'terribly phoney', as cinematographer Robert Krasker observed, yet they show Olivier making a considered filmic response to the play's complex exploration of theatrical artifice. 'Though you are in a cinema,' Olivier seems to tell us, 'I shall make the same appeal as the Chorus made to the play's first audiences: "Let us . . . on your imaginary forces work."'

Dramatically, the sets are aptly insubstantial backdrops for one-dimensional performances: Harcourt Williams's French King is a half-senile fool who swoons when Exeter warns of Henry's approach. His knights are even more effete and vain than the text suggests, and, in true propaganda style, such caricatured villains could never be a match for Olivier's monarch in shining armour. Despite talk of exhausted English troops and impossible odds, despite Olivier's soaring Harfleur and Saint Crispian speeches, this storybook treatment lacks tension and it is a relief when it gives way to the open-air realism of the Agincourt battle (shot in eight weeks in Ennis Kerry, Ireland). Galloping French knights are brought down by arrows unleashed with an unforgettable 'whoosh' by the English archers (whom Shakespeare does not even mention) and there is messy hand-to-hand combat, all spurred on by William Walton's orchestral crescendo.

Victory secured, Olivier goes into reverse gear. We return to studio sets for our last glimpse of fearless, fiery Fluellen (the beetle-browed Esmond Knight, with the broadest of Welsh accents), and Henry's faltering wooing of Renee Asherson's demure Katharine. As the couple join hands, we dissolve back to the Globe, the actors bow and the camera repeats its opening bird's-eye view of an elaborate model of Elizabethan London.

With British troops dying in France, Olivier felt 'shadowed' by patriotic duty, and, though it meant softening Shakespeare's brutally uncompromising exploration of kingship, eliminated everything that might tarnish Henry's image: the treacherous Earls are absent; Harfleur surrenders without Henry threatening to leave its 'naked infants spitted upon spikes'; there is no mention of Bardolph's execution, no order from Henry that 'every soldier kill his prisoners'.

Yet this sanitised, Technicolor vision of war must have stirred its 1944 audiences – all with relatives, friends or acquaintances in the armed forces – in ways that peacetime viewers can only imagine, especially when Henry celebrates the glory of fighting for one's country, or listens to a young infantryman count the gruesome cost of war and conclude 'there are few die well that die in a battle'. *Henry V*'s opening title offers a reminder of historical circumstances that make it unique among Shakespeare films: 'To the commando and airborne troops of Great Britain, the spirit of whose ancestors it has been humbly attempted to recapture in some ensuing scenes, this film is dedicated.'

Dir/Prod: Laurence Olivier; **Scr:** Alan Dent, Laurence Olivier; **DOP:** Robert Krasker; **Editor:** Reginald Beck; **Score:** William Walton; **Main Cast:** Laurence Olivier (Henry V), Leslie Banks (Chorus), Nicholas Hannen (Exeter), Esmond Knight (Fluellen), Roy Emmerton (Bardolph), Robert Newton (Pistol), Harcourt Williams (King Charles VI of France), Renee Asherson (Katharine), Ivy St Helier (Alice), Max Adrian (Dauphin).

Henry V
UK, 1989 – 137 mins
Kenneth Branagh

From a first-timer of twenty-eight, Kenneth Branagh's *Henry V* was a
stunning debut, winning him Oscar nominations as director and actor,
and the BAFTA for Best Direction. More importantly, *Henry V* took
double its $9m budget in America and Britain; after more than fifteen
years of neglect on both sides of the Atlantic, Shakespeare's cinematic
renaissance had begun.

Accused of hubris by the media for daring to emulate Olivier, Branagh
delivered a film utterly unlike his predecessor's, the immense contrast
never clearer than when the English army retreats to Calais. Richard
Briers's Bardolph stands on a cart in tattered clothes, blood streaked
across his bulbous nose and a noose around his neck. A brief flashback to
Henry IV, Part 1, shows him boozing with Henry and Falstaff at the Boar's
Head. Then, close to tears, the King gives a signal and Bardolph is hauled
aloft, jerking horribly as he dies. Shakespeare deals with this execution by
report only; Olivier omits it. Its depiction by Branagh typifies his bold,
moving concentration on the human cost of war, rather than heroism.
The gritty realism was designed to reflect British ambivalence to military
expeditions seven years after the controversial Falklands conflict, and
though Olivier's film was made in wartime, it is Branagh who more clearly
reveals how Shakespeare's play laid down a template for countless war
movies about twentieth-century conflict.

Many Hollywood and British screenwriters have used a comparable
structure: the build-up to the mission; a comparatively small-scale early
battle (Harfleur); intimate, 'calm-before-the-storm' conversation (Henry's
disguised encounter with Williams and Bates) as prelude to a larger,
climactic burst of action (Agincourt). Like Shakespeare, some war movies
personalise their story with a three-tier dramatis personae: the leaders
making strategic decisions (Henry and Exeter), the junior officers (Fluellen,
MacMorris, Jamy and Gower) and their 'grunts' (Pistol, Nym and the

soldiers who meet the disguised King), preferably leavening life-and-death moments with comic regional tensions (Welsh, Irish, Scottish and English accents compete in Shakespeare; in a Hollywood script it might be New Yorkers vs. Iowa hicks).

Parts of Branagh's night-time Harfleur sequence evoke *All Quiet on the Western Front*, as MacMorris and Fluellen take cover from explosions in a trench, while Agincourt (filmed on a field behind Shepperton Studios) recalls the Shrewsbury carnage in *Chimes at Midnight* (1966, p. 54), as knights and soldiers hack away in agonised slow-motion, the sordid Pistol and Nym loot the dead, and Nym is killed as he steals. The victorious army's overwhelming relief and exhaustion are captured in a magnificent, three-minute tracking shot, which follows Branagh as he carries the murdered Robin (fifteen-year-old Christian Bale) across the corpse-strewn field, and the 'Non Nobis' hymn swells on the soundtrack.

Henry's ragged soldiers look as 'sick and famished' in Phyllis Dalton's Oscar-winning costumes as Shakespeare suggests, and as they trudge through the rain, cinematographer Kenneth MacMillan gives the countryside a murky, medieval feel in tune with Tim Harvey's production design, which includes a spartan French court and grubby Boar's Head, where Judi Dench delivers a heart-rending account of Falstaff's death.

Despite this earthy realism, Branagh confidently has Derek Jacobi's excitable Chorus draw our attention to cinematic illusion, mirroring Shakespeare's highlighting of theatrical artifice. In modern dress, Jacobi turns on the lights of a Shepperton soundstage during his opening speech, appears at Harfleur, after Bardolph's execution and at Agincourt (three moments when voiceovers would have made his contributions less intrusive) and closes the set doors to end the film. Like Olivier with his storybook production design, Branagh keeps faith with the Chorus's opening speech, acknowledging that despite its ability realistically to depict events far beyond the scope of a 'wooden O', film, like theatre, is still illusion.

As actor, Branagh delivers a thoughtful, understated performance,

(*Next page*) 'When I come to woo ladies, I fright them.': the King (Kenneth Branagh) seeks the hand of Princess Katharine (Emma Thompson) in Branagh's *Henry V*

based on his Henry for the Royal Shakespeare Company in 1984. Slight, boyish and, when not rousing his troops, quietly spoken, he is a God-fearing, inexperienced man who initially depends heavily on Canterbury and Exeter, and attains heroic stature almost in spite of himself. He demonstrates Henry's ruthlessness, violently condemning the Southampton conspirators and yelling spittle-flecked threats at the Harfleur governor (though he avoids the 'war crime' of prisoner execution at Agincourt).

He has sterling support, notably from Ian Holm's fierce, tearful Fluellen, Brian Blessed's bellicose Exeter, Paul Scofield's wary French King, and Emma Thompson's skittish Katharine (Thompson and Branagh married soon afterwards). Henry's awkward wooing is amusing *and* affecting, because we know what he has endured. Olivier's King was essentially the same man from first to last; Branagh's undergoes profound transformation.

However, the ending – courtly diminuendo after battlefield crescendo – feels cinematically anti-climactic. When Agincourt is fought on stage with, say, two minutes of carefully rehearsed swordplay or flag-waving flourishes, the drop in dramatic temperature from battle to the (now tedious) comedy of Fluellen and Pistol's leek-eating and the wooing is much less pronounced than on the big screen, where the vivid and prolonged battles of Olivier and Branagh (who cuts the Fluellen/Pistol exchange) feel like natural climaxes, perhaps to be followed by a caption explaining that Henry married Katharine, uniting France and England, and the end credits. Indeed, when 'Non Nobis' started up at one New York screening, some viewers started heading for the exits. This is not to denigrate Shakespeare's beautifully modulated ending, rather to illustrate the contrast between cinemagoers' expectations of *Henry V* the war film, compared to theatregoers' expectations of *Henry V* the history play.

Dir/Scr: Kenneth Branagh; **Prod:** Bruce Sharman; **DOP:** Kenneth MacMillan; **Editor:** Michael Bradsell; **Score:** Patrick Doyle; **Main Cast:** Kenneth Branagh (Henry V), Derek Jacobi (Chorus), Brian Blessed (Exeter), Ian Holm (Fluellen), Richard Briers (Bardolph), Robert Stephens (Pistol), Paul Scofield (King Charles VI), Emma Thompson (Katharine), Geraldine McEwan (Alice), Michael Maloney (Dauphin), Judi Dench (Mistress Quickly).

Julius Caesar (play synopsis)

Roman Emperor Julius Caesar has virtually become a dictator. Infuriated by his excessive power, senators Cassius and Brutus lead a conspiracy against him. After an ominously stormy night, the conspirators meet in Brutus's orchard in the early hours and resolve to kill Caesar in the Senate later that day. Portia, Brutus's wife, begs him to reveal what is going on, and he promises to do so.

Caesar's wife, Calpurnia, has dreamed of his murder and pleads with him to stay at home. Despite having also been warned by a soothsayer to beware this day, the Ides of March, he proceeds to the Senate where the conspirators stab him to death. Brutus, his close friend, is last to strike.

Brutus manages to persuade the angry citizens gathered in the Forum that this was a just assassination. Then Marc Antony, a staunch ally of Caesar's who took no part in his murder, convinces them that Caesar loved ordinary Romans and reveals that the Emperor has bequeathed his estate to them. He turns the mob to violence against the conspirators, who flee Rome. In the ensuing riot, Cinna the poet is mistaken for his namesake, one of Caesar's assassins, and murdered.

Marc Antony joins forces with Octavius, Caesar's nephew and heir, and after deciding which conspirators are to be executed, they pursue Brutus and Cassius's legions to Philippi, in Macedonia. Brutus, who has learned of Portia's suicide, argues with Cassius about honour and is then visited by Caesar's ghost, who says they will meet at Philippi. Cassius leads his troops against Antony and is routed. Brutus, despite initial success against Octavius, is also defeated. Cassius orders his slave to kill him; Brutus throws himself upon his sword. Marc Antony eulogises Brutus as 'the noblest Roman of them all'.

Julius Caesar
US, 1950 – 93 mins (B&W)
David Bradley

Shot on 16mm for just $15,000, the first English-language feature
version of *Julius Caesar* was rightly hailed by the *Los Angeles Daily News*
as 'a triumph of ingenuity and imagination'. David Bradley had already
produced a film of *Macbeth* (1946) at Northwestern University, Chicago,
and again used fellow students as cast and crew, fitting eighteen-hour
shooting days around campus commitments for six months.

His masterstroke was to use Chicago's Romanesque architecture: the
long colonnade of Soldier Field Stadium as the Coliseum; the Rosenwald
Museum of Science and Industry as the Forum; the Elks Veterans
Memorial rotunda as the Senate chamber. All this marble creates a far
more authentic backdrop than the sets built for the 1953 and 1970
*Caesar*s, and Bradley and professional cinematographer Louis McMahon
use it imaginatively, often dwarfing the protagonists against imposing
classical structures. They favour high angles, natural light and shadowy
contrasts, and deliver arresting, varied imagery from the opening shot, a
swirling soothsayer repeating 'Beware the Ides of March!', to the final
silhouette of Marc Antony standing over Brutus's corpse.

Only during the battle sequence, shot on desolate dunes beside Lake
Michigan and driven forward by fanfares and timpani, does Bradley's tiny
budget become obvious. He can deploy only a dozen extras, their
'Roman' helmets remodelled from GI surplus, yet the horrors are more
visceral than in many epics, with brief snatches of close combat and an
almost abstract final montage of fallen soldiers' heads, hands, chests,
discarded swords, shields.

As adapter, Bradley trims intelligently, makes only one damaging cut
(without the debate in Brutus's orchard the conspiracy feels too easily

(*Opposite page*) 'Cry "Havoc", and let slip the dogs of war.': Marc Antony (Charlton
Heston) contemplates revenge in David Bradley's *Julius Caesar*

cemented) and splits the action into two parts, separated in American cinemas by an intermission: 'The Death of Caesar', which ends on Marc Antony crying 'Let slip the dogs of war', and 'The Revenge of Caesar'.

He makes selective, telling use of voiceovers for soliloquies and asides and as narration for flashbacks showing Cassius rescuing Caesar from drowning and the Emperor rejecting the crown. All the men speak with impeccable diction, like so many Edward R. Murrows, and move with statesmanlike grace, although Bradley's monotonous delivery and doughy, Dan Aykroyd-like features make for a weak Brutus. Neither he nor the lean, hollow-eyed Cassius of Grosvenor Glenn seem comfortable with an unquestionably homoerotic take on their impassioned exchange after the revelation of Portia's death. Charlton Heston, a recent Northwestern graduate who was the only actor to be paid ($50 a week) delivers a restrained yet charismatic performance that helped him win his star-making contract from Hal Wallis.

Julius Caesar shared top prize at the Locarno Film Festival and earned Bradley a directing contract from Dore Schary at MGM, but after leaving the studio he made only low-grade fare such as *Dragstrip Riot* (1958). He became a distinguished instructor in Film History and Aesthetics at UCLA and died in 1997.

Dir/Prod/Scr: David Bradley; **DOP:** Louis McMahon; **Score:** John Becker; **Main Cast:** Charlton Heston (Marc Antony), Grosvenor Glenn (Cassius), David Bradley (Brutus), Mary Sefton Darr (Portia), Harold Tasker (Caesar), Helen Ross (Calpurnia), William Russell (Casca).

Julius Caesar
US, 1953 – 120 mins (B&W)
Joseph L. Mankiewicz

In 1952, MGM coupled its substantial $1.7m investment in Shakespeare with one of the most inspired casting decisions in Hollywood history. A year after stunning audiences as macho, mumbling Stanley Kowalski in *A Streetcar Named Desire*, Marlon Brando was to play the 'wise and valiant' Marc Antony. Columnists expressed astonishment, TV comedians impersonated Kowalski's rendition of 'Friends, Romans, countrymen', but the star, declaring himself 'sick to death of being thought of as a blue-jeaned slobbermouth', had decided that *Julius Caesar* must kill his *Streetcar* image. He spent hours imitating recordings by great British Shakespeareans such as Olivier; then, after a disastrous cast read-through, asked Gielgud to record Marc Antony's lines.

Instructed by Mankiewicz to 'stopy copying the goddamn Limeys', he eventually concluded that he must also temporarily set aside the Method insistence on playing emotional subtext, because with Shakespeare 'the *text* is everything'. Thus liberated, suggested producer John Houseman, Brando was able to let the language express all emotion and thought, peaking in the funeral oration.

The first half, however, belongs to the conspirators. In the role that taught him to appreciate 'the fascinating subtleties of screen acting', John Gielgud makes a suitably 'lean and hungry' Cassius and condemns Caesar with such furious eloquence that you cannot blame James Mason's aloof, well-intentioned Brutus, or Edmund O'Brien's cynical, nervy Casca for succumbing. Six-foot-five Louis Calhern gives an ironic edge to the power play: the tallest, most outwardly confident Roman is revealed to be the weakest. Deborah Kerr and Greer Garson can do little with one scene each, though the fault lies not with the stars but with Shakespeare, for giving scant attention to his politicians' wives.

Mankiewicz's taut and assured direction respects Houseman's pre-production injunction not to 'distort Shakespeare's text with cinematic devices'. He does not show Caesar's fainting fit or the conspirators' flight from Rome, eschews adventurous camerawork, and uses Miklós Rózsa's score sparingly, between scenes, so music never distracts from the speeches. He spices the urgent, coldly reasoned plotting with supernatural dread, notably when the blind soothsayer rises up from a crowd and during the spectacular storm before the conspirators' meeting. During the assassination there are no shouts from the killers, nor screams from Caesar, and the silence is as shocking as the sight of these civilised men's pristine togas suddenly stained with blood. Enter Brando to wrest control of plot and film.

Decisively set apart from the other conspirators by his comparative youth, dark robes and tanned, muscular build, Brando first stands beside Caesar's body, steeling himself for revenge. Then, after Mason's Brutus has convinced about 250 braying citizens that the Emperor deserved to die, they give a collective gasp and we see Brando carrying the corpse down the Senate steps.

For the next ten minutes Brando brings Shakespearean rhetoric to life with irresistibly charismatic acting as reaction shots show the rough-looking plebeians falling under his spell. That the remainder of the film cannot sustain the intensity of the conspiracy, the assassination and its aftermath has much to do with a play whose second half feels as anti-climactic here as in every stage and screen production I have ever seen.

There is, nonetheless, much to admire in the second hour. Mankiewicz stages a Western-style Battle of Philippi, as archers and cavalry take up positions high above a valley floor and swoop down on Brutus and Cassius's infantry like Apaches ambushing a wagon train. Gielgud and Mason bring dignity and poignancy to the defeated leaders' suicides.

Great credit must go to Houseman. Having agreed to MGM's demand for budget savings by re-using sets and costumes from its last Roman epic, *Quo Vadis?* (1951), he successfully resisted front-office pressure to shoot in colour. Monochrome photography and austere (and ultimately Oscar-winning) art direction were better suited than lush colour to Shakespeare's cool, clinical drama, and footage of Roman legionaries marching behind eagle-topped standards would, Houseman hoped, remind audiences of newsreels of Fascist and Nazi rallies in Italy and Germany.

When the film opened, the *New York Times* said it surpassed Olivier's *Hamlet* and in Britain the *News Chronicle*'s critic found it 'maddening' to concede that Hollywood had made 'the finest film version of Shakespeare yet'. It lost the Best Picture Academy Award to *From Here to Eternity*, and William Holden in *Stalag 17* beat Brando to Best Actor.

Dir/Scr: Joseph L. Mankiewicz; **Prod**: John Houseman; **DOP**: Joseph Ruttenberg; **Editor**: John Dunning; **Score**: Miklós Rózsa; **Main Cast**: Marlon Brando (Marc Antony), John Gielgud (Cassius), James Mason (Brutus), Deborah Kerr (Portia), Louis Calhern (Caesar), Greer Garson (Calpurnia), Edmund O'Brien (Casca).

Julius Caesar
UK, 1970 – 117 mins
Stuart Burge

'As flat and juiceless as a dead haddock,' said the *New York Times* of
Stuart Burge's second screen *Caesar* (after a 1959 BBC production), and
the *Daily Telegraph* attacked its 'hotch-potch of styles, both acting and
visual'. Unsubtle and garish where Bradley's and Mankiewicz's versions
were thoughtful and restrained, it convinces neither as political thriller
nor historical epic.

Burge was hamstrung by disastrous trans-Atlantic casting. Producer
Peter Snell hoped that including Robert Vaughn and Richard
Chamberlain would bring in fans of their television hits, *The Man from
U.N.C.L.E.* and *Dr Kildare*, yet both men are embarrassingly out of their
depth, and Vaughn's 'English' accent makes him sound like a shifty Cary
Grant. In minor roles, this pair are merely distracting; Jason Robards turns
'the noblest Roman of them all' into the dullest, delivering Shakespeare's
intricate verse as though it were leaden prose, and even managing to
ruin Brutus's two head-to-heads with Cassius (Richard Johnson), scenes
so brilliantly written they should be foolproof. His uninflected American
whine jars against Johnson's measured, Royal Shakespeare Company-
trained English. Robards appears disinterested, Johnson suggests an
empire is at stake.

Twenty-five years later, Charlton Heston would write of Robards's
Brutus in his autobiography, 'I have never seen a good actor so bad in a
good part', though his own performance as Marc Antony is not beyond
reproach. In 1950 we had Heston the aspiring actor, serving the text, in
1970 we have Heston the Academy Award-winning star, playing up to
his reputation by declaiming from the Senate steps like Moses down
from the mountain and (as he would do again in his *Antony and
Cleopatra* (1972, see p. 2) showing off his athletic heroism by
dispatching half-a-dozen enemy soldiers from horse-back during the
Battle of Philippi (an overlong, clumsily edited sequence shot in Spain).

Heston suffers as much as anyone in the absurd costume parade, obliged for the Roman scenes to wear a virulent green number, which, like the pale blue togas and golden cloaks of Brutus and Cassius and the cardboard scenery would look more at home in a stage production of *A Funny Thing Happened on the Way to the Forum*. Burge's direction is equally crude, full of superfluous images and action, and drenching moments of high drama with shamelessly manipulative music. So, when Jill Bennett's almost hysterical Calpurnia describes her dream, the words recap what we've already seen as she writhed in bed: dreadful, superimposed images of rioting and a bust of Caesar weeping blood. Octavius and Antony receive massages as they single out the names of those conspirators who are to be executed, giving Heston a gratuitous opportunity to show off his physique.

The assassination of the vain, pliant Emperor (the least impressive of John Gielgud's screen Shakespeare performances) is a collection of clichés: the camera's vision blurs as Caesar loses consciousness, heartbeats thump on the soundtrack, composer Michael Lewis supplies an overdose of shrill flutes and frantic xylophone. Like everything else in the film, the flashing blades and copious, ketchupy blood have a fraction of the impact achieved in the *Caesar*s of 1950 or 1953.

Dir: Stuart Burge; **Prod:** Peter Snell; **Scr:** Robert Furnival; **DOP:** Ken Higgins; **Editor:** Eric Boyd-Perkins; **Score:** Michael Lewis; **Main Cast:** Charlton Heston (Marc Antony), Richard Johnson (Cassius), Jason Robards (Brutus), Diana Rigg (Portia), John Gielgud (Caesar), Jill Bennett (Calpurnia), Robert Vaughn (Casca).

King Lear (play synopsis)

The ageing King Lear wishes to divide his kingdom between his daughters, Goneril, Regan and Cordelia. Enraged by Cordelia's refusal to match her elder sisters' fawning declarations of love, Lear banishes his youngest child and gives her share to Goneril and Regan. The King of France takes Cordelia as his queen.

Edmund, bastard son of the Duke of Gloucester, convinces him that his legitimate heir, Edgar, is plotting to kill him; Edgar flees. The Duke of Kent, banished by Lear for criticising his rash treatment of Cordelia, disguises himself as a servant and rejoins the King and his beloved Fool, who are staying with Goneril and her husband, the Duke of Albany. When Goneril asks Lear to dismiss most of his 100 knights, he curses her ingratitude and heads for Regan's castle.

Regan and her husband, the Duke of Cornwall, evade Lear by staying with Gloucester. They place Kent in the stocks for beating Goneril's treacherous steward, Oswald. Lear cannot bear this insulting treatment of one of his men, nor Regan's ingratitude. Descending into madness, he strides into the countryside, pursued by Kent and the Fool. Seeking shelter from a storm, they encounter Edgar, disguised as 'Poor Tom', a madman.

Edmund informs Cornwall that Gloucester is in league with Cordelia, who has landed at Dover with a French army. Cornwall gouges out Gloucester's eyes and is fatally wounded by an outraged servant. Oswald is killed by Edgar, who leads his blinded, dying father to Dover.

Albany and Edmund lead British forces to victory against the French. Albany learns by letter of Goneril's lust for Edmund and forces him to fight a challenger. Goneril, knowing that Regan is also desperate to marry Edmund, poisons her. Edgar answers the challenge and fatally wounds Edmund. Regan dies. Goneril, denounced by Albany, kills herself. Edmund dies just before Lear's entry carrying the dead Cordelia, hanged on Edmund's orders. Wailing at her loss, he dies.

King Lear (Korol Lir)
USSR, 1970 – 137 mins (B&W)
Grigori Kozintsev

This outstanding Soviet epic presents *King Lear*'s tragedy as a domestic tale of fathers and children and a political tale of a monarch's relationship to his people. The latter is the key to Kozintsev's approach; cinematically and emotionally, Lear begins as his subjects' god and ends as their helpless equal.

In the quasi-biblical opening sequence, hundreds of shuffling, hooded peasants congregate on rocky ground outside Lear's castle (Ivangorod Fortress, on the Russian/Estonian border). After Yuri Yarvet, slight and white-haired, has divided the kingdom, he appears above the main gate and the masses bow down as to a messiah. During the storm, the hovel one expects to house only 'Poor Tom' is already crammed with

'I think this lady to be my child Cordelia.': Lear (Yuri Yarvet), centre, is reunited with Cordelia (Valentina Shendrikova), as Kent (Vladimir Yemelyanov) looks on, in Grigori Kozintsev's *King Lear*

shivering vagabonds (rather than the drowned rats of Peter Brook's film, p. 82), and Lear suddenly realises that he has shamefully neglected these 'poor naked wretches'. This shattering self-knowledge completes the descent into madness initiated by filial ingratitude.

On a desolate mountain road, Lear passes refugees fleeing homes torched by Edmund's troops, and after their defeat he and Cordelia are cast adrift in a tide of bewildered peasants. This is *Lear* refracting Russia's obsession with the hungry, oppressed proletariat, and on the film's UK release the *Sunday Telegraph* welcomed 'a remarkably successful translation of the play into Communist terms'. Yet, as in his *Hamlet* (1964, p. 31), Kozintsev's great compassion, and some unforgettable performances, renders Shakespeare's family tragedies as forcefully as the national catastrophe, what the director called his 'generalised picture of civilisation heading towards doom' (Kozintsev, 1977).

Yarvet, an Estonian who had to learn Russian to deliver his lines, which were then dubbed by a Moscow actor, Zinovi Gerdt, is cinema's most affectingly restrained Lear. He starts off light-footed, with quick wits and a fierce temper that makes courtiers cower, and his sparkling eyes seem to fade as his life and kingdom disintegrate. With his daughters, the youth and ethereal beauty of Valentina Shendrikova's Cordelia has clearly been resented for years by Galina Volchek's fat, frumpish Regan and Elsa Radzin's sour-faced Goneril; both are shockingly callous.

Oleg Dal's Fool, with the shaven head and half-starved body of 'a boy from Auschwitz' (Kozintsev's words), haunts the film and the director was even fonder of him than Lear; his one notable change to Shakespeare being to bring the Fool back into the story by ending on a shot of the weeping Dal, playing his recorder as soldiers carry Lear's corpse from the battlefield.

Throughout, Kozintsev has a wondrous eye for intelligent detail (for instance, the King of France relies on a whispering interpreter to comprehend the division scene), matched by his control of large-scale action, most notably during the final scenes. The tall, handsome half-brothers, Leonard Merzin's blond, dazed Edgar and Regimastas

Adomaitis's dark, menacing Edmund, fight a thrilling duel, encircled by hundreds of soldiers. Then the officers rushing to save Cordelia are stopped in their tracks by Lear's howls and a shot of her hanging from the noose. Shostakovich's score adds immeasurably to the despair, with its increasingly ironic trumpet fanfare for Lear, fearsome energy in the storm and five-bar 'Call of Death' to greet each character's demise.

All this was the product of extraordinary effort: a year of casting, rehearsals and location-scouting, followed by a freezing, muddy shoot in Ivangorod, the mountains of the Crimea and on a plain near the Caspian Sea. 'What hell it all was!', recalled Kozintsev in his *King Lear: The Space of Tragedy*, one of the great books on film-making and the culmination of his relationship to a play he had first directed on stage in 1941. It was published in Russian in 1973, the year in which Kozintsev died, aged sixtyseven, leaving behind unrealised plans to film *As You Like It*, *Measure for Measure* and *The Tempest*.

Dir/Editor: Grigori Kozintsev; **Prod:** Lenfilm; **Scr:** Grigori Kozintsev, from Boris Pasternak's *King Lear* translation; **DOP:** Ionas Gritsus; **Score:** Dmitri Shostakovich; **Main Cast:** Yuri Yarvet (King Lear), Elsa Radzin (Goneril), Donatas Ban (Albany), Galina Volchek (Regan), Aleksandr Vokach (Cornwall), Valentina Shendrikova (Cordelia), Oleg Dal (Fool), Vladimir Yemelyanov (Kent), Karl Sebris (Gloucester), Leonard Merzin (Edgar), Regimastas Adomaitis (Edmund).

King Lear
UK/Denmark, 1971 – 132 mins (B&W)
Peter Brook

In his second screen *Lear*, following a seventy-five-minute live production
for CBS Television in 1953 (starring Orson Welles), Peter Brook uses
Jutland to make the divided realm of Paul Scofield's bear-like Lear one of
the coldest, most barren places on Earth: dark, windswept, blanketed
with greying snow. Men and women wear thick furs against blizzards
and freezing rain, and inside Goneril and Gloucester's spartan wooden
castles, roaring fires appear to give off little warmth.

In this environment, cruelty seems as much a product of landscape
and climate as human nature. It is not surprising to find savagery here,
and Brook's treatment of violence does not distinguish between villainy
and the 'just' killings committed by Edgar, who dispatches the squealing
Oswald like a caveman sticking a wild boar. Brook cuts Albany's
challenge, which on stage (and in Kozintsev, p. 79) makes Edgar's
appearance thrillingly chivalrous; here he is a black-helmeted avenger
sinking his axe into Edmund's neck. The sisters' off-stage deaths are
shown and, instead of poisoning Regan, Goneril brains her against a
seaside boulder, then hurls herself against a rockface, followed by a
shocking glimpse of Cordelia's neck snapped by a noose. As Lear dies,
further along the beach, Scofield slips slowly out of the film's last shot.

Devoid of music, Brook's approach numbs where it should move,
extinguishing any of the hope inherent in the courageous, humane
interventions of Edgar, Kent and, belatedly, Albany; the *New Yorker*
compared the film to a nihilistic zombie classic: 'Peter Brook's *Night of
the Living Dead*.'

Though the production design is realistic, the camerawork,
composition and editing indicate that for Brook the only appropriate
response to *Lear*'s horrors was fragmentary abstraction. Characters
appear at weird angles or drift in and out of frame and focus, and there
is some forced symbolism. As 'Poor Tom', Edgar resembles Jesus on the

cross, wearing loincloth and crown of hay, though nothing in his character suggests martyrdom. During the storm, as the focus blurs to indicate Lear's mental fog, the 'poor naked wretches' who prick his conscience are drowned rats, not fellow men (as in Kozintsev), so does he (or Brook) now equate humans with vermin? As Cornwall scoops out Gloucester's eye, the screen goes completely dark; at other moments we see only blankness while characters continue speaking, voices from a pitiless void, anticipating the final shot, when nothing has come of 'nothing'.

The film's predominant sound is Scofield's parched, reverberating growl. He had starred in Brook's Royal Shakespeare Company *Lear* in 1962, which, the director's biographer Michael Kustow writes, banished forever 'the archetype of the poor old white-haired patriarch', and his screen portrayal of dementia eschews all sentimentality. You initially feel sympathy for his daughters; playing host to this demanding old man and his raucous knights would be a nightmare. Irene Worth's Goneril is an exceptional performance, her chilly demeanour thawed by feral lust for Ian Hogg's brutish Edmund, whereas Susan Engel's Regan seems too civilised for this primitive world. Jack MacGowran's middle-aged, Irish Fool, who laughs in order not to cry, and Tom Fleming's gruff Kent are the best supporting performances and it is impossible not to admire the unwavering commitment of cast and director to a deeply idiosyncratic interpretation, which inevitably divided critics. *Newsweek* detected 'a kind of fractured greatness'. The *New York Times* accused Brook of doing 'anything for an effect, however nonsensical, as long as every frame proclaims his supremacy over Shakespeare.'

Dir/Scr: Peter Brook; **Prod:** Michael Birkett; **DOP:** Henning Kristiansen; **Editor:** Kasper Schyberg; **Main Cast:** Paul Scofield (King Lear), Irene Worth (Goneril), Cyril Cusack (Albany), Susan Engel (Regan), Patrick Magee (Cornwall), Annelise Gabold (Cordelia), Jack McGowran (Fool), Tom Fleming (Kent), Alan Webb (Gloucester), Robert Lloyd (Edgar), Ian Hogg (Edmund).

Ran
Japan/France, 1985 – 160 mins
Akira Kurosawa

As this dazzlingly photographed transposition of *King Lear* unfolds on the mountain slopes and volcanic plains of Kyushu, Akira Kurosawa astonishes again with the spectacular action that earned him a Best Director Oscar nomination and made *Ran*, at the time, the most expensive Japanese film ever, surpassing the benchmark established by his previous sixteenth-century epic, *Kagemusha* (1980). What makes *Ran* a masterpiece, however, is the skill with which, as in *Throne of Blood* (1957), Kurosawa tailors Shakespeare to Japanese history and culture.

He had pondered the legend of Motonari Mori, a sixteenth-century warlord whose three sons were paragons of goodness, and wondered what might have been if Mori's children had been less virtuous. He found his answer in Shakespeare. Lear's daughters become the three sons of warlord Hidetora, aged seventy (as was Kurosawa when he began the script): Taro is equivalent to Goneril, though lacks her implacable malice; Jiro is as ruthless as Regan and Cornwall; Saburo is the recalcitrant yet devoted Cordelia.

Saburo and Tango, a Kent-like retainer, are banished for challenging Hidetora's decision to cede power to Taro in an open-air division of the kingdom. With the rival factions colour-coordinated by Emi Wada's Academy Award-winning costumes and hierarchically arranged in a circle, this is the first of many scenes in which, as Donald Richie points out in his masterly study, *The Films of Akira Kurosawa* (1996), *Ran*'s compositions are reminiscent of the groupings of figures in Noh theatre. Parts of Toru Takemitsu's score copy the percussion and pauses of Noh music and, as Hidetora, the formidable Tatsuya Nakadai's stylised make-up is based on Noh masks.

Soon after the division, Taro makes his father sign away all power at the immense First Castle – a humiliation utterly contrary to *giri*, Japan's complex system of interpersonal obligations, which places great emphasis

Lear and his fool: Hidetora (Tatsuya Nakadai) and Kyoami (Peter) wander the countryside as outcasts in Akira Kurosawa's *Ran*

on children's respect for elderly parents. In Japanese eyes, Taro's ingratitude is perhaps even more offensive than Goneril's and it is emulated by Jiro, who treats Hidetora with disdain at Second Castle.

By now it has become clear that, unlike Lear, Hidetora is not 'more sinned against than sinning'. His downfall is retribution for having spilled 'an ocean of blood' while suppressing rival families, and Kurosawa summons great pity for two of his victims: Jiro's deeply religious wife, Sué, who watched Hidetora burn her parents alive, and her beautiful brother, Tsurumaru (an amalgamation of Edgar and Gloucester), whose eyes were gouged out by Hidetora, and who finds some solace playing his *fué* (Noh flute). Though they have ample cause to see Hidetora suffer, their profound Buddhist faith has enabled them both to forgive, and it is Taro's wife, Kaede, played by Mieko Harada with extraordinary, quiet menace, who turns this *Lear* into revenge tragedy. Hidetora murdered her father and brother and drove her mother to suicide and, like a younger, sexier version of Asaji in *Throne of Blood*, she manipulates Taro into mistreating his father and, after Jiro has had her husband killed, seduces and marries him so that she can complete Hidetora's destruction.

Yet while the King languishes in the countryside, attended by thirty knights, a dozen concubines and his androgynous, graceful fool, Kyoami (Peter, a transvestite singer hugely popular on Japanese television), a happy ending remains possible. He need only follow Tango's advice and live with Saburo at the home of his father-in-law, Fujimaki (equivalent to the King of France). Having misjudged his son so badly, however, Hidetora asks Tango: 'How could I face him?' The Japanese obsession with not losing face prevents reconciliation, and this twist on the Lear/Cordelia relationship seals Hidetora's fate.

Taking refuge in the Third Castle, he is attacked by his elder sons' troops, and his men are wiped out in an astonishing ten-minute battle. We can only see, not hear, terrible carnage: men hit by musket rounds and flaming arrows, Hidetora's concubines committing *sepuku*. Takemitsu's trumpets, strings and muffled timpani (modelled, at Kurosawa's insistence, on Gustav Mahler's First Symphony) are the only sounds until Taro is shot in the back by Jiro's wily lieutenant, Kurogane (Hisashi Igawa), and the cacophony is suddenly audible. Hidetora staggers from the burning fortress like a soul descending into hell – the most potent and obvious of *Ran*'s many metaphorical images and sounds (distant, ominous thunder in the division scene; blood-red sunsets; Hidetora lost in fog).

In the *Lear*-like storm that follows, Nakadai's make-up changes, the fierce visage of the opening hour gains a deeply lined forehead and red-rimmed eyes, speaking more eloquently of his torment than the script, which gives Nakadai only the briefest of speeches and when Lear's lines are paraphrased at greater length, it is Kyoami who delivers them. Hidetora sows the seeds of the tragedy but is seldom its central figure, and the Expressionistic presentation of his mental decline led Richie to suggest, perceptively, that 'he becomes a visible idea' rather than the 'believable person' created by Shakespeare.

After the outcast pair find short-lived refuge in Tsurumaru's hut, Kurosawa choreographs a second remarkable battle, involving 1,200 extras and 200 horses, in which Saburo's musketeers decimate Jiro's cavalry. Hidetora and Saburo are briefly, movingly reunited, before a climax even more harrowing than *Lear*'s. Saburo is shot dead and Hidetora dies of a broken heart. The army of a rival warlord, Ayabe (effectively *Lear*'s Burgundy), attacks First Castle. Kaede, having engineered the beheading of Sué, is herself beheaded by Kurogane, who joins Jiro in suicide.

It falls to Tango, addressing the grieving Kyoami, to sum up the film's view of humanity: 'Men – they are so stupid that they believe that survival depends upon killing. No, not even the Buddha can save us.' The apocalyptic final shot – Tsurumaru helpless on the edge of a precipice, silhouetted against the last of those morbid sunsets – underlines why Kurosawa chose *Ran* as his title; it can mean 'chaos', 'rebellion' or, more aptly for *Lear* and this adaptation, 'desolation of the soul'.

Dir/Editor: Akira Kurosawa; **Prods:** Masato Hara, Serge Silberman; **Scr:** Akira Kurosawa, Hideo Oguni, Masato Ide; **DOPs:** Takao Saito, Masaharu Ueda, in collaboration with Asakazu Nakai; **Score:** Toru Takemitsu; **Main Cast:** Tatsuya Nakadai (Hidetora Ichimonji), Akira Terao (Taro Ichimonji), Mieko Harada (Lady Kaede), Jinpachi Nezu (Jiro Ichimonji), Yoshiko Miyazaki (Lady Sué), Daisuke Ryo (Saburo Ichimonji), Peter (Kyoami), Masayuki Yui (Tango), Takeshi Nomura (Tsurumaru), Hitoshi Veki (Fujimaki), Hisashi Igawa (Kurogane).

A Thousand Acres
US, 1997 – 101 mins
Jocelyn Moorhouse

This adaptation of Jane Smiley's 1991 Pulitzer Prize-winning novel sees the raw power of *King Lear* diluted into the familiar upheavals of rural melodrama. In 1990s' Iowa, Smiley's *Lear* surrogates, headed by revered, irascible widower Larry Cook (Jason Robards), live in an outwardly perfect world of whitewashed farmhouses and sunny cornfields. When Larry decides for tax reasons to give his three daughters joint ownership of his fertile farm, the idea is embraced by the married children who help run it: naive, caring Ginny, languishing in a childless marriage to Ty (a mild-mannered Albany figure), and frustrated Rose, whose volatile husband Pete is the story's Cornwall. However, when the youngest daughter, Caroline, a city lawyer, wavers, Larry instantly disowns her.

Rose and Ginny turn against Larry, who sexually abused them as teenagers, and both begin affairs with Jess (a selfish Edmund clone), who quarrels with his farmer father, Harold (a perfunctory Gloucester substitute; there is no Edgar). Rose's adultery drives Pete to suicide. Larry and Caroline unsuccessfully sue to reclaim the farm; Ginny leaves Ty, and we jump forward two years to her reunion with Rose, who has been abandoned by Jess and is dying from breast cancer. Lange's mawkish narration reveals that Larry has died of a heart attack.

Where *Lear* and Smiley's 370-page novel both give fully developed characters time to undertake convincing emotional journeys, Laura Jones's screenplay is overloaded with thinly sketched, unsympathetic figures (despite copious emoting from Jessica Lange and Michelle Pfeiffer) and clichéd revelation, ploddingly orchestrated by Jocelyn Moorhouse. The talents of exceptional actors are wasted as six months' worth of soap opera are crammed into 100 minutes.

Dir: Jocelyn Moorhouse; **Prods:** Marc Abraham, Steve Golin, Lynn Arost, Kate Guinzburg, Sigurjon Sighvatsson; **Scr:** Laura Jones, from the novel by Jane Smiley; **DOP:** Tak Fujimoto;

Editor: Maryann Brandon; **Score:** Richard Hartley; **Main Cast:** Jason Robards (Larry Cook), Jessica Lange (Ginny Cook Smith), Keith Carradine (Ty Smith), Michelle Pfeiffer (Rose Cook Lewis), Kevin Anderson (Peter Lewis), Jennifer Jason Leigh (Caroline Cook), Pat Hingle (Harold Clark), Colin Firth (Jess Clark).

My Kingdom
UK, 2001 – 116 mins
Don Boyd

In the press notes for this relentlessly grim Liverpool crime saga, Don
Boyd insisted it had 'no other serious parallels' with *King Lear* apart from
'the basic familial device'. This was disingenuous. From opening caption
(Gloucester's 'As flies to wanton boys, are we to th' gods . . .') to
climactic slaughter, the play exerts a constant influence.

Richard Harris's silver-haired crime lord, Sandeman, dotes on his wife
Mandy (interesting to see Lear, briefly, as loving husband). A black
addict, Delroy, mugs the couple and Sandeman's hubristic defiance leads
to Mandy being shot dead – a collateral victim of Sandeman's drugs
trade. His sins initiate his destruction, and his adored youngest daughter,
Jo (the slight, pretty Emma Catherwood), a crack-addicted prostitute-
turned-psychology student, understandably rejects ill-gotten gains when
told to assume nominal ownership of his assets. Grieving and insulted,
Sandeman cedes control to his scheming daughters and sons-in-law:
brothel-owner Kath and her husband, Dean, and Tracy, a promiscuous
tramp married to Jug, a psychopathic Sikh who tortures Delroy to death.

As with gangster *Macbeth*s (pp. 100–27), the absolute power, strict
hierarchy and immense wealth shared by high-ranking criminals and
ancient royals makes this central sextet adequate *Lear* substitutes, though
clichéd dialogue and over-the-top performances from Louise Lombard,
Lorraine Pilkington and Jimi Mistry push Kath, Tracy and Jug towards
caricature.

My Kingdom falters when it introduces substitutes for the Fool,
Edmund and Gloucester. Kath's young son Jamie is referred to as 'Boy'
because that is what Lear calls the Fool. He follows the homeless
Sandeman into the urban wilderness and is senselessly killed by Jug's
minders, so that we see the hero bear an innocent's corpse: Sandeman
with Boy instead of Lear with Cordelia. Does corrupt vice-squad detective
Puttnam (Aidan Gillen) lust after Kath and let Tracy bed him because the

character might plausibly do so, or because Edmund must be sexually involved with Goneril and Regan? Similar contrivance is needed to make a cancer-ridden customs investigator, Quick (Tom Bell), resemble Gloucester (he has his eyes put out by Jug), and both officers drift awkwardly through a plot that hinges on Sandeman's importing of Dutch cows with supposedly drug-filled stomachs.

This reaches a rushed, muddled climax when Sandeman abruptly recovers his wits to engineer a double-cross that sees Dean and Jug killed (the latter by Delroy's father) and Kath and Tracy kill each other. Sandeman and Jo are reconciled, although Boyd and co-writer Nick Davies frustratingly evade the question of what he has learned from his ordeal, and whether he and Jo will reject crime.

Eschewing even dark humour, Boyd supplies an antidote to the glib antics of 1990s' British gangster films, led by Guy Ritchie's flashy *Lock, Stock and Two Smoking Barrels* (1998), while relying on a Ritchie-esque plot. Uniformly cold and grey Liverpool locations (rundown streets and docksides, the choppy Mersey) and horribly realistic violence reflect the post-industrial deprivation and underworld horrors exposed by Davies in his book *Dark Heart: The Shocking Truth about Hidden Britain* (1997). It is implicit that Sandeman has prospered from urban decay, yet Boyd and Davies unwisely have Quick editorialise about Liverpool's descent into moral chaos and quote Albany's 'Humanity must perforce prey upon itself'. *My Kingdom* is dragged down by its failure to reconcile genre ingredients (stake-outs, interrogations, dodgy cops, shootings), social conscience and Shakespearean allusions, and took less than £30,000 in the UK.

Dir: Don Boyd; **Prods:** Neil Weisman, Gabriela Bacher; **Scr:** Don Boyd, Nick Davies; **DOP:** Dewald Aukema; **Editor:** Adam Ross; **Score:** Deirdre Gribbin, Simon Fisher Turner; **Main Cast:** Richard Harris (Sandeman), Lynn Redgrave (Mandy Sandeman), Louise Lombard (Kath), Paul McGann (Dean), Lorraine Pilkington (Tracy), Jimi Mistry (Jug), Emma Catherwood (Jo), Reece Noi (The Boy), Tom Bell (Quick), Aidan Gillen (Sgt Puttnam), Otis Graham (Delroy).

King of Texas
US, 2002 – 95 mins (TVM)
Uli Edel

Retaining every major character from *King Lear* except Kent, this strongly cast TV movie successfully combines the play with two types of Western: films dealing with the Alamo and the Texas War of Independence, and patriarchal ranch sagas, notably the *Lear*-like *Broken Lance* (1954) and the long-running TV series *The High Chaparral* (1967–71).

In late 1830s' Texas, Patrick Stewart's white-haired, bearded Lear is an 'ornery', self-made tyrant who ruthlessly defends his 200,000 acres (he hangs two starving Mexicans for stealing a cow). Every inch was 'paid for in blood', including that of his beloved son, who fell helping to win Texan independence. So, like Hidetora in *Ran* and Sandeman in *My Kingdom* (p. 84 and p. 90), the hero has a backstory driven by his violent rise to power, and, after Lear banishes his youngest daughter, Claudia, for refusing to fawn at the division of his kingdom, we view the destructive ingratitude of Marcia Gay Harden's ice-cold Susannah (Goneril), Lauren Holly's demurely malicious Rebecca (Regan) and her sadistic husband, Highsmith (Patrick Bergin with a bizarre Scottish accent), as punishment for Lear's imperial and familial crimes: 'You worked our mother to death and never took no notice of Rebecca or me,' cries Susannah.

Claudia takes refuge with her Mexican lover Menchaca (Steven Bauer, as the story's King of France), a landowner whose father died at the Alamo and whom Lear calls 'the enemy of our blood', injecting a dash of *Romeo and Juliet*'s forbidden romance into the gathering storm.

Lear declines into madness, attended by his black slave Rip (a sardonic performance from David Alan Grier), the middle-aged 'Fool' cherished as 'the only son of a bitch can make me laugh'. Highsmith and Susannah take advantage of her benevolent husband Tumlinson's absence on government business in Austin to attempt to grab back territory ceded by Lear to Menchaca in the Tex-Mex peace treaty of

1836. They fail to enlist Lear's fellow Alamo veteran Westover (Roy Scheider), a horse-breeder whose bastard elder son, Emmett, murders two men while framing his good-hearted half-brother, Thomas, for 'stealing' their stock. (Thomas then disappears, with no equivalent of Edgar's 'Poor Tom' disguise or Act V heroics.) Emmett betrays his father to Highsmith, who blinds Westover for warning Menchaca of the impending attack and is shot dead by one of Lear's horrified cowboys.

Stephen Harrigan's banal dialogue (occasionally poeticised by a few words from *Lear*), Uli Edel's low-key direction and an incongruously romantic orchestral score make it hard for Stewart and his fine co-stars to shine, until, almost from nowhere, the climactic battle demanded by Western convention and the *Lear* plot becomes surprisingly moving.

At Menchaca's hacienda, Emmett, Claudia and Susannah's racist ranch-hand, Cornell (equivalent to Oswald), are all killed. Lear, looking like an Old Testament prophet, attains tragic self-knowledge in renouncing violence at the point when Shakespeare's King kills the man who hanged Cordelia. He walks past dead men, women and children, crying 'Stop!', and dies of a broken heart beside Claudia's corpse, watched by Menchaca, Rip and Tumlinson, who escorts the bodies to Lear's ranch, arrests Rebecca and allows Susannah to shoot herself. That *King of Texas* was produced for the TNT cable channel explains why this finale can afford to be bleaker and more violent than the generally bland movies made for artistically cautious American TV networks (such as *The Tempest*, p. 262), although it is undermined by a sunny, sentimental coda showing the blind Westover contentedly returned to horse-breeding, the devoted Thomas at his side.

Dir: Uli Edel; **Prod**: Art Levinson; **Scr**: Stephen Harrigan; **DOPs**: Paul Elliott, Guillermo Rosas; **Editor**: Mark Conte; **Main Cast**: Patrick Stewart (John Lear), Marcia Gay Harden (Susannah Lear Tumlinson), Colm Meaney (Mr Tumlinson), Lauren Holly (Rebecca Lear Highsmith), Patrick Bergin (Mr Highsmith), Julie Cox (Claudia Lear), David Alan Grier (Rip), Roy Scheider (Henry Westover), Liam Waite (Thomas Westover), Matt Letscher (Emmett Westover), Steven Bauer (Menchaca).

Love's Labour's Lost (play synopsis)

At the court of the King of Navarre he and three companions, Longaville, Dumaine and Berowne, sign an oath: for three years they will renounce female company and devote themselves to study. Costard the clown is assigned to take care of their guest, Don Armado, who loves country wench Jaquenetta; so does Costard, who is arrested for breaking the vow by talking to her.

The Princess of France arrives at court to discuss a France–Navarre finance settlement, accompanied by three ladies-in-waiting, Rosaline, Maria and Katharine. Though the men hesitate to make contact, mutual attraction follows: Princess matched with King, Rosaline with Berowne, Maria with Longaville, Dumaine with Katharine.

Armado entrusts Costard with a letter to Jaquenetta and Berowne gives him the poem he has written for Rosaline. The four friends overhear each other penning poetry to their beloveds and Berowne mocks them, only for the pedantic schoolmaster, Holofernes, to enter bearing Berowne's own poem, which, like Armado's letter, Costard has misdirected. The quartet resolve to research love by wooing their women while disguised as Russian visitors.

They attend the pageant organised by Holofernes and featuring Sir Nathaniel, the curate, Dull, the constable, Armado and his page, Moth. Also in the audience are the ladies, who, aware of the men's ruse, are themselves disguised and wearing each other's jewels. In the ensuing confusion, the performance has to be abandoned.

When a messenger brings news that the Princess's father has died the ladies prepare to leave court. The Princess tells Navarre that they must spend a year apart and he may then, if he has remained faithful, resume his suit. Her ladies give their men the same instruction and the play ends with songs of spring and winter as the two groups go their separate ways.

Love's Labour's Lost
UK/France/US, 2000 – 93 mins
Kenneth Branagh

After using every line of *Hamlet* (1996, p. 45), Kenneth Branagh went in the opposite direction with *Love's Labour's Lost*, cutting almost 75% of the text and incorporating what remained into an old-fashioned musical featuring 1930s' standards from Irving Berlin, Cole Porter and the Gershwins. An £8.5m budget helped him recapture the glossy escapism of Hollywood's Fred Astaire/Ginger Rogers classics, and you come away humming the tunes, or replaying the dance routines. The problem with *Love's Labour's Lost* as Shakespeare is that you struggle to recall a single scene from the play.

Witty, Movietone-style newsreels, plummily voiced by Branagh, are used to summarise omitted Shakespeare scenes, and the first introduces us to a 1939 fantasy Oxbridge college (superb sets by Tim Hatley) and four freshmen, two Americans, Navarre (the serene Alessandro Nivola) and Longaville (preppy Matthew Lillard), and two Brits, Dumaine (suave Adrian Lester) and Berowne (Branagh at his most relaxed). Gathered in a mini-Bodleian library they sign their oath of abstinence and launch into 'I'd Rather Charleston', a gasp-inducing moment, topped by Timothy Spall's absurdly pompous, 'Spaneesh'-accented Armado expressing his love for Jaquenetta with an hilarious 'I Get a Kick out of You' music video.

The Princess and ladies-in-waiting arrive by punt in a dreamy night-time scene and Branagh reinvents Holofernes as a whimsical tutor, Holofernia (Geraldine McEwan); Costard, the innuendo-prone clown, becomes Nathan Lane's vaudevillian. They, like Spall, have little to do, as Branagh gives the lovers seven of the ten songs chosen because he believed they equalled Shakespeare in conveying 'how silly, wonderful, stupid and agonising' love is. Berowne's long speech in praise of love segues into 'Cheek to Cheek'; the girls sing 'No Strings (I'm Fancy Free)' while swimming in synchronised homage to Busby Berkeley, and join their paramours for a pulsating, masked 'Let's Face the Music and Dance'.

All this is captivating – if you can excuse the slightly amateurish edge to the singing and hoofing from everyone except award-winning musical theatre stars Lester and Lane, who sing 'There's No Business Like Showbusiness' in the pageant. The shifts from 1930s' lyrics or newsreel commentary back into lofty Elizabethan metaphor are, however, an insuperable problem. By the time you have readjusted, the next musical number may be seconds away; Shakespeare is reduced to filler material.

Such verse as remains is well handled by all except the miscast Alicia Silverstone, who is left breathless, if not quite *Clueless*, as the Princess, outshone by the regal grace of Natascha McElhone's Rosaline. After Silverstone has struggled through her farewell speech, the couples drive to a *Casablanca*-inspired airfield farewell. The vapour trail from the Princess's plane spells out the last line of the play: 'You that way, we this way.' It's a perfectly bittersweet finale, ruined by Branagh's feelgood epilogue: a sentimental newsreel montage of the characters' World War II heroism, ending with joyous VE-Day reunion.

An understandably confused marketing campaign (unsure whether to brand the film as Branagh Shakespeare or retro-Hollywood musical) and some scathing reviews contributed to its very poor box-office performance in Britain and America (a combined gross of just $1.16m). Ultimately, you wonder why Branagh did not try to emulate *The Boys from Syracuse* (1940, p. 14) and *Kiss Me Kate* (1953, p. 237), abandoning Shakespeare's language and, as solo writer or in a partnership, creating a stylistically coherent compilation musical whose book complemented the lyrics and Anglo-American cast with waspish Noël Coward-meets-Philip Barry dialogue.

Dir/Scr: Kenneth Branagh; **Prods:** David Barron, Kenneth Branagh; **DOP:** Alex Thomson; **Editor:** Neil Farrell; **Score:** Patrick Doyle; **Main Cast:** Kenneth Branagh (Berowne), Natascha McElhone (Rosaline), Alessandro Nivola (King), Alicia Silverstone (Princess), Matthew Lillard (Longaville), Carmen Ejogo (Maria), Adrian Lester (Dumaine), Emily Mortimer (Katharine), Nathan Lane (Costard), Timothy Spall (Armado), Stefania Rocca (Jaquenetta), Geraldine McEwan (Holofernia).

Macbeth (play synopsis)

Scotland. Returning from victory over rebels opposed to King Duncan, Macbeth, Thane of Glamis, and his friend, Banquo, encounter three witches, who prophesy that Macbeth will become Thane of Cawdor and then King, and that Banquo's heirs will become kings.

Duncan has Cawdor executed for treason and appoints Macbeth in his place, then stays the night at Macbeth's castle, with his sons Malcolm and Donalbain. Goaded into action by Lady Macbeth, Macbeth stabs the sleeping Duncan and then kills the two bodyguards whom his wife has drugged, and blames them for the King's murder. Malcolm and Donalbain flee separately to England and Ireland and are suspected of ordering Duncan's death. Macbeth is crowned King.

Fearful of losing the crown to Banquo's heirs, Macbeth has him murdered, but his son, Fleance, escapes. Banquo's ghost torments Macbeth at a banquet. Macbeth revisits the witches, who conjure apparitions who warn him to beware Macduff, reassure him that no man born to a woman can harm him and that he will be invincible until Birnam Wood advances on Dunsinane. But he is also shown eight generations of Banquo's descendants, each as King.

Macbeth sends murderers to kill the wife and young children of Macduff, who has fled to England to join Malcolm, who is raising an army to reclaim the crown. Lady Macbeth is obsessed with washing her hands clean of Duncan's blood, and a waiting-gentlewoman and a doctor observe her delirious sleepwalking. As Malcolm's army prepares to attack, Lady Macbeth dies, apparently by her own hand. Malcolm has his soldiers camouflage themselves with tree branches – so Macbeth sees Birnam Wood marching on Dunsinane. In battle, Macbeth kills Siward, a young nobleman, but is beheaded by Macduff, who was 'from his mother's womb untimely ripp'd.' Malcolm is crowned King.

Macbeth
US, 1948 – 107 mins (B&W)
Orson Welles

Made in just twenty-three days, Welles's black-and-white experiment
combines cinematic visuals with theatrical acting and design and a radio
director's emphasis on the verse. His production of *Macbeth* at the Utah
Centennial Festival in May 1947 was effectively a dress rehearsal for the
movie, which began shooting a month later on a tight $700,000 budget
from Hollywood B-movie studio, Republic.

Welles could only afford abstract sets: the jagged walls of Macbeth's
castle resemble quick-dried volcanic lava; its courtyard has the
unmistakable smoothness of a studio floor. The bewildering costumes
range from Scottish traditional (tartan capes for Dan O'Herlihy's robust,
stagey Macduff and Roddy McDowall's boyish Malcolm) to science fiction
(Macbeth's *Flash Gordon*-like silver jerkin), and Welles would later regret
sporting such bizarre crowns (one made him look like the Statue of
Liberty).

Copious thunder, lightning and wind effects enhance the artifice,
and yet there is great visual poetry when the camera closes in on
Macbeth's feverish face as he sees a crowded banquet table suddenly
empty, save for Banquo's ghost, or when a ten-minute take follows the
build-up to and aftermath of Duncan's murder (Welles could shoot such
long takes without worrying about off-camera interruptions because the
cast had pre-recorded their dialogue in Scottish accents, and acted to
playback).

Welles's Macbeth towers above his co-stars in low-angle close-ups (as
he would in *Othello,* p. 165), murders Duncan in a virtual trance and as King
deadens reality by remaining perpetually drunk; sobriety returns only when
he faces death. The impression that Macbeth is enduring a nightmarish, out-
of-body experience is strongest when Welles, in a fine burr, delivers the most
important soliloquies in voiceover and, as in Welles's radio Shakespeare, his
thoughts belong as much to the audience as to the speaker.

Jeanette Nolan's Lady Macbeth, with a *Bride of Frankenstein* hairdo and shrill voice, lusts after husband and power with equal fervour, though her inexperience in front of the camera explains her stiff performance. Lady Macbeth's guilt and our sense of the couple's complicity is deepened by some interpolated appearances, such as when Welles gives her some of Lady Macduff's lines with which to engage Macduff's doomed son (played by Welles's then eight-year-old daughter, Christopher).

His main conceptual addition is to make the preposterous, white-haired witches the last representatives of paganism, opposed to early Christianity in the form of the blonde, pigtailed Holy Father (the imposing Alan Napier), who speaks most of Ross's lines. Early on, the Father leads a service in which Duncan, Malcolm and the Macbeths swear to renounce Satan, and marches in the vanguard of Malcolm's invading soldiers who are driven forward by Jacques Ibert's martial score and carry staffs topped with a Celtic cross. The forces of darkness achieve a partial victory when Macbeth kills the Father with a well-aimed spear.

The meaning of this half-baked addition was presumably lost on the Republic executives who so hated Welles's original cut that they obliged his assistant, Richard Wilson, to hack it to eightysix minutes, with redubbed American accents. Released in the US in September 1950, this version made Republic a small profit. In Britain the *Observer* branded it 'uncouth, unscholarly, unmusical'. Only in 1980, when Wilson restored the excised footage and Scottish dialogue for a re-release, was *Macbeth* judged as Welles had intended it, as 'a violently sketched charcoal drawing of a great play.'

Dir/Prod/Scr: Orson Welles; **DOP:** John L. Russell; **Editor:** Louis Lindsay; **Score**: Jacques Ibert; **Main Cast:** Orson Welles (Macbeth), Jeanette Nolan (Lady Macbeth), Edgar Barrier (Banquo), Dan O'Herlihy (Macduff), Erskine Sandford (Duncan), Roddy McDowall (Malcolm), Alan Napier (a Holy Father).

Joe Macbeth
UK, 1955 – 90 mins (B&W)
Ken Hughes

Consummate and prolific genre screenwriter Philip Yordan already had
crime yarns such as *Dillinger* (1945) and a *King Lear*-influenced Western
(*Broken Lance*, 1954) on his CV when *Joe Macbeth* made him the first of
many writers to uncover the common ground between Shakespeare's
thanes and twentieth-century gangsters. Both groups swear absolute
loyalty to King/Godfather; both practise summary execution of traitors
and 'whack' anybody who stands in their path to power.

Yordan's entertaining, blackly comic screenplay, shot in Britain with a
mostly American cast, carefully harvested aspects of *Macbeth* that would
plausibly fit Hollywood's tried-and-tested mould: trench-coated, chain-
smoking hoodlums plotting in dimly lit offices, dining out with glamorous
molls and gunning each other down.

Our middle-aged hero, Joe (burly Paul Douglas), is short on smarts
but has brawn to spare, making him an effective and obedient enforcer
for Mr del Duca (Grégoire Aslan), the cigar-chomping Italian kingpin of
New York gangland. Joe rubs out Duca's 'number one boy', Tommy
(equivalent to Cawdor), in the opening scene, and the boss rewards him
with a diamond ring for his gorgeous, domineering new bride, Lily (Ruth
Roman, a tough-gal specialist).

The couple's celebration dinner is interrupted by Rosie (diminutive
Minerva Pious), an actress-turned-flower-seller who once played a witch
in a Broadway *Macbeth*. Her Tarot reading says Joe will become 'Lord of
the Castle' and 'King of the City'. Seconds later, Duca walks in to greet
Joe as his new right-hand man and proffers the key to Tommy's Gothic,
lakeside mansion. Cue ominous brass and the Macbeths' rise to power
begins.

After we meet Joe's pal, Banky (Sid James, playing it shockingly
straight compared to his *Carry On* . . . roles), and Banky's son, Lennie
(the pale, fidgety Bonar Colleano), Yordan breaks away from *Macbeth*.

Duca orders Joe, Banky and Lennie to eliminate a bloated grotesque named Dutch (Harry Green). Though he employs a stuttering food taster to make sure his gargantuan meals are safe, he is so eager to guzzle his crêpes suzettes that he plunges straight in. With a touch of Jacobean revenge tragedy, Joe has had the pancakes poisoned; so much for Dutch.

Lily uses this episode to convince Joe that Duca is only ever going to treat him as dispensable muscle and that they will languish as 'stooges playing big-shots' unless Joe kills the King (making them newlyweds puts a neat spin on Lady Macbeth's manipulation). After another prophecy from Rosie ('So long as you have no fear, nothing shall stop you.'), Joe agrees to murder Duca.

At the Macbeths' house-warming party, Duca, who has designs on Lily, invites her for a dawn dip in the lake. He swims out, followed by

Joe (Paul Douglas), left, receives a wedding gift from boss Duca (Grégoire Aslan), right, watched by Banky (Sid James) in Ken Hughes's *Joe Macbeth*

Joe, who hauls him underwater and stabs him, sending birds screeching into the air – a very *Macbeth*-like image. Joe takes control and the violence returns to the Shakespearean model.

Joe's hired guns shoot Banky but miss Lennie, whose wife and baby make him an amalgamation of Fleance and Macduff. The appearance of Banky's ashen-faced ghost at Joe's dinner table sees Douglas indulge in some B-movie 'madness'. Joe dispatches his hitmen to pressure Lennie's wife into making him leave town and they end up killing her and her baby; a glimpse of this carnage drives Lily insane (though Roman is denied a sleepwalking scene).

At the mansion, Joe accidentally shoots Lily, thinking she is Lennie. Moments later, Lennie kills Joe and is then cut down, off screen, by the police. Last man standing is Angus, the sardonic butler, memorably played by Walter Crisham as a mixture of Jeeves and *Macbeth*'s Porter.

Ken Hughes, best known for *Chitty Chitty Bang Bang* (1968), switches proficiently between the violent action, comedy and Gothic elements; it is just a pity that he did not have stronger lead actors. Made ten years earlier with James Cagney as Joe, Barbara Stanwyck as Lily and Edward G. Robinson as Duca, *Joe Macbeth* might have been a noir classic instead of a cherishable oddity. Nonetheless, it has an increasingly valuable place in Shakespeare film history, as godfather to a burgeoning, multinational family of gangster *Macbeth*s, four of which follow in this chapter.

Dir: Ken Hughes; **Prod:** M. J. Frankovich; **Scr:** Philip Yordan; **DOP:** Basil Emmott; **Editor:** Peter Rolfe Johnson; **Score:** Trevor Duncan; **Main Cast:** Paul Douglas (Joe Macbeth), Ruth Roman (Lily), Sid James (Banky), Bonar Colleano (Lennie), Nicholas Stuart (Duffy), Grégoire Aslan (Mr del Duca), Harry Green (Dutch), Walter Crisham (Angus).

Throne of Blood (*Kumunosu-jo*)
Japan, 1957 – 110 mins (B&W)
Akira Kurosawa

Washizu, Akira Kurosawa's wild-eyed samurai Macbeth, has all his Shakespearean counterpart's courage, none of his eloquence. Played by Toshiro Mifune at his fiercest, he rarely says more than a dozen words, his language as plain as his castle's floorboards. Yet while there is no poetry in *Throne of Blood*'s sparse dialogue, and little subtlety in its characterisation, its pace, atmosphere and imagery are utterly Shakespearean.

Kurosawa's vision of fifteenth-century Japan follows on from his rain-swept 1954 action epic *Seven Samurai* (both are traditional *jidai-geki*, period films) and, like *Macbeth*, is characterised by bestial omens and foul weather: a horse's distress presages its master's murder; galloping warriors are buffeted by wind and water, or shrouded in mist and fog. Linguistic rhythms are replaced by the woodwind and percussion of Masaru Sato's distinctively Japanese score.

The film begins with a shot of a monument marking the site of Cobweb Castle (the 'Kumunosu-jo' of the title), as a male chorus sings of its destruction. Next we see the castle in its former glory, as Tsuzuki (Duncan) learns of heroic exploits by Washizu and his best friend, Miki (Kurosawa stalwart Minoru Chiaki as a jovial, trusting Banquo), against Inui (Norway) and the treacherous Fujimaki (Cawdor).

Meanwhile, in a marvellously eerie scene, Washizu and Miki become lost in the maze-like Cobweb Forest, and meet an aged 'Evil Spirit' (Chieko Naniwa), whose white make-up resembles the ghost-masks of Noh theatre (the ancient Japanese form adored by Kurosawa). She prophesies in the husky, expressionless tones of Noh actors: Washizu, commander of Fort One, will rule North Mansion and then Cobweb Castle, while Miki will take over Fort One, and his son will one day rule the castle.

Tsuzuki installs Washizu and his wife, Asaji (the mesmerising Isuzu Yamada), in North Mansion, and Kurosawa immediately uses Noh to associate his Lady Macbeth so closely with the forest spirit that you suspect they are accomplices. Yamada's long, oval face is like a Noh mask, she walks heel to toe, like Noh actors, and adopts an expressionless voice to suit Asaji's pitiless ambition. She convinces the unambitious Washizu that Tsuzuki and Miki are plotting his death and that he must strike while Tsuzuki is their guest.

Washizu (Toshiro Mifune) is about to die in the hail of arrows fired by his own soldiers at the climax of Akira Kurosawa's *Throne of Blood*

Kurosawa now devises a night-time sequence of such stealth that it perfectly distils the dreadful tension of Duncan's murder. For seven minutes, from Asaji's promise to give Tsuzuki's guards refreshment until her cry of 'murder', no words are spoken or necessary: the horror of the deed is writ large on Mifune and Yamada's faces.

The 'guilty' flight of Kunimaru (Malcolm), Tsuzuki's son, and Noriyasu (Macduff) makes Washizu lord of the castle, and from hereon the script works ironic variations on *Macbeth*. The childless Washizu has promised to let Miki's son, Yoshiteru, inherit the castle, until Asaji declares: 'I am with child.' Miki and Yoshiteru must die, and Kurosawa boldly decides not to show a murder that is depicted on stage. At Fort One, Miki's horse refuses to be saddled, but he ignores this sign and sets off for Washizu's feast. When his mount returns riderless we know he is dead *before* his dazed ghost appears at the feast.

Months pass, Asaji's child is still-born and the realisation that Yoshiteru, who escaped his father's assassin, will still inherit prompts Washizu to cry 'Fool! Fool!' – the closest Mifune comes to soliloquy.

With the crazed Asaji ceaselessly washing her hands and his enemies, including Yoshiteru, gathering, the forest spirit promises Washizu invincibility 'until Cobweb Forest comes to Cobweb Castle'. His soldiers see an army of pines approaching through the mist and we reach the ultimate twist on *Macbeth*: Washizu is killed by his own men. Dozens of whistling arrows pierce his armour, turning Mifune into a staggering pincushion, until one last arrow transfixes his neck and he collapses. Noriyasu's men prepare to raze the castle and the screen fades back to the opening shot of the monument.

Kurosawa and his co-writers, by keeping to the spirit of their source while introducing modified or original elements, miraculously transplant *Macbeth* in such a way that it retains deep roots in Shakespeare and in Japanese history (feuding warlords) and theatre (Noh). Fifty years after its premiere *Throne of Blood* still causes many to react like the Russian director of *Hamlet* and *King Lear* (pp. 31 and 79), Grigori Kozintsev: 'One caught one's breath at the greatness of Shakespeare and at the same time the greatness of cinema.'

Dir/Editor: Akira Kurosawa; **Prods:** Shojiro Motoki, Akira Kurosawa; **Scr:** Shinobu Hashimoto, Ryuzo Kikushima, Hideo Oguni, Akira Kurosawa; **DOP:** Asakazu Nakai; **Score:** Masaru Sato; **Main Cast:** Toshiro Mifune (Washizu), Isuzu Yamada (Asaji), Minoru Chiaki (Miki), Akira Kubo (Yoshiteru), Takashi Shimura (Noriyasu), Takamaru Sasaki (Tsuzuki), Yoichi Tachikawa (Kunimaru), Chieko Naniwa (Evil Spirit).

Macbeth
UK, 1971 – 140 mins
Roman Polanski

The production of Roman Polanski's *Macbeth* was mired in notoriety. Some 60% of the $2.5m budget came from *Playboy* founder Hugh Hefner, and newspapers also dwelt on Polanski's decision to begin visualising the savage slaughter of Macduff's wife and children less than a year after his young, heavily pregnant wife, Sharon Tate, had been murdered at their Los Angeles home by members of Charles Manson's 'Family' cult. This personal tragedy and the director's childhood memories of Nazi atrocities in Poland can only have increased his determination to bring out the play's full horror, and this most gruesome of original-text

'What's done is done.': Lady Macbeth (Francesca Annis) tries to comfort her husband (Jon Finch) in Roman Polanski's *Macbeth*

*Macbeth*s is also the first English-language screen treatment to prove that *Macbeth* reads more like a film script than any other Shakespeare play.

In comparatively short scenes, Polanski and Shakespeare cross-cut between numerous interior and exterior locations, including the blasted heath, Forres Castle, Macduff's castle, Dunsinane Castle and Birnam Wood, punctuating the story with frequent bursts of supernatural or violent action. Polanski opens out *Macbeth* impressively, shooting on beaches, hills and mountains (Welsh rather than Scottish) and in real fortresses (Lindisfarne Castle and Bamburgh Castle, Northumberland) and convincing you that a whole nation's fate is at stake.

Devised sequences, such as Duncan's funeral procession and Macbeth's coronation, strengthen our understanding of this primitive culture, and spacious, detailed castle chambers, built at Shepperton Studios, bristle with crude vitality.

True to his promise 'to show [*Macbeth*'s] violence the way it is', because 'if you don't show it realistically then that's immoral and harmful', we see all the deaths that occur off stage, and more: Cawdor's execution; Macbeth stabbing Duncan; the slit throat of Banquo's ghost weeping blood; Macbeth beheaded by Macduff. This gore is justified by the blood-drenched poetry and, by allowing breathing space for the Macbeths' more reflective moments, Polanski does not allow carnage to overwhelm philosophy.

The Third Ear Band's distorted bagpipes and bass guitars fuel the supernatural mood, particularly in a wildly over-the-top sequence for Macbeth's second encounter with the three witches, who are joined by a dozen more, all grotesquely naked. Their foul brew sends Jon Finch's Macbeth on an acid trip: special-effects-laden hallucinations, including a baby torn from a womb.

Finch, then a relative unknown aged twenty-eight, suits Polanski's conception of Macbeth as 'a young, open-faced warrior', starting out neurotic and short of confidence, imbued with utter conviction once crowned, and just as swiftly wearied by power and what he must do to maintain it. He is spurred into action by tearful, almost girlish reproaches from Francesca Annis (who at twenty-five thought herself too young for the role). Her flawless porcelain beauty and inner malice seem to embody the witches' 'Fair is foul, and foul is fair' and she sleepwalks nude (which must have pleased Hugh Hefner). Though the script leaves the soliloquies largely intact, Polanski imposes a distractingly inconsistent technique on Annis and Finch: the bulk of a speech's lines are delivered in voiceover, a few are spoken out loud at random points.

Martin Shaw's intelligent, sober Banquo, and Terence Bayler's stoical Macduff head a solid supporting cast (all of whom share the Macbeths' English accents). The most intriguing characterisation is the smiling menace of John Stride's Ross. Polanski and Tynan follow a radical interpretation from an obscure Victorian essay to make one of the play's 'good guys' a merciless opportunist who, substituting for the Third Murderer, tries to kill Fleance, then leaves the gates of Macduff's castle open to his family's killers. Only when Macbeth refuses to reward his vicious loyalty does he join Duncan in England, echoing Buckingham's defection in *Richard III*, and the script also turns Donalbain (Paul Shelley), an innocent in the play, into a Richard III-in-waiting, seething with resentment at Malcolm's elevation. With men like these at his side, the new king should not feel secure, and a silent epilogue shows Donalbain riding to the witches' lair to hear his fortune. The cycle of violence is about to recommence.

Dir: Roman Polanski; **Prod:** Andrew Braunsberg; **Scr:** Roman Polanski, Kenneth Tynan; **DOP:** Gilbert Taylor; **Editor:** Alastair McIntyre; **Score:** The Third Ear Band; **Main Cast:** Jon Finch (Macbeth), Francesca Annis (Lady Macbeth), Martin Shaw (Banquo), Terence Bayler (Macduff), Nicholas Selby (Duncan), Stephan Chase (Malcolm), John Stride (Ross), Paul Shelley (Donalbain).

Men of Respect
US, 1991 – 107 mins
William Reilly

William Reilly takes the gangster premise from *Joe Macbeth* and by slavishly retaining virtually every aspect of *Macbeth* digs himself and a formidable cast into a very deep hole. A movie that wants to be taken seriously ends up providing the most risible chunks of modernised Shakespeare in screen history.

Reilly's Macbeth, low-ranking wiseguy Mike Battaglia (John Turturro), walks into a crowded restaurant and blows away the Greek who has been threatening the New York empire of his Godfather, Charlie D'Amico. Fleeing the scene, Mike and his best pal, loanshark Bankie Como (the reliable Dennis Farina), stumble improbably into the derelict home of an elderly gypsy fortune-teller, her husband and their weird male companion. To Misha Segal's embarrassingly crude synthesizer score, she tells Mike he will be promoted and become Godfather, as will Bankie's son, Phillie. D'Amico (Rod Steiger, in mercifully low-key mood) promptly elevates Mike to 'Man of Respect' status.

Goaded by his wife, Ruthie (Katherine Borowitz), Mike stabs D'Amico as he sleeps in the guest house attached to the Battaglias' Greenwich Village trattoria, setting off a series of murders faithfully copied from *Macbeth*, though directed in turgid, low-budget style.

Mike's henchmen gun down Bankie, but miss Phillie, ludicrously portrayed as a bespectacled MBA graduate. The wife and young son of Mike's enemy, Duffy (a disinterested-looking Peter Boyle), are blown up by a car bomb. Duffy joins forces with D'Amico's sons, Mal and Don, and, on the night that Ruthie slits her throat, leads a revenge attack. Duffy, born after his mother died in childbirth, kills the seemingly invincible Mike, and Mal takes over as Godfather.

While Turturro's edgy, haunted persona suits Macbeth's psychological peaks and troughs, and Borowitz's glacial good looks suit perhaps the only screen Mafia wife who wants her husband to be *more* violent, both are poorly served by Reilly's script. Quentin Tarantino, rumoured to have been preparing a film of *Macbeth* in 1995, might have created stylised Mob blank verse, but Reilly deals in expletive-heavy clichés. His version of one of *Macbeth*'s key philosophical questions (does fate or free will drive the action?) goes no deeper than Mike's last words: 'Shit happens.' Bathos is another problem. For Lady Macbeth's attempt to wash away Duncan's blood, Reilly gives Borowitz a can of bleach and has her scrub the bath in which she cleaned Mike's clothes after the D'Amico murder; suicidal remorse and housework do not mix.

The familiar mob setting assumes an intriguingly spooky aspect when Bankie's ghost enters (imagine one of Michael Corleone's victims interrupting a *Godfather* family dinner), but the other supernatural elements become unintentionally hilarious because of Reilly's determination not to ditch Shakespeare's most outlandish imagery. How does he replicate the witches' brew made from 'eye of newt' and 'lizard's leg'? The gypsies watch a TV chef outlining, in gruesome close-up, her recipe for lamb's head stew. Since Greenwich Village has no equivalent for Birnam Wood, the gypsy has prophesied that Mike will be safe until 'the stars fall from the heavens'. As the climactic shootout begins, fireworks start exploding near the restaurant, and one of Mike's goons declares: 'You'd think the stars were dropping.' Plot contrivance has rarely been this shameless.

Dir/Scr: William Reilly; **Prods:** Efraim Horowitz, Gary Mehlman; **DOP:** Bobby Bukowski; **Editor:** Elizabeth King; **Score:** Misha Segal; **Main Cast:** John Turturro (Mike Battaglia), Katherine Borowitz (Ruthie Battaglia), Dennis Farina (Bankie Como), Peter Boyle (Duffy), Rod Steiger (Charlie D'Amico), Stanley Tucci (Mal).

Macbeth
UK, 1997 – 129 mins
Jeremy Freeston

Funded by Grampian Television and more than 300 private individuals whose donations earned them an Associate Producer credit, Jeremy Freeston's low-budget feature début is inferior in every respect to Polanski's *Macbeth* (1971), though indebted to its use of real locations and sexy young leads.

Blackness Castle, Falkirk, and Warwick Castle serve convincingly for Dunsinane, while Dunfermline Abbey doubles for Scone at the coronation of Jason Connery's Macbeth. Comfortable with the battlefield heroics, he hurries uncomprehendingly through his lines, never suggesting dawning self-knowledge. Helen Baxendale fares better, though her Lady Macbeth's harrowing descent into madness is lent redundant extra motivation by a horror-movie trick: when she goes to 'smear the sleepy grooms' with Duncan's blood the King revives and she stabs him repeatedly.

Freeston includes about an hour of Paul Farrer's wretchedly clichéd score (*Psycho* strings for horror; a spectral choir for supernatural moments), at such volume that it sometimes drowns out a supporting cast of competent, unremarkable Scottish actors. Clumsy hand-held camerawork blunts intimate interior dialogues, and the scenes separately credited to Brian Blessed, featuring the elderly, middle-aged and young witches, resemble 1980s' heavy-metal videos, all midnight blue lighting and dry ice.

Most frustratingly, a film that retains a very full text is guilty of confusing omissions. We do not know who Macbeth's army defeats in the opening battle scene or why Cawdor dies. Despite laying on the gore for Duncan's murder and Banquo's bleeding zombie appearance at the feast, Freeston shows neither the murders of Macduff's wife and son, nor his harrowing grief, so that Macbeth's nemesis seems thinly drawn. Instead of confirming Scotland's fate after the tyrant's death, Freeston ends by hinting at an imminent reunion in the afterlife: Connery closes his eyes and in voiceover we hear again Baxendale's 'Hie thee hither' from her first appearance.

Dir: Jeremy Freeston; **Prod:** Shona Donaldson; **Scr:** Bob Carruthers, Jeremy Freeston; **DOP:** Dave Miller; **Editors:** Chris Gormlie, Owen Parker; **Score:** Paul Farrer; **Main Cast:** Jason Connery (Macbeth), Helen Baxendale (Lady Macbeth), Graham McTavish (Banquo), Kenny Bryans (Macduff), John Corvin (Duncan), Ross Dunsmore (Malcolm), Iain Stuart Robertson (Ross).

Makibefo
UK, 2000 – 73 mins (B&W)
Alexander Abela

In October 1998, English-born oceanographer-turned-film-maker
Alexander Abela and Danish sound recordist Jeppe Jungersen arrived
with 350kg of equipment in Faux Cap, a remote fishing village on the
southern tip of Continent Island, Madagascar. The villagers, members of
the Antandroy tribe, had never seen a film, nor heard of Shakespeare;
yet they agreed to take part in an adaptation of *Macbeth*, and had a
huge influence in shaping its scenario. Abela completed post-production
in 2000 and the following year French critics acclaimed this stunning
feature début on its limited theatrical release.

It alternates between scenes in the Antandroy's Malagasy dialect and
bridging extracts from *Macbeth*, delivered in English to camera or in
voiceover in a thick French accent by a narrator (the lean, handsome Gilbert
Laumord, from Guadaloupe), who sits on a beach beside four thin totem
poles and also delivers an English-language Prologue summarising the story.

Makibefo (the tall, intimidating Martin) and his younger friend,
Bakoua, recapture a fugitive traitor, Kidoure, and meet a witchdoctor
who promises Makibefo glory before metamorphosing into a snake. The
peace and harmony created by venerable, grey-haired King Danikany are
threatened when his hot-headed son Malikomy defies his father and
executes Kidoure, precisely as the witchdoctor has foretold.

The King and his young warriors dine with Makibefo and his wife,
bringing long-horned Zebu oxen as reward for his loyalty. His wife, who
has eagerly embraced the prophecy and drugged her guests, cannot
abide her husband's hesitation and is about to stab the King when
Makibefo takes the dagger from her, ushers her outside and strikes (as
with all the violence, we see the blows fall but not land).

(*Opposite page*) Makibefo (Martin) emerges after killing his king, Danikany, in Alexander
Abela's *Makibefo*

Makidofy discovers the murder, Malikomy flees by boat and Bakoua is killed on Makibefo's orders in a sequence reminiscent of the assassination of Colonel Kurtz and the slaughter of the water buffalo at the end of *Apocalypse Now* (1979), as Abela cuts between Bakoua's murder and the sacrifice of a Zebu ox (killed in the director and Jungersen's honour, rather than as a pre-scripted incident). Makibefo holds the ox's head aloft and cries 'I am your new King!'

Soon afterwards, his hysterical reaction to Bakoua's ashen-faced ghost disrupts a relaxed village dinner, attended by men, women and children and a fine example of how Abela (as in 2004's *Souli*, p. 184) creates a vivid, documentary sense of community. He has written that although *Makibefo* is a costume drama, with the villagers wearing simple clothing of a type last worn by their ancestors more than fifty years ago (today they wear jeans or T-shirts), it also depicts aspects of contemporary life in Faux Cap.

The village's unhurried pace determines Abela's leisurely direction (he is content to hold for seconds on a character's progress across a beach, and fades to lingering black between some scenes) and the village intimacy, compared to the nationwide scope of, say, Polanski's *Macbeth*, is turned to dramatic advantage. With everyone living so close together, Makibefo need not send men to raid Makidofy's home; he and a warrior can stroll there in minutes. He hauls his enemy's wife, baby and two young boys to the shore as Makidofy flees, gloatingly yells 'Look!' and Makidofy glances back from his canoe to see all four butchered.

Swiftly abandoned by the rest of the villagers, and widowed by his wife's suicide, Makibefo confronts Malikomy and Makidofy's twelve-strong landing party on the beach, dancing defiance until he lays down his spear and accepts death.

Even though Makibefo and his wife speak no more than 300 words between them, the imagery movingly articulates their dehumanising journeys. Abela shows that 'the milk of human kindness' initially flows through Makibefo's veins by having him gently salve Kidoure's spear wound, and balances the couple's brutality with marital tenderness, notably when Makibefo comforts her sleepless guilt: 'Calm yourself . . . come back to bed.' This complements the moving addition of two women not in *Macbeth*: Kidoure's wife, who begs Danikany to spare her husband and howls over his corpse, and Danikany's wife, traumatised by seeing the murdered King.

The villagers' artless 'performances', the spare dialogue and the storyteller device all help turn Shakespearean tragedy into morality play, and in this context the Narrator's use of complex Jacobean imagery feels more effective as commentary for scenes without dialogue than at the occasionally jarring moments when simple, subtitled Malagasy segues directly into Shakespeare.

Above all, this is a film of intense visual and aural contrasts: black skin against clear skies, pristine white sand and robes; the soothing background of waves lapping the shore juxtaposed against the awful sound of metal tearing flesh.

Dir/Prod/Scr/DOP: Alexander Abela, in collaboration with Jeppe Jungersen; **Editor:** Douglas Bryson; **Score:** Bien Rasoanan Tenaina; **Main Cast:** Martin (Makibefo), Noeliny (Makibefo's wife), Randria Arthur (Bakoua), Jean-Felix (Danikany), Bien Rasoanan Tenaina (Malikomy), Jean-Noël (Makidofy), Boniface (Kidoure), Victor (Witchdoctor), Gilbert Laumord (Narrator).

Bleeder (Sangrador)
Venezuela, 2000 – 86 mins (B&W)
Leonardo Henriquez

Shakespeare's juxtaposition of the fantastical with realistic horrors is central to *Macbeth*'s impact, and Leonardo Henriquez's *versión liberrima* ('very free version'), inspired by Polanski and Kurosawa, replicates this combination to astonishing effect.

Made for less than $300,000, his third feature divides the story into ten chapters, with titles such as 'Three Witches', 'Assassins' and, finally, 'The Wood Walks!', and his very spare script mixes original dialogue with Shakespearean quotation and paraphrase. The setting is Mérida, western Venezuela, in the early 1900s, where the portly Duncan figure, Durán, looking like a tin-pot *presidente*, leads a ragged gang of lazy bandits who launch raids on local coffee barons from their 'castle', an Andean village reached via a rope bridge and portcullis-like metal gate. Durán has one son, Damián, who horrifically botches the execution of traitor Cardozo (Cawdor) and is dismissed as a 'foolish moron with no guts' by the diminutive, peasant-like Macedonio (Macduff, with elements of Ross).

Daniel Alvarado's brutish hero, Max, seems drawn from a Sergio Leone Western, his dark beard, poncho and savage nature contrasted with the white suit of Francisco Alfaro's suave, placid J. B. (Banquo), who has a young son, Florenzo. Max's wife, dressed in figure-hugging silk and hauntingly portrayed by tall, fine-boned Karina Gómez (a leading figure in avant-garde Colombian theatre), reminds him that he has 'enjoyed' killing more than thirty men, so why should he hesitate to kill Durán and fulfil the prophecy delivered in giggling unison by three beautiful, naked young witches?

Once the carnage begins, Henriquez and cinematographer Cezary Jaworski deliver a series of indelible scenes. They delight in picking faces from the darkness with candles or flaming torches, and as Max murders Durán, killer and victim are shadows on the wall, like something from

Murnau's *Nosferatu*. The two assassins hired by Max scurry down a slope covered with squat *frailejon* bushes to dispatch Macedonio's wife and two children with scythe and pikestaff and when Henriquez abruptly cuts to Macedonio's howl of anguish more than 100 lines of Shakespeare have been harrowingly compressed into ten seconds of film.

Max's wife hangs herself from a bell-tower, which chimes erratically with each swing of her corpse, and Max becomes a grim reaper, strapping on the assassin's scythe to behead an attacker before surrendering to Macedonio, now backed by coffee barons who tolerated the moderate losses inflicted by Durán's regime, but are sick of Max's indiscriminate pillaging.

Shockingly realistic moments complement boldly reworked, stylised characterisations. Max's hired killers are a blackly comic, bickering double-act whose motto, hugely ironic in light of Max's self-delusion, is 'No one is immortal.' His wife sleeps covered in Calla lilies, beside a shrine to Saint Michael (a potent Catholic icon in Mérida) and, believing that 'urine of virgin' cleanses all human stains, has four young girls and

Covered in Calla lilies, Max's wife (Karina Gómez) sleeps beside a shrine to Saint Michael in Leonardo Henriquez's *Bleeder*

her sexy young maid pee on her 'bloody' hands. The lascivious Farmhand (a combination of *Macbeth*'s Porter and Doctor) has sex with a donkey, and the witches share their lair with a naked, caged man and their matronly queen, Hecaté. When Max visits them, one witch seems to give birth and strangle her baby with its umbilical cord. This sounds like laughable Ken Russell excess, yet because it is presented without a hint of camp, and because black-and-white tones down what might otherwise seem lurid, Henriquez not only carries off the most extravagant moments, he can successfully explore a new seam of irony in the witches' role. Hecaté reprimands her apprentices, 'old moody women . . . disguised as beautiful whores', for meddling with Max when they were supposed to disrupt someone else's life; so not only was the hero's strutting and fretting as futile as in Shakepeare, it was also a mistake.

After Macedonio has thrust Max's neck onto a giant, spear-tipped trepanner we see Hecaté and her charges in kaleidoscopic split-screen. 'What now, sisters?' she asks and, as with Polanski, we assume more horrors are imminent. The final shot of the bizarre execution machine pointing skywards pays homage to Hieronymus Bosch and recalls the end of *Throne of Blood* (1957); fittingly so, for *Bleeder* is the most visually potent translation of *Macbeth* since Kurosawa's masterpiece.

Dir/Scr: Leonardo Henriquez; **Prod:** Alberto Arvelo; **DOP:** Cezary Jaworski; **Editors:** Leonardo Henriquez, Alberto Arvelo; **Score:** Nascuy Linares; **Main Cast:** Daniel Alvarado (Max), Karina Gómez (Max's wife), Francisco Alfaro (J. B.), José Sánchez (Macedonio), Gerard Longo (Farmhand), Jacinto Cruz, Freddy Torres (Assassins), Leonardo Villalobos (Damián), Alfonzo Rivas (Durán).

Scotland, PA
US, 2001 – 104 mins
Billy Morrissette

On the *Scotland, PA* DVD, writer–director Billy Morrissette recalls encountering *Macbeth* in high school in the 1970s and immediately thinking 'it should be played as comedy in a fast food restaurant, because I was working in one and hated my boss and really wanted to kill him.' That teenage impulse inspired this likeable comedy-thriller, which generated mixed reviews and grossed $380,000 on its US-only theatrical release.

In the town of Scotland, Pennsylvania, in 1975, Pat (Maura Tierney, Nurse Abby Lockhart in *ER*,1994–) and Joe 'Mac' McBeth (James LeGros, blessed with lazy charm and Jon Bon Jovi looks) are the waitress and chef exploited by officious burger king Norm Duncan (James Rebhorn). Morrissette replicates Macbeth's courage and Cawdor's treachery as Mac ejects two rowdy diners and then, tipped off by nerdy best friend and fellow chef 'Banko', exposes the pilfering assistant manager, Doug. Norm promotes Mac, and Pat urges him on: 'We're not bad people, Mac. We're just under-achievers that have to make up for lost time,' she says, in lines as central to Morrissette's sympathetic portrayal of his protagonists as Norm's semi-accidental murder. Mac intends to stab him after clearing out his safe at knife-point, but instead Norm falls head-first into the deep-fat fryer (splashed oil scalds Pat's left hand, replacing the 'damned spot' of blood).

The McBeths frame an elderly vagrant for the crime, buy the restaurant from Norm's slacker sons – Malcolm, an aspiring rock guitarist, and Don, a closet-homosexual high-school student – and business booms. Orange-clad staff serve 'McBeths with Cheese'; cars queue at the drive-thru invented with tips from the pot-smoking hippy 'witches' (two men and a woman, whose supernatural role in the story is slightly fudged) and these nods to the rise of McDonald's dominate a loving evocation of 1970s' styles (notably the men's tight jeans, shaggy hair and wide collars) and pop culture, with five songs by Bad Company on the soundtrack and an action sequence from TV cop show *McCloud* (1970–7) playing under the opening titles.

A vegetarian detective, Lieutenant Ernie McDuff (Christopher Walken, applying his uniquely offbeat, menacing delivery to innocuous lines), investigates Norm's death and after he releases the vagrant for lack of evidence, the Shakespearean cycle of violence gives way to routine police procedural.

McDuff treats this as just another case and Malcolm and Don rejoice at losing their authoritarian pop and blowing their inheritance, so the Shakespearean parody benefits from this trio's disinterest in comparison to the equivalent *Macbeth* characters' impassioned quest for vengeance. Morrissette, who is married to Tierney, emphasises the McBeths' tragicomic love story, as remorse destroys their previously easygoing natures and boundless mutual passion. After Mac kills 'Banko' and the vagrant, the deranged Pat dies chopping off the hand whose 'scar' only she sees and McDuff and Mac's climactic fight ends with Mac impaled on the bull horns attached to his car bonnet. Ernie quits the force and McBeth's becomes McDuff's, home to the veggie Garden Burger.

Morrissette has acknowledged that Joel and Ethan Coen's *Fargo* (1996), with eccentric small-town characters embroiled in comically gruesome robbery and murder, was his most important source after *Macbeth*, though his feature début lacks the Coens' quirky dialogue and poise in switching between tenderness and violence. *Scotland, PA* may, in turn, have influenced Peter Moffat, writer of the BBC's 'Shakespeare Retold' *Macbeth* (2005), whose hero, Joe, is a brilliant chef at the swish Scottish restaurant where his wife is the ambitious *maître d'*.

Dir/Scr: Billy Morrissette; **Prods**: Richard Shepard, Jonathan Stern; **DOP**: Wally Pfister; **Editor**: Adam Lichtenstein; **Score**: Anton Sanko; **Main Cast**: James LeGros (Joe 'Mac' McBeth), Maura Tierney (Pat McBeth), Kevin Corrigan (Anthony 'Banko' Banconi), Christopher Walken (Lieutenant Ernie McDuff), James Rebhorn (Norm Duncan), Tom Guiry (Malcolm Duncan), Geoff Dunsworth (Donald Duncan), Josh Pais (Doug).

Maqbool
India, 2003 – 132 mins
Vishal Bhardwaj

In present-day Mumbai, gravel-voiced Godfather Jahangir Khan, known as Abbaji, is a short, paunchy widower with a young actress mistress, Nimmi (Tabbu). Abbaji and loyal right-hand man, Miyan Maqbool (bulging-eyed, taciturn Irfan Khan), are like father and son, much closer than Duncan and Macbeth, but what makes *Maqbool*'s characterisation truly radical is Miyan's bachelor status; he is destroyed by desire for Abbaji's queen, not his crown.

By making his hero fall for the boss's girl, Bhardwaj emulates James M. Cain and umpteen other crime writers, and although Tabbu does not evince the dangerous sexuality needed to carry off femme fatale lines like 'There are twelve moles on my body. Do you want to count them?', *Maqbool* adds a secondary layer to the tension of *Macbeth*'s first two Acts: 'Will-they-or-won't-they kill Abbaji *and* sleep together?'

While their passion simmers, Bhardwaj explores real-life Mumbai's unholy alliances between underworld, Bollywood, politics and police. The enforced suicide of Abbaji's treacherous brother-in-law, Asif (Cawdor), sees Maqbool inherit the gang's film interests (stars paying to secure juicy roles), and Abbaji's hold over the justice minister means he can have the gung-ho cop who has dared to arrest him summarily transferred. He also employs Inspectors Purohit and Pandit (a joyful double-act by veterans Naseeruddin Shah and Om Puri) as informants and occasional hit men. It is Pandit who expertly divines Miyan's shifting fortunes in *kundali* (astrology) charts, which, like the Tarot in *Joe Macbeth* (1955), keep a realistic urban context free of explicitly supernatural intervention. Pandit's use of sand, leftover curry, sweets and even blood to make the charts becomes a droll running gag.

Nimmi pressures Miyan by revealing that Abbaji's daughter Sameera is in love with gang member Guddu (Fleance), rash son of Kaka (Banquo), warning him that 'the son-in-law becomes next in line', and, after Abbaji orders Sameera and Guddu to marry and humiliates Nimmi by taking a second mistress, she and Miya finally make love, at his house. The following night, after Miyan has hosted Sameera's engagement party (the only occasion when major characters follow Bollywood convention and burst into pre-recorded song), Nimmi watches Miyan shoot Abbaji, blood splashing her face, and kills his inebriated bodyguard. Miyan inherits queen, castle and kingdom.

We are eighty minutes in, and while this comparative delay creates a stronger emotional connection to Abbaji than to Duncan, it also exposes Bhardwaj's unbalanced structure. After the pivotal murder in Polanski's original-text *Macbeth*, we have 100 minutes to observe Macbeth's reign of terror and the couple's psychological disintegration; here, only fifty minutes remain, the plot resolution is confusingly rushed and, even without knowing the play, Miyan and Nimmi's development would feel unsatisfactory. They have almost as little to say as Washizu and Asaji in *Throne of Blood* (1957), and Bhardwaj cannot deliver sufficient visual poetry to compensate for minimal self-expression.

Miyan has Kaka killed and is tortured by suspicions that Abbaji is the father of the baby Nimmi is carrying. Guddu abducts Sameera, murders Miyan's lieutenants and forces him into a doomed drug deal to raise cash and maintain political control. After Nimmi gives birth prematurely the couple prepare to flee, but she dies from demented guilt and physical trauma (has Abbaji's child avenged him?). At the hospital, Miyan finds Sameera and Guddu claiming the baby. Numbed, he walks outside and the story comes full circle when he is shot dead by Boti, son of a gangster murdered on Miyan's orders in the opening sequence.

Though Bhardwaj integrates Shakespearean and Indian elements (especially production numbers and local politics) more successfully in *Omkara* (2006, p. 188), his storytelling still has a poise that is a cut above most commercial Hindi films, perhaps explaining why *Maqbool* was less of a hit with Indian cinemagoers than with critics.

Dir/Score: Vishal Bhardwaj; **Prod:** Bobby Bedi; **Scr:** Abbas Tyrewala, Vishal Bhardwaj; **DOP:** Hemant Chaturvedi; **Editor:** Aarif Sheikh; **Lyrics:** Gulzar; **Main Cast:** Irfan Khan (Miyan Maqbool), Tabbu (Nimmi), Pankaj Kapoor (Abbaji), Om Puri (Insp. Pandit), Naseeruddin Shah (Insp. Purohit), Piyush Mishra (Kaka), Masumi Makhija (Sameera), Ajay Gehi (Guddu).

Macbeth
Sweden/Norway, 2004 – 83 mins
Bo Landin, Alex Scherpf

Based on the *Macbeth* staged by Norwegian director Alex Scherpf at the Ice Globe Theatre in Jukkasjärvi, Swedish Lapland, in January 2004, and performed in the Sámi language, this eccentric production's emphasis on landscape and wildlife owes more to co-director Bo Landin's background in natural history documentaries than to Shakespeare. Footage of hundreds of galloping reindeer and the aurora borealis, and helicopter views of snow-covered pine forests, are initially captivating, before giving way to cumbersome symbols as, for example, we cut between Macbeth killing Duncan and a lone wolf prowling the snow.

More damagingly, the contrast between documentary realism and stylised production design jars whenever the action moves indoors. The exterior of the Macbeths' castle is the circular Ice Globe and its cramped, frozen interiors (filmed inside the Ice Globe and the nearby Ice Hotel) make the actors' breaths condense, and allow Toivo Lukkari's fierce, red-bearded Macbeth to be pictured through or mirrored in ice blocks at suitably reflective moments. He and the other dreadlocked warriors wear cartridge bandoliers across their fur jackets, yet their weapons of choice are lengths of chain or daggers and swords made from ice. With clown-face make-up and shredded white costumes, the witches (two of whom double as Lady Macduff and her son) resemble circus refugees; Anitta Suikkari's operatic Lady Macbeth sports a Jean Paul Gaultier-style scarlet and black bustier and the letter-reading scene implies that she may herself be a witch.

Severe editing reduces the longer speeches to just a few lines and significant characters to walk-ons and omits, among others, Donalbain, the Porter, Doctor, Seyton and the Siwards. The sing-song patterns of Sámi give a distinctive rhythm to the verse, the textual localisations are quaint (Banquo tells Macbeth that 'If my reindeer is not fast I must borrow an hour of night') and some added lines are insightful, as when

Lady Macbeth challenges her husband: 'Are you afraid to be the same
man in an act of valour as you are in desire?'

Dirs: Bo Landin, Alex Scherpf; **Prod/Scr**: Bo Landin; **DOP**: Jens Jansson; **Editor**: Robert
Nordh; **Score**: Björn J:son Lindh [sic]; **Main Cast**: Toivo Lukkari (Macbeth), Anitta Suikkari
(Lady Macbeth), Nils Henrik Buljo (Banquo), Sven Henriksen (Macduff), Per Henrik Bals
(Duncan), Mikkel Gaup (Malcolm).

Macbeth
Australia, 2006 – 109 mins
Geoffrey Wright

Ten years after Baz Luhrmann's *William Shakespeare's Romeo + Juliet*, Australian Geoffrey Wright fused his compatriot's use of original-text Shakespeare in a modern setting with the *Joe Macbeth* gangster formula and produced this disappointingly flat, extremely violent thriller, which flopped in Australia in September 2006.

Sam Worthington's handsome young Macbeth drives an Aston Martin. His pale, slender wife (Victoria Hill) wears gaudy designer outfits and snorts cocaine in their mansion, Dunsinane. Middle-aged, sleek-suited Melbourne gang lord Duncan (Gary Sweet) finances luxury property developments with drug deals, including one with a double-crossing oriental crew, which explodes into the second scene's gun battle and car chase. The sequence ends with Macbeth and Banquo victorious at the Cawdor nightclub, where Macbeth's dance-floor encounter with three flame-haired schoolgirl witches is shot like a music video, and as he is drunk and high on drugs, and Banquo is vomiting in the toilet and does not see the girls, we wonder if their prophecy was produced by Macbeth's stoned subconscious. Wright similarly makes us suspect sexual fantasy when the witches invade Dunsinane, naked, and Macbeth learns of his 'invincibility' while having sex with all three, desire stoked because his wife's grief for their dead son has eradicated her libido. Hill weeps at the boy's graveside in the opening scene and later stares at an empty swing in their garden, powerfully underpinning lines such as 'I have given suck . . .'. Her loss and his implied auto-suggestion are, however, the only thoughtful interpretive strokes until the last scene.

Though the script sometimes tweaks the text ('castle' becomes 'house') or matches it to modern props (Macbeth asks Banquo 'Ride you with Fleance?' when he sees their motocross bikes), Wright and Hill could and should have rewritten more, because the production design lacks the *Romeo + Juliet* (see p. 223) stylisation that made Shakespeare's archaic language palatable within Luhrmann's 'created' world. This constantly creates the same problems as Michael Almereyda's *Hamlet* (2000, p. 47): every 'Worthy Sir' from leather-jacketed, pistol-packing hardmen, every reference to swords when we see guns, jars. Worse still, everyone speaks with little regard for rhythm, punctuation or meaning; Hill is strident, Worthington tosses away the soliloquies in voiceover.

Most damagingly, the criminalised revenge plot loses credibility in the last third. Malcolm (there is no Donalbain) forms an alliance not with fellow mobsters who might profit from Macbeth's removal (one of the elements that makes perfect sense in *Men of Respect* (1991, p. 110), but two detectives whom we have seen staking out Dunsinane with night-vision video cameras. Attaching invented lines to the names of minor characters from Act V, Malcolm introduces this pair to Macduff as 'My lords Caithness and Menteith, angels of the law, companions to our cause' but there is no additional dialogue to explain the deal they must have made with Malcolm (a cut of the drugs trade, maybe, or payback for the murder of a brother officer?), so we must blindly accept that the cops are happy to supply Macbeth's enemies with assault rifles and join their climactic night-time assault on Dunsinane. Even if you do not know the play, this is lazily inadequate scriptwriting.

Macduff does for Macbeth in a slow-motion firefight, illuminated by laser-sight beams, gunshots muted in favour of orchestral requiem, after which Wright has the adolescent Fleance enter the Macbeths' bedroom intending to finish off the dying hero and mistakenly shoot dead the housekeeper – a first kill en route to his predicted reign. Macduff then leads him paternally into the dawn, suggesting that both have swiftly adopted replacements for their murdered son and father.

Dir: Geoffrey Wright; **Prod:** Martin Fabinyi; **Scr:** Geoffrey Wright, Victoria Hill; **DOP:** Will Gibson; **Editor:** Jane Usher; **Score:** John Clifford White; **Main Cast:** Sam Worthington (Macbeth), Victoria Hill (Lady Macbeth), Steve Bastoni (Banquo), Lachy Hulme (Macduff), Gary Sweet (Duncan), Matt Doran (Malcolm), Damian Walshe-Howling (Ross).

The Merchant of Venice (play synopsis)

In Venice, a young nobleman, Bassanio, is determined to win the wealthy heiress, Portia, who in Belmont sets her suitors a challenge: they must open one of three caskets, gold, silver and lead, and whoever chooses the one containing Portia's portrait will marry her.

To finance his mission, Bassanio borrows 3,000 ducats from his merchant friend, Antonio, who himself borrows this sum from Shylock, a Jewish moneylender, despite their past enmity. Antonio offers as surety the imminent return of his cargo ships. Shylock insists that he may cut off a pound of Antonio's flesh if the merchant forfeits.

The Princes of Morocco and Aragon choose, respectively, the gold and silver caskets; both lose. Shylock's daughter, Jessica, is in love with a Christian, Lorenzo, and Bassanio's friend Gratiano helps him steal her away from Shylock's house, taking money and jewels. Shylock's servant, Launcelot Gobbo, leaves him to work for Bassanio.

In Belmont, Bassanio finds Portia's portrait in the lead casket. Her lady-in-waiting, Nerissa, accepts Gratiano's marriage proposal. Jessica, Lorenzo and Antonio's friend, Solanio, bring news that Antonio's ships have been wrecked and Shylock has had him arrested. Bassanio and Gratiano leave immediately after their weddings to free Antonio with Portia's money. She and Nerissa follow in secret, disguised as a young lawyer, 'Balthasar', and 'his' clerk.

At the trial, Shylock rejects all offers of money, and Balthasar's eloquent pleas for mercy. The lawyer challenges him to cut the flesh without spilling blood, as blood is not mentioned in the bond. He cannot. The Doge seizes half his wealth and gives the rest to Antonio, who insists that Shylock become a Christian. He leaves, shattered. The lawyer and his clerk persuade Bassanio and Gratiano to pay them with the rings Portia and Nerissa gave them. In Belmont, the wives ask for the rings and reveal the truth of their disguise. Antonio learns that three of his ships have returned home safely.

The Merchant of Venice (Der Kaufman von Venedig)
Germany, 1923 – 103 mins (UK version: 71 mins)
Peter Paul Felner

Peter Paul Felner's film combines the *Merchant*, Giovanni Fiorentino's fourteenth-century novella *Il Pecorone* (one of Shakespeare's main sources) and much invention. It was released in Britain as *The Jew of Mestri* (the only name given to Fiorentino's moneylender), probably, suggests Robert Hamilton Ball in his indispensable *Shakespeare on Silent Film* (1968), 'in fear lest the public might stay away from another Shakespeare film.' My assessment is based on that shortened British version.

In June 1565, the careworn Mordecai (Werner Krauss, infinitely more convincing than as Iago, see p. 161), lives in luxury with his solemn wife (Frida Richard) and pigtailed, withdrawn daughter, Rachela. When Mordecai and Tubal (Albert Steinrück) agree that Rachela will shortly marry Tubal's rabbinical son, Elias, this enforced betrothal makes her and Lorenzo's secret plan to elope more urgent than in the *Merchant*, and Elias's presence mirrors the romantic rivalry in the film's 'Portia' storyline.

In this, wealthy merchant Benito (Antonio) escorts wild-eyed, 'ne'er do well' nobleman Giannetto (Bassanio) to a vast palace overlooking the Grand Lagoon, home to the sprightly and flirtatious Lady of Belmont, Beatrice (Henny Porten, Germany's most popular film actress). Benito presents his friend as Venice's richest trader, a worthy rival to Beatrice's most eligible suitor, the Prince of Aragon, an absurd popinjay (Ferdinand von Alten, Roderigo in *Othello,* 1922). Beatrice falls for Giannetto, but announces her engagement to Aragon after he exposes Giannetto's lie.

Her presence within walking distance of the Rialto removes the *Merchant*'s contrast between Belmont and Venice, but Felner makes spectacularly varied use of the latter, giving us wide, high-angle shots of Beatrice's dining hall and gardens, St Mark's Square, and canals and bridges choked with gondolas and masked revellers as Rachela elopes. Before then, however, comes the most arresting departure from Shakespeare.

Needing cash for Rachela's wedding feast, Mordecai sends his wife to collect a loan from Giannetto, but he and Benito mock her. Cursing them ('Wastrels, knaves!'), she collapses, is carried home by Mordecai (looking like Lear with Cordelia) and later dies. So when some of Benito's ships are wrecked and he must borrow to sustain his friend's feigned wealth, Tubal urges Mordecai: 'They killed your wife, they will steal your child, now is your chance for revenge.' In seeking the pound of flesh, Mordecai is an out-and-out avenger, his 'villainy' more sympathetic and less complex than Shylock's response to years of insults and oppression and the loss of Jessica.

Rejoicing when further disasters prevent Benito from repaying, Mordecai learns that Rachela has converted to Christianity and sits *shiva* for his 'dead' daughter. Elias drowns himself and the two fathers become brothers in sorrow, leading to an astonishing scene when Rachela approaches Tubal and Mordecai and, after almost an hour, finally has her first lines, beseeching her father not to do 'this awful thing', meaning exact the forfeit – and making one wonder how Shakespeare might have handled a comparable Shylock–Jessica reunion.

The Jew's defeat is a breathlessly edited courtroom epic, as hundreds of extras throng the Senate and the Doge presides from on high. The disguised Beatrice (having laughed off Giannetto's confession of penury) intervenes like Portia, though Mordecai's pantomime gloating ('Revenge is sweeter meat than gold!') is of course no substitute for the ebb and flow of the *Merchant*'s trial. After Beatrice reveals her disguise and forgives Giannetto for giving away her ring, we cut from her and Rachela's joint wedding celebrations on the canal to Mordecai's desolate face – the film's only extreme close-up and a transition that distils perfectly Samuel Johnson's definition of the Shakespearean world 'in which, at the same time, the reveller is hasting to his wine, and the mourner burying his friend.'

Dir/Prod: Peter Paul Felner; **DOPs:** Axel Graatkjaer, Rudolph Maté; **Main Cast:** Werner Krauss (Mordecai), Lia Eibenschütz (Rachela), Heinz-Rolf Münz (Lorenzo), Carl Ebert (Benito), Harry Liedtke (Giannetto), Henny Porten (Beatrice), Cläre Rommer (Nerissa), Albert Steinrück (Tubal), Ferdinand von Alten (Prince of Aragon).

The Maori Merchant of Venice (*Te Tangata Whai Rawa*)
New Zealand, 2002 – 153 mins
Don C. Selwyn

Don Selwyn had spent decades directing and training Maori actors when he used Shakespeare to make the first ever Maori-language feature: this slow, fitfully engaging production with the feel of a community television play.

The script is Dr Pei Te Hurinui Jones's 1945 translation of the play into poetic Maori, first used by Selwyn in a 1990 stage *Merchant*, and Waihoroi Shortland reprises his surprisingly amiable Hairoka (Shylock). In skull cap and gaberdine, a bald, bearded and portly Shortland is dwarfed by stylish young Christians built like seventeenth-century All Blacks. Venetian architecture is represented by Italianate buildings in Auckland and the canal and Rialto by inner-harbour waterways and the Herald Island wharf.

There is no apparent parallel for the Christian/Jew divide within Maoridom (as with, say, an Indian *Merchant* pitting Hindus against a Muslim), so it is gratuitous to have Hairoka and Anatonio (Antonio) agree terms in a gallery while celebrated Maori artist Selwyn Muru dabs at a grim painting that repeats the word 'Holocaust'. The cultural translation focuses instead on Belmont, which becomes the lush, oddly magical kingdom of Pomona. Conch-blowers and flying *turehu* (fairies) greet the Prince of Morocco, and Pohia (Portia) is surrounded by Maori music, dance and song.

Selwyn's casting of non-professionals (he hoped to inspire young Maori to take up the language) brings inevitably mixed results. The verse-speaking is declamatory and as Anatonio, lecturer Scott Morrison has a first-timer's stiffness. Radio newsreader Ngarimu Daniels makes a spirited Pohia, and actor and student Sonny Kirikiri steals the film as Karatiano (Gratiano), contrasting early bonhomie with Haka-like fury at the trial, which is shot in Auckland's Holy Sepulchre Church (venue for Selwyn's

1990 production). Christians fill one bank of pews, Jews the other, chorusing 'Yea, a Daniel!' or 'Good Shylock!' as their 'team' scores legal points. A 'community play' policy means every extra is named in the end credits.

Dir: Don C. Selwyn. **Prod:** Ruth Kaupua Panapa; **Scr:** Dr Pei Te Hurinui Jones; **DOP:** Davorin Fahn; **Editor:** Bella Erikson; **Score:** Hirini Melbourne (Maori music), Clive Cockburn; **Main Cast:** Waihoroi Shortland (Hairoka), Reikura Morgan (Tiehika), Te Arepa Kahhi (Roroneto), Scott Morrison (Anatonio), Te Rangihau Gilbert (Patanio), Ngarimu Daniels (Pohia), Veeshayane Armstrong (Nerita), Sonny Kirikiri (Karatiano).

William Shakespeare's The Merchant of Venice
UK/Luxembourg/Italy/US 2004 – 131 mins
Michael Radford

Michael Radford's adaptation, the first English-language sound feature of the *Merchant*, is a graduate of the Zeffirelli school, its beautifully crafted, historically authentic production design (including BAFTA-nominated costumes) following a template established by the Italian in 1967–8 with *The Taming of the Shrew* and *Romeo and Juliet* (see pp. 239 and 218). Radford, cinematographer Benoît Delhomme and production designer Bruno Rubeo distinguish admirably between settings. With a seamless combination of Luxembourg studio sets and location filming, they make Venice a place of danger for Jews and sexual and gastronomic indulgence for privileged Christians. The day-time interiors are hazy, and as claustrophobic as the torch-lit canals and narrow streets of the night-time scenes. Belmont is a spacious and sunny lakeside idyll, which Jocelyn Pook fills with harp music.

Radford begins with a lengthy prologue contextualising the religious animosity. Captions explaining that in 1596 'intolerance of the Jews was a fact of life' are intercut with shots of a Jew denounced as 'Usurer!' and hurled from a bridge into the canal by an angry mob, observed by Tubal, Shylock and Antonio, who returns Shylock's greeting with spittle (establishing the credibility of 'You . . . spit upon my Jewish gaberdine' in the bond scene). We see Antonio praying in church and Shylock and Jessica in a synagogue. Seven minutes have elapsed before we hear the play's first lines and thereafter Radford cuts less savagely than Zeffirelli, pruning carefully and respecting the play's structure. A handful of crude, Zeffirelli-esque insertions add spurious 'colour' (a topless whore tauntingly invites Shylock to 'taste my Christian flesh!') and the Italian might well also applaud the 'show-and-tell' tactics adopted whenever

(*Opposite page*) 'Hath not a Jew eyes?': Al Pacino as Shylock in Michael Radford's *The Merchant of Venice*

Radford feels the language needs reinforcement. Sometimes this is evocative (cutaways to Jessica and Lorenzo buying a monkey emphasise Shylock's torment as Tubal describes their wasteful revelry), at others heavy-handed: Shylock devises the 'flesh' clause after buying meat shown in several close-ups as it is cut, weighed and wrapped, lest we worry that his 'merry sport' might have lacked direct inspiration.

Al Pacino, looking older than in any other screen role, highlights Shylock's keen sense of irony and flashes of wit, proving that to be joyless is not to be humourless. On trial, however, he suggests that his livelihood is at stake, not his soul and the honour of his tribe, and in a mid-Atlantic accent with hints of *Mittel Europa* he cannot prevent his American rhythms from working against the pentameter, occasionally marring verse and prose with trademark over-emphasis ('We will resemble you in THAT!').

Jeremy Irons's superlative Antonio personifies Solanio's belief that the merchant 'only loves the world' because it contains Joseph Fiennes's Bassanio, a graceless leather-clad libertine who pouts and smoulders. Antonio savours a kiss on the lips from his grateful friend, so stressing the homoeroticism that the *Observer* described him as 'a sad, rheumy-eyed old queen', while in the trial you feel he might have died content, his love tragically unrequited but ennobled by the sacrifice that brought Bassanio happiness.

Reliable character actors fill the mature supporting roles, with John Sessions and Gregor Fisher memorably turning Salerio and Solanio into over-fed clubmen. Apart from Mackenzie Crook's droll, bug-eyed Launcelot, however, the juvenile actors are uniformly weak. Charlie Cox's bland Lorenzo praises his beloved as 'wise and fair', despite Zuleikha Robinson's Jessica meriting only the latter adjective, and her American accent is as incongruous as that of Lynn Collins's Portia. Collins looks the part (fine, pale features framed by red Botticelli curls) without conveying Portia's formidable intellect, either in the withering dismissals of her suitors (Radford does not let her dismiss the Prince of Morocco with 'Let all of his complexion choose me so') or the trial, when her rhetoric sounds like over-rehearsed recitation.

After dutifully retaining the tiresome rings comedy, Radford follows the happy couples' exits by dwelling finally on Antonio's solitary future (denied even the consolation of his ships' safe return), shows Shylock barred from a Venetian synagogue and returns to Jessica, alone in regretful contemplation – all this as counter-tenor Andreas Scholl sings Pook's haunting 'With Wand'ring Steps'. This melancholy sequence ends a respectable entertainment, which for all its outward virtues and some fine performances, reveals much less of the play than the straightforward video record of Trevor Nunn's outstanding National Theatre production from 1999.

Dir/Scr: Michael Radford; **Prods:** Cary Brokaw, Michael Cowan, Barry Navidi, Jason Piette; **DOP:** Benoît Delhomme; **Editor:** Lucia Zucchetti; **Score:** Jocelyn Pook; **Main Cast:** Al Pacino (Shylock), Zuleikha Robinson (Jessica), Charlie Cox (Lorenzo), Jeremy Irons (Antonio), Joseph Fiennes (Bassanio), Lynn Collins (Portia), Heather Goldenhersh (Nerissa), Kris Marshall (Gratiano).

A Midsummer Night's Dream (play synopsis)

Ancient Athens. Duke Theseus is about to marry Hippolyta, Queen of the Amazons, whom he conquered in battle. Bottom the weaver and his fellow craftsmen plan to perform a play, *Pyramus and Thisby*, as part of the wedding celebrations. Young lovers Hermia and Lysander defy Hermia's father, Egeus, and Theseus, who order her to marry Demetrius on pain of death or a vow of chastity. The couple flee into the woods, chased by Demetrius, who is pursued by Helena, who is hopelessly in love with him.

In the woods, the Fairy King, Oberon, has quarrelled with his Queen, Titania, over her refusal to give him her beloved 'changeling' boy. He orders his mischievous sprite, Puck, to gather juice from a magic plant that will make Titania fall in love with the next creature she sees. This turns out to be Bottom, who thanks to Puck has acquired the head of an ass, a transformation that sent his horrified fellows fleeing from their rehearsal in the wood.

Using the same juice, Puck mistakenly makes Lysander transfer his passion to Helena, to her great distress, instead of making Demetrius fall for Hermia as Oberon intended. Oberon sprinkles more magic juice on Demetrius, with the result that he, too, declares his love for Helena.

After Bottom has enjoyed a night of bliss with Titania, and the four lovers one of bewildering chaos, Titania and Oberon are reconciled and the Athenians, thanks to Puck's final sprinkling of the love juice, are correctly paired off: Hermia with Lysander, Helena with Demetrius. They are married in Athens alongside Theseus and Hippolyta. Bottom, restored to human shape, and his fellows farcically perform the tragic *Pyramus and Thisby* before leaving the newlyweds to retire to bed. Puck, Oberon, Titania and their fairies process through Theseus's palace blessing the couples and promising them contented and fertile futures.

A Midsummer Night's Dream
US, 1935 – 117 mins (B&W)
Max Reinhardt, Wilhelm Dieterle

The hugely influential Austrian-born director Max Reinhardt had already
staged *A Midsummer Night's Dream* ten times in Europe when, in 1934,
he fled the persecution of Jews in Nazi Germany and sought refuge in
Los Angeles. His first assignment there was an acclaimed open-air *Dream*
for 15,000 spectators at the Hollywood Bowl and soon afterwards
Warner Bros. hired him to direct a film version intended to show cinema-
knocking 'snobs' that the studio could produce more than Westerns and
gangster movies.

'When thou wakest . . .': Puck (Mickey Rooney) applies love juice to restore the sleeping
Lysander's (Dick Powell) passion for Hermia in Reinhardt and Dieterle's *A Midsummer
Night's Dream*

They gave him a huge budget, $1.5m, but disliked his early footage, replacing the original cinematographer and installing Wilhelm Dieterle, a former Reinhardt collaborator with several feature films to his credit, as co-director. Together they deliver Shakespeare on the grandest scale, and from the opening scene, showing Theseus leading his gilded army in a triumphant homecoming parade, drama takes a back seat to spectacle.

The woodland action begins with a seven-minute ballet, accompanied by Mendelssohn's 1826 *Dream* overture. Blonde ballerina fairies in ethereal lace emerge from the mist and gambol around a giant oak, which appears rooted in the sky. A goblin orchestra plays manically. Filters make the air sparkle around black-clad Oberon (a declamatory Victor Jory), whose bald-headed minions use their sinewy wings to round up the terrified fairies.

At the heart of this pageant is thirteen-year-old Mickey Rooney as Puck, a hyperactive blond cherub in a grass skirt, masking his sketchy grasp of the language with whooping laughter and enjoying the best of the special effects, as he soars above the trees and belches fog. Reinhardt uses him to enhance the play's latent family appeal, and does the same with the 'changeling boy'. Not required, and seldom shown, on stage, this turbaned little fellow rides a unicorn, weeps when briefly abandoned by Titania (the angelically serene Anita Louise), and is eventually kidnapped by Oberon. Rather than merely providing motivation for the royal feud that inspires the *Dream*'s confusion, he becomes the sentimental key to unlocking Titania and Oberon's volatile relationship.

Less than a decade into the sound era, the effects showcased what cinema was now capable of, and *Variety* hailed 'unquestionably the loveliest fantastic imagery the screen has yet produced'; to contemporary eyes it is overkill, while the emotional core of the play – the plight of the Athenian lovers – becomes a tiresome, broadly acted series of shouting matches (years later, Dick Powell admitted that he had never really understood Lysander's lines).

Shakespeare is slightly better served by the mechanicals. As Bottom, James Cagney distanced himself from his habitual tough-guy roles with a slow-witted turn, enhanced by a magnificent ass's head. He enjoys a necessarily chaste night with Titania (the merest hint of sex between 'donkey' and fairy queen would have been unthinkable), then, in the chaotic *Pyramus and Thisby* performance, spars enjoyably with his dim, seed-munching Flute (Joe E. Brown, fondly remembered as the millionaire who woos Jack Lemmon in *Some Like It Hot*, 1959).

Not even this fine double-act could prevent a wave of hostile British reactions, as the *Sunday Times* concluded 'Poor old Shakespeare!' and John Gielgud wrote to a friend that watching the film was 'like having an operation'. American critics were kinder, cinematographer Hal Mohr and editor Ralph Dawson earned Oscars and Reinhardt earned a nomination for Best Picture. He had finally realised the long-held ambition 'of doing this play with no restriction on my imagination', yet disappointing attendance figures led Warners to shelve its plan for him to direct more Shakespeare films.

Dirs: Max Reinhardt, Wilhelm Dieterle; **Prod:** Max Reinhardt; **Scr:** Charles Kenyon, Mary McCall Jr; **DOP:** Hal Mohr; **Editor:** Ralph Dawson; **Score:** Felix Mendelssohn, arranged by Erich Wolfgang Korngold; **Main Cast:** Ian Hunter (Theseus), Verree Teasdale (Hippolyta), Olivia De Havilland (Hermia), Dick Powell (Lysander), Jean Muir (Helena), Ross Alexander (Demetrius), James Cagney (Bottom), Anita Louise (Titania), Victor Jory (Oberon), Mickey Rooney (Puck).

A Midsummer Night's Dream
UK, 1969 – 124 mins
Peter Hall

In pre-release interviews for his Royal Shakespeare Company *Dream*, Peter Hall took a dig at Max Reinhardt's 1935 Hollywood version, dismissing its 'fairies in little white tutus, skipping through gossamer forests'. Offering a text-driven antidote to studio-bound fantasia, he banished all shots without dialogue and filmed in autumn daylight, in the grounds of Compton Verney (a seventeenth-century manor house near the RSC's base in Stratford-upon-Avon).

We see a great deal of what Puck calls the 'dank and dirty ground', and, tracked by a hand-held camera through tangled undergrowth, the Athenian lovers, vain Carnaby Street youths in dainty, 1960s' outfits, become cold, muddy and bewildered, their ordeal closer to *The Blair Witch Project* than Reinhardt's *Dream*. Diana Rigg's Helena is a neurotic brunette who towers over Helen Mirren's blonde, girlish Hermia, whose furious 'How low am I, thou painted maypole?' can seldom have had such apt casting. As Lysander, the blond David Warner has a physical and intellectual edge over the dark-haired, haughty Demetrius of Michael Jayston. The lovers' shifting romantic allegiances, suggested several critics, were in tune with late 1960s' sexual promiscuity and vibrant performances ensure that the quartet live up to Shakespeare's description of 'quick bright things'.

Hall's treatment of the fairy world, however, is disastrous. Titania, Oberon and Puck are covered from head to toe in sickly, silvery-green make-up and little else (a topless Judi Dench's modesty is protected by a few leaves). Woeful lighting continuity means they and their equally verdant urchin-like minions change colour alarmingly from shot to shot. 'Special effects' means fairies appearing and vanishing via jump-cuts or making speeded-up exits to cartoonish whizzes. There is no visual magic to go with the magical verse, eloquently delivered by Dench, suitably spellbound for her one-night stand with Bottom (a tiresomely loud Paul

Rogers), Ian Richardson's careworn Oberon and Ian Holm's Puck, all boyish energy. Derek Godfrey's benevolent, man-of-the-world Theseus, and Barbara Jefford's sultry Hippolyta (dressed in knee-length leather boots and miniskirt) enliven the opening and closing scenes inside the manor house.

The cast, many of them retained from Hall's stage *Dream*s, speak in close-up in perhaps eight out of ten shots because of the director's conviction that 'Shakespeare's text only has film value in close-up'; his wish to stress words over images also led him to have the actors post-synch every line 'in the peace and concentration of a studio'. Initially distracting, this dubbing is soon forgotten, and you relish hearing every word so precisely weighted – making this perhaps the only Shakespeare film that offers greater rewards if watched with eyes shut.

Its theatrical release in Britain in February 1969 elicited a chorus of derision ('Drab, mundane and shockingly inept,' fumed the *Observer*). A week later, a deal with CBS enabled Shakespeare to knock *Mission: Impossible* off America's prime-time Sunday schedule and twenty-five million viewers tuned in – enough to have filled the RSC's largest auditorium every night for thirty years.

Dir: Peter Hall; **Prod**: Michael Birkett; **DOP**: Peter Suschitzky; **Editor**: Jack Harris; **Score**: Guy Woolfenden; **Main Cast**: Derek Godfrey (Theseus), Barbara Jefford (Hippolyta), Helen Mirren (Hermia), David Warner (Lysander), Diana Rigg (Helena), Michael Jayston (Demetrius), Paul Rogers (Bottom), Judi Dench (Titania), Ian Richardson (Oberon), Ian Holm (Puck).

A Midsummer Night's Dream
UK, 1996 – 99 mins
Adrian Noble

Adrian Noble's film serves as an adequate small-screen record of his acclaimed 1994 production for the Royal Shakespeare Company, but should never have been released in cinemas, where it was savaged by critics and became such a box-office disaster that in the fierce media and industry debate about wasteful National Lottery funding of British features in the 1990s it was cited as one of the worst offenders: its £2.3m budget included £750,000 of Lottery funding; it took less than £10,000 in the UK.

Noble's *Alice in Wonderland*-like framing device makes this the *Dream* of a blond pre-adolescent (Osheen Jones, later to play a comparable role in *Titus*, 1999 p. 265), who tumbles in striped pyjamas from his Victorian home into Anthony Ward's stylised studio design, where garish costumes and rudimentary special effects betray a hotchpotch of influences. Fairies float into a lightbulb-filled sky on large umbrellas (*Mary Poppins*, 1964) and sport candy-floss wigs and fuzzy trousers in *Sesame Street* colours. To bursts of flatulent brass, the rude mechanicals gather in a Nissen hut like off-duty Home Guards (*Dad's Army*). Bicycle and motorbike riders are silhouetted racing across a brilliant moon (*E.T. The Extra-Terrestrial*).

Noble's muddled direction sometimes has the Boy as an invisible spectator, his smiles or gasps reassuring us that we should feel amused or shocked, or his presence is tacitly acknowledged by the characters. The commonplace theatrical doubling of Theseus/Oberon and Hippolyta/Titania (Alex Jennings and Lindsay Duncan, suitably majestic in both guises) is so comprehensively extended that Athens and the fairy wood are put forward as mirror images, with Barry Lynch as Philostrate and Puck, and Starveling, Quince and Flute confusingly returning as Cobweb, Mustardseed and Peasblossom to feed Bottom, as though Puck had transformed them, too. Alongside four charmless, poorly spoken

lovers, the only actors who impress are Jennings, Duncan and Desmond
Barrit as Bottom, braying in ecstasy as he makes rough love to Titania.

Dir/Scr: Adrian Noble; **Prod:** Paul Arnott; **DOP:** Ian Wilson; **Editors:** Paul Hodgson, Peter
Hollywood; **Score:** Howard Blake; **Main Cast:** Alex Jennings (Theseus/Oberon), Lindsay
Duncan (Hippolyta/Titania), Monica Dolan (Hermia), Daniel Evans (Lysander), Emily Raymond
(Helena), Kevin Doyle (Demetrius), Desmond Barrit (Bottom), Barry Lynch (Puck/Philostrate),
Osheen Jones (The Boy).

William Shakespeare's A Midsummer Night's Dream
US/Germany, 1999 – 116 mins
Michael Hoffman

Twentieth Century-Fox's attempt to capitalise on its huge success in 1996 with *William Shakespeare's Romeo + Juliet* (p. 223) by financing this star-studded, heavily promoted *Dream* brought artistic and commercial disappointment (grosses of $16m in America and $2m in Britain). Michael Hoffman, who had directed the play twice on stage, apes the Anglo-American casting formula of Kenneth Branagh's *Much Ado About Nothing* and, to make the play more accessible, moves the story from ancient Athens to the fictional Monte Athena, Tuscany, in the 1890s. The marriage of Sophie Marceau's dreamy, scarcely intelligible Hippolyta (her French accent turns 'admirable' into 'hot mirror ball') and David Strathairn's strait-laced Theseus at his *palazzo* becomes a prudent match between European aristocrats, not conqueror and captive, while the young lovers acquire the buttoned-up fashions and romantic conventions familiar from Merchant/Ivory costume dramas such as *A Room with a View* (1986).

Before inhibitions are cast off in the fairy wood, however, Hoffman introduces his big idea: giving Bottom a backstory. In a bustling market square, we see Kevin Kline in straw boater and cream suit, pretending to be a gentleman and avoiding his furious wife, who yells in subtitled Italian: 'Where's my husband? Where's that worthless dreamer?' The two scenes showing Bottom yearning to escape lowly status and unhappy marriage deepen our sense of his inner life; yet Kline, an experienced stage Shakespearean, squanders this advantage with a performance of wearying self-regard, especially once bright Tuscan locations are replaced by a cramped, sanitised wood (built at Rome's Cinecittà studios).

Sporting ass's ears and whiskers, Kline strains too hard to make us sigh at the contrast between his home life and his ecstatic night in the arms of Michelle Pfeiffer's glittering Titania. Pfeiffer scarcely seems enamoured of either Bottom or Rupert Everett's bare-chested Oberon, and while King and Queen are breathtakingly beautiful they are as engaging as perfume models; indeed, the film's cosmetic tone was symbolised by its tie-in deal with Max Factor, who launched a limited edition 'Midsummer Night's Dream Collection', including Cobweb Nail Varnish.

Only Stanley Tucci's Puck energises proceedings. Bald, Spock-eared and sardonic, he would rather be boozing or seducing one of Titania's gorgeous attendants than chasing after the Athenians. Perky Anna Friel and her cocksure admirers, Dominic West and Christian Bale, are adequately ardent, though you never believe these civilised Brits belong to the same century, let alone community, as Helena, played by Calista Flockhart as a more neurotically exasperating version of her title role as a Boston attorney in TV comedy-drama Ally McBeal (1997–2002, then at the peak of its popularity). As the quartet cycle and stumble across unconvincing sets, Hoffman's uncertain direction generates neither confusion nor enchantment. His idea of physical comedy is to have Flockhart and Friel mud-wrestle, and the effects shots of vanishing fairies scarcely improve on the 1935 Dream.

Tucci excepted, no one has as much zest as the score, which includes bustling original themes by Simon Boswell, and extracts from several Italian operas, including the drinking song from Verdi's La Traviata as the mechanicals' signature tune. When they launch into their shambolic performance in Theseus's private theatre, Hoffmann does not trust us to laugh unaided, so each amateurish gaffe extracts canned laughter from a largely unseen audience.

Dir/Scr: Michael Hoffman; **Prod:** Michael Hoffman, Lesley Urdang; **DOP:** Oliver Stapleton; **Editor:** Garth Craven; **Score:** Simon Boswell; **Main Cast:** David Strathairn (Theseus), Sophie Marceau (Hippolyta), Anna Friel (Hermia), Dominic West (Lysander), Calista Flockhart (Helena), Christian Bale (Demetrius), Kevin Kline (Bottom), Michelle Pfeiffer (Titania), Rupert Everett (Oberon), Stanley Tucci (Puck).

The Children's A Midsummer Night's Dream
UK, 2001 – 113 mins
Christine Edzard

This laudable, uneven experiment offers a fine introduction to
Shakespeare for young viewers. Made for £1.3m, it involved 360 pupils
aged eight to twelve from eight state schools in Southwark and filmed
for six months at Sands Films' studio in Rotherhithe on school-day
afternoons. It begins with children in a mocked-up Elizabethan court
theatre, watching marionettes begin the *Dream*. They speak with pre-
recorded, patrician voices (including Derek Jacobi as Theseus), until, in a
terrific coup, Jamie Peachey leaps up from her stalls seat, shouts Hermia's
'I would my father but looked with my eyes.' and she and John Heyfron's
Demetrius and Danny Bishop's Lysander interact with the puppets. The
audience boo Theseus's threats before dispersing as the scene ends (they
return to watch *Pyramus and Thisby*).

Edzard inserts some location scenes, including Helena in her
bedroom, about to phone Demetrius, then the theatre floor gains thick
foliage and dry ice to become the fairy wood. The lovers reappear in
ornate Elizabethan costumes, matched by those for Oberon, Titania, Puck
and the fairies, who vanish in jump-cuts and sometimes appear to play
the harps, hurdy-gurdy and other instruments of Michael Sanvoisin's
Handel-like score.

It is illuminating to see aspects of the play suit such young
performers: the mechanicals' Act I casting session feels like team
selection for a playground kickabout, Oliver Szczypka's pleasure in
performance is perfect for Bottom's childlike nature, and the Athenian
quartet's puppy-love tantrums come across superbly. Much of their
energy and enthusiasm is, sadly, offset by their inevitable struggles with
Shakespeare's language, and Edzard's attempt to create coherent line
readings by splicing words or phrases from different takes often makes
her cast sound like androids: 'Why art thou here?' emerges as 'Why. Art
thou. Here?' Only when Bottom dons his ass's head and we cannot see

his lips move do language and performance work in tandem, not competition.

Dir: Christine Edzard; **Prod/Editor:** Olivier Stockman; **DOP:** Joachim Bergamin; **Score:** Michael Sanvoisin; **Main Cast:** Derek Jacobi (Theseus; voice only), Samantha Bond (Hippolyta; voice only), Jamie Peachey (Hermia), Danny Bishop (Lysander), Jessica Fowler (Helena), John Heyfron (Demetrius), Oliver Szczypka (Bottom), Rajouana Zalal (Titania), Dominic Haywood-Benge (Oberon), Leany Lyson (Puck).

Midsummer Dream (*El Sueño de una noche de San Juan*)
Spain/Portugal, 2005 – 85 mins
Ángel de la Cruz, Manolo Gómez

Labelled by *Variety* magazine as '*Shrek* meets Shakespeare', *Midsummer Dream* shares *Shrek*'s computer animation and fairytale quest, but replaces inventive scriptwriting and action with simplistic dialogue and repetitive knockabout. Shakespeare's *Dream* supplies characters' names, some relationships and the basic structure: mortals' adventures in fairy land book-ended by city scenes.

In Oniria, Duke Theseus, an incorrigible dreamer obsessed with grand architectural schemes, his stuffy butler, Philostratus, and his financier, Demetrius, a moustachioed cad suavely voiced by Toby Stephens, all appear Victorian, and yet the cars and motorbikes suggest the 1930s and the Duke's feisty daughter, Helena, and clumsy assistant-cum-inventor, Lysander, have twenty-first-century clothes and attitudes.

Demetrius threatens to cut off Theseus's building loans unless he is given Helena in marriage. The Duke refuses and falls gravely ill, murmuring 'Titania, Queen of the Fairies', whereupon the Spanish folklore surrounding Saint John's Night (hence the original title), when humans may enter the supernatural world, sends Helena, Demetrius and Lysander into a garishly coloured realm of forests and waterfalls. They team up with Puck, who resembles a plastic troll, and the bearded, barrel-chested Oberon, long separated from the ailing Titania, to save Theseus and the fairy queen.

With no rude mechanicals (though a carpenter, tinker, tailor and cobbler make token appearances in Oniria), and no Hermia to complicate the Lysander–Demetrius rivalry, the quest is more Tolkien than Shakespeare, as the fellowship of the *Dream* brave mountain paths and an icy labyrinth. Demetrius joins forces with three vengeful witches banished by Titania and borrowed from *Macbeth*. Bland songs, tiresome arguments and muddled confrontation leave Demetrius imprisoned in fairy land, Titania and Oberon reconciled, Theseus restored to health and Helena warming to Lysander. *Midsummer Dream* lacks Shakespearean enchantment and *Shrek*-like sophistication and fared poorly in Spanish cinemas in 2005.

Dirs: Ángel de la Cruz, Manolo Gómez; **Prod:** Manolo Gómez; **Scr:** Ángel de la Cruz, Beatriz Iso Soto; **Editors:** Ángel de la Cruz, Mercedes Arcones Schallmoser, Juan Galinanes; **Score:** Arturo B. Kress, Artur Guiamaraes; **English Voice Cast:** Bernard Hill (Theseus), Romola Garai (Helen), Rhys Ifans (Lysander), Toby Stephens (Demetrius), Miranda Richardson (Titania), Brian Blessed (Oberon), Billy Boyd (Puck).

A Midsummer Night's Dream
UK, 2005 – 89 mins (TVM)
Ed Fraiman

Television dramatist Peter Bowker's extensive credits include *The Miller's Tale*, from the contemporary *Canterbury Tales* (2003) series that inspired the BBC's *Shakespeare Retold*, and his *Dream* was the most intelligent and entertaining of those four modernised adaptations (see pp. 158 and 244).

We are in Dream Park, a Center Parcs-like woodland resort, and in the first of numerous sardonic speeches to camera, Dean Lennox Kelly's scruffy, louche Puck, coming across like a Mancunian drug dealer, explains that he, Oberon and Titania use their fairy powers as marriage guidance counsellors. Their latest 'clients' are gruff Scots businessman Theo Moon (Theseus) and downtrodden, Northern-accented wife Polly (Hippolyta), whose relationship is suffering a clichéd midlife slump (Polly: 'I'm sick of your sarcasm and the fact that you never listen to me') as they prepare for a party celebrating their daughter Hermia's engagement to childhood friend James Demetrius. Entertainment is to be provided by the rude mechanicals, four security guards who will be promoted to full-time performers if the Moons enjoy their variety show: Snug as magician, Quince on acoustic guitar with the female Flute (Mina Anwar) on vocals and Bottom (obese stand-up comic Johnny Vegas) as a comedian-impressionist.

Their big chance is jeopardised when the very posh Xander (Lysander) and the earthy, Northern Hermia make their secret love public, leaving her best friend Helena to console James while Theo rages. Puck's misdirected love juice and transformation of Bottom spark a night of familiar chaos, dominated by recriminatory banter between Oberon and Puck, and Vegas's beautiful timing. 'Where did you learn to make love like that?' gasps Titania. 'Dedication,' replies Bottom. 'I've studied lots of books and videos.'

Ed Fraiman directs energetically, helped by a strong cast, speeded-up flash-forwards or flashbacks when magic juice is applied, bursts of the

Searchers' 'Love Potion Number 9' and some enchanting guitar and glockenpsiel in Charlie Mole's score.

Instead of keeping his Theseus and Oberon so separate that they are frequently doubled on stage, Bowker brings them together with rewarding results. A bemused barman watches Theo talk to the invisible Oberon about their first meeting, at his wedding to Polly in 1979, and the pair compare their marital woes over late-night cigars. Theo and Polly renew their vows, Oberon learns from human foolery and promises Titania 'no more stupid rage, no more jealousy, because I've seen the damage it does' and Bowker neatly embellishes Shakespeare's *Dream* structure: four couples, two middle-aged and two young, quarrel and are reconciled, rather than three in the play.

At Hermia and Xander's sunlit, lakeside engagement bash, Oberon, Titania and Puck are invisible guests. Puck makes Snout's faltering magic tricks sparkle and when Bottom's lame jokes are heckled, Titania's spell sends the audience into hysterics. By replacing *Pyramus and Thisby* with solo turns, this becomes the only screen adaptation I know that prevents the mechanicals' performance feeling overly theatrical and anti-climactic.

When directors of original-text *Dream*s feel obliged to cut back and forth between the play-within-the-film and the watching Athenians' interjections, *Pyramus and Thisby* never gains the comic momentum that should build in the theatre, where Theseus and co. become an extension of the paying audience, who simply continue to switch their attention from actor to actor. Here, the variety show invites audience participation, is inherently fragmented, and, unlike *Pyramus*, does not need to work up a head of steam, enabling Bowker and Fraiman's five-minute finale to stay true to the *Dream*'s ending with a fluent economy that original-text versions of the play can only dream of.

Dir: Ed Fraiman; Prod: Piers Wilkie; Scr: Peter Bowker; DOP: Tony Miller; Editor: Mark Thornton; Score: Charlie Mole; Main Cast: Bill Paterson (Theo Moon), Imelda Staunton (Polly), Zoe Tapper (Hermia), Rupert Evans (Xander), Michell Bonnard (Helena), William Ash (James Demetrius), Johnny Vegas (Bottom), Sharon Small (Titania), Lennie James (Oberon), Dean Lennox Kelly (Puck), Mina Anwar (Flute).

Much Ado About Nothing (play synopsis)

Messina, Sicily. The local governor, Leonato, plays host to Don Pedro, Prince of Aragon, who arrives with his bastard brother, Don John, and his followers, the lords Benedick and Claudio. Claudio falls in love with Hero, Leonato's daughter, and Don Pedro woos her on his friend's behalf. Leonato's niece, Beatrice, spars verbally with Benedick, a confirmed bachelor.

Don John sets out to disrupt Claudio and Hero's marriage with his aides, Borachio and Conrade. At night, Borachio flirts with Hero's maid, Margaret, on Hero's balcony, while down below Don John makes the listening Claudio believe that his bride-to-be is betraying him. Two night-watchmen hear Borachio and Conrade talking about this deceit, arrest them and hand them over to the constable, Dogberry, and his assistant, Verges. Meanwhile, Pedro, Claudio and Hero make Beatrice and Benedick overhear separate, contrived conversations, which convince them that each is secretly in love with the other.

Claudio denounces Hero as a whore during their wedding ceremony. She faints, and a friar advises Leonato, Benedick and Beatrice to keep pretending that she is dead until they can explain Claudio's behaviour. Beatrice tells Benedick to kill Claudio to convince her of his love. He challenges his friend to a duel, but before they can fight, Dogberry makes Borachio confess to his role in the plot laid by Don John, who has fled. Leonato tells Claudio to make amends by marrying his other 'niece' and at this ceremony Claudio is astonished to discover that his second bride is Hero brought back to life. Benedick finally silences Beatrice's repartee by kissing her and they agree to marry.

Much Ado About Nothing
UK/US, 1993 – 111 mins
Kenneth Branagh

Much Ado About Nothing has the most uplifting opening of any
Shakespeare film. On a sunny Italian hillside, the leisurely picnic enjoyed
by Beatrice, Hero and their companions is interrupted when they spy Don
Pedro and his brothers-in-arms galloping back from distant conflict. The
women sprint to Leonato's villa and they and the horsemen are captured

Don Pedro (Denzel Washington) and Don John (Keanu Reeves) ride in the opening
sequence of Kenneth Branagh's *Much Ado About Nothing*

in a slow-motion homage to *The Magnificent Seven* (1960), accompanied by Patrick Doyle's brassy score. The women hurriedly shower and change into white cotton dresses even cleaner than the ones they discard; the soldiers strip off, plunge into fountains to scrub away the trail dust and emerge with their dark leather trousers and cream tunics looking as good as new. Both groups march in formation into a courtyard: let the battle of the sexes commence.

This is exuberant, economical film-making. In five minutes, Branagh establishes location and tone, introduces the principals and hooks his audience. He had mentally storyboarded the sequence while playing Benedick on stage in 1988 and around that time also decided that *Much Ado . . .* (previously filmed in East Germany in 1963 and twice in Russia, in 1956 and 1973) would come most vividly to life in a verdant landscape, a view triumphantly vindicated by his decision to shoot in Tuscany, instead of the more arid Messina, in southern Sicily (the play's specified location).

All but a handful of scenes take place in the landscaped grounds of the fourteenth-century Villa Vignamaggio, Chianti, beneath perfect blue skies or on balmy nights filled with masked revels, creating an irresistible combination of beautiful scenery, perfect weather and (mostly) gorgeous people in a flimsy plot that hinges on *five* cases of eavesdropping.

The improbable twists are much less important to the play's popularity than the 'merry war' between Beatrice and Benedick, and the deep desire for love and companionship that flows beneath their wit, and Branagh and Emma Thompson, then one of Britain's highest-profile showbiz couples, enjoy their verbal jousts. As always when directing himself, Branagh could be less self-conscious, especially in his soliloquies, and at this point, long before his unforgettable television performances in *Conspiracy* (2001) and *Shackleton* (2002) and on film in *Rabbit-Proof Fence* (2002), he was a less assured screen performer than Thompson, who balances Beatrice's pleasant, spirited intelligence with her fear of being left on the shelf.

With one eye on the American market (the $8m budget came from the Samuel Goldwyn Company), Branagh established the Anglo-

American casting model that he was to repeat with *Hamlet* (1996), *Love's Labour's Lost* (2000) and *As You Like It* (2006), only achieving complete success with the most recent attempt. The other Brits include Branagh regulars Richard Briers, quietly benevolent, and Brian Blessed, all lusty, theatrical guffaws as Leonato's brother, Antonio, alongside reliable character players such as Imelda Staunton as Margaret and Gerard Horan as Borachio. Among the Americans, only Denzel Washington matches Thompson's star quality, delivering a typically regal portrayal as Pedro. Robert Sean Leonard makes a blandly handsome partner for Kate Beckinsale's Hero, while Keanu Reeves is characteristically wooden as Don John, happily for the actor's sake a man 'not of many words'.

Branagh inexcusably over-indulges Michael Keaton's grotesque Dogberry, all matted hair, foul teeth and scarcely intelligible accent (Welsh-Irish-American, with a dash of Long John Silver). Keaton leers, gurns and, like Ben Elton's equally absurd deputy, Verges, clops around on an imaginary horse. Mercifully, his four, excruciating appearances put only a shallow dent in the surrounding joy and sexual energy.

Much Ado became a smash hit, taking $8m in the UK and $22m in America, where its release was able to capitalise on the publicity surrounding Thompson's Best Actress Oscar for *Howards End* (1992) six weeks earlier. It became the highest-grossing British film of 1993 – commercial success that helped Branagh to find American finance for his full-length *Hamlet* (p. 45), and *Much Ado*'s co-producers Stephen Evans and David Parfitt to raise the budget for Trevor Nunn's *Twelfth Night* (1996, p. 273).

Dir/Scr: Kenneth Branagh; **Prods:** Stephen Evans, David Parfitt, Kenneth Branagh; **DOP:** Roger Lanser; **Editor:** Andrew Marcus; **Score:** Patrick Doyle; **Main Cast:** Kenneth Branagh (Benedick), Emma Thompson (Beatrice), Richard Briers (Leonato), Michael Keaton (Dogberry), Denzel Washington (Don Pedro), Robert Sean Leonard (Claudio), Keanu Reeves (Don John), Kate Beckinsale (Hero), Brian Blessed (Antonio), Ben Elton (Verges).

Much Ado About Nothing
UK, 2005 – 90 mins (TVM)
Brian Percival

This woefully scripted entry in the BBC's *Shakespeare Retold* series of modernised adaptations transplants *Much Ado…* into an inhospitable new environment and reduces it to a mirthless amalgam of second-rate sitcom and soap opera.

David Nicholls, writer of *Cold Feet* (1997–2003) and *Starter for Ten* (2006), presents Beatrice (Sarah Parish) and Benedick (Damian Lewis) as joint anchors of Bournemouth-based evening news magazine *Wessex Tonight*. Three years after Ben abruptly dumped Bea, her regular co-presenter has a heart attack and producer Leonard (Martin Jarvis) reunites the pair on screen, alongside his bubbly daughter and TV weathergirl, Hero (Billie Piper), and her soon-to-be fiancé, Claude (Tom Ellis), a tall, dark and dim sports reporter.

The slimmed-down dramatis personae accommodates Margaret (sexy floor manager), Ursula (dowdy production assistant) and Peter (equivalent to Don Pedro), the director brought in to replace the malicious Don, whose recent divorce and worsening drink problem cause Leonard to demote him. Dogberry and Verges become the diminutive, jobsworth security manager, Mr Berry, and his gawky young assistant, Vincent.

As the team dupe Bea and Ben into rekindling their love, and the pair bicker on the studio sofa, you sense that Nicholls hoped to emulate the sexual/professional tension and TV newsroom banter of *Switching Channels* (1988), the remake of Howard Hawks's vastly superior *His Girl Friday* (1940), with its 'merry war' between newspaper editor Cary Grant and his ex-wife and star reporter Rosalind Russell. Yet instead of the Hawks film's acidic one-liners, the best Nicholls can offer is Bea telling Ben: 'You really do put the "w" into anchorman.'

Nicholls ticks off the play's key incidents (a fancy dress ball, his-and-hers eavesdropping, a wedding ceremony), while sacrificing the deep bonds between Shakespeare's characters. In the play, Pedro has Don

John as-brother and Benedick and Claudio as loyal companions. Beatrice and Hero are devoted cousins, both adored by Leonato and his brother, Antonio. Nicholls preserves only the father–daughter bond and Jarvis shows great tenderness towards the perkily radiant Piper. Otherwise we see professional colleagues who fail to convince as individuals and scarcely care about one another, so why should we care about them? Pete has no relationship with Ben or Don, who has been stalking Hero since they shared a one-night stand and, on the eve of the wedding, convinces Claude that they are still lovers. Nicholls turns Shakespeare's Beatrice into a shallow 'chick-lit' singleton who switches absurdly from finding Hero insufferable to staunchly defending her honour. One moment Benedick is mocking Claude's stupidity, the next he is his Best Man.

Brian Percival's pacing is monotonous, his soundtrack choices from the literal-minded romcom catalogue (James Brown's 'I Feel Good' for Ben's triumphant return to the studio) and he draws cartoonish performances from a talented cast. There are even some glaring continuity errors.

Yet I doubt anyone could have negotiated the lurch from broad comedy into life-threatening melodrama, which feels as though the last twenty pages from another, more serious film script have been arbitrarily attached. Claude's Othello-like jealousy is ridiculous and, when he denounces Hero during their wedding, we are presented with a tired rehash of the bride/groom-abandoned-at-the-altar scenario from umpteen soap episodes. The end follows with merciful speed. Don knocks Hero to the ground, leaving her unconscious. She revives after the briefest of hospital comas and a 'Sometime in the Future' epilogue shows her and Claude leading separate lives and Bea and Ben about to marry.

Dir: Brian Percival; **Prod:** Diederick Santer; **Scr:** David Nicholls; **DOP:** Peter Greenhalgh; **Editor:** Kristina Hetherington; **Score:** Tim Atack; **Main Cast:** Sarah Parish (Beatrice), Damian Lewis (Benedick), Billie Piper (Hero), Tom Ellis (Claude), Martin Jarvis (Leonard), Derek Riddell (Don), Michael Smiley (Peter), Nina Sosanya (Margaret), Olivia Colman (Ursula).

Othello (play synopsis)

Venice. Desdemona, daughter of Venetian senator Brabantio, has secretly married Othello the Moor, an heroic general. In the Senate, Brabantio accuses Othello of bewitching her, but she confirms that she loves him. Brabantio warns Othello that she may deceive him as she deceived her father. The Doge sends Othello to defend Cyprus against the Turkish fleet.

Iago, Othello's 'honest' Ensign, promises Roderigo, a gullible nobleman, that he can help him win Desdemona, with whom Roderigo is hopelessly in love. Iago plans to destroy Othello for promoting Cassio to Lieutenant ahead of him, and he also suspects that Othello has slept with his wife, Emilia, Desdemona's maid.

Othello arrives, victorious, on Cyprus, to join Desdemona. That night, Iago engineers a fight between a drunken Cassio and a disguised Roderigo, which leads Othello to demote Cassio and make Iago his Lieutenant.

Iago encourages Cassio to enlist Desdemona's help in regaining his position, then tells the Moor that Desdemona and Cassio are lovers. He refuses to believe it but when Desdemona appeals for Cassio's reinstatement, he becomes insanely jealous. Iago obtains Othello's first gift to Desdemona, a handkerchief, places it in Cassio's bedroom and tells the Moor that Cassio kisses it and whispers lovingly of Desdemona in his sleep. He helps Othello overhear Cassio apparently laughing about Desdemona's passion for him when he is actually referring to his mistress, Bianca. Othello vows to kill Desdemona and Iago promises to kill Cassio.

On the night before Othello is due to return to Venice, Roderigo ambushes Cassio on Iago's orders and wounds him; Iago kills Roderigo. Othello wakes Desdemona, condemns her for adultery and suffocates her. Emilia discovers Desdemona's body, realises Iago has caused the tragedy and denounces him. Iago kills her, flees but is captured. Realising his terrible mistake, Othello wounds Iago, then kills himself. Cassio becomes Governor of Cyprus and Iago is taken to Venice to be punished.

Othello
Germany, 1922 – 93 mins
Dimitri Buchowetzki

Drawing on Shakespeare's principal source (Cinthio's *Hecatommithi*) as well as the play, Dimitri Buchowetzki's *Othello* was a box-office hit in New York City, where *Film Daily* greeted 'a highly intelligent and compelling interpretation . . . masterfully handled and wholly absorbing' (this essay evaluates that eighty-minute American version). A tense opening in a packed Senate indicates that Iago is motivated solely by professional resentment (anticipating *Omkara*, 2006, p. 188). Werner Krauss's absurd-looking Ensign – slicked-down black hair, caterpillar moustache and figure-hugging black one-piece (later augmented by a vampiric cape) – stands beside Ica von Lenkeffy's angelic, blonde Desdemona and Ferdinand von Alten's wide-eyed, kiss-curled Roderigo, absolutely certain that Othello will promote him. When the Moor chooses Cassio, he instantly vows revenge and his machinations unfold in largely familiar fashion, though his methods are cruder than in the play and, in Bianca's absence, the scarcely glimpsed Cassio becomes a purer figure than in Shakespeare.

The film is dominated by Krauss (more credible as Shylock the following year, see p. 130) and Emil Jannings, still celebrated for *The Blue Angel* (1930), where as Professor Rath he played another decent man destroyed by his passion for a younger blonde, albeit one of very different character. In turban and elaborately decorated, heavy robes, he towers over his nemesis (much as Orson Welles dwarfs Micheál MacLiammóir; see p. 165) and, compared to Krauss and von Alten's eye-rolling gesticulations, he is, initially, stillness personified, with pride, dignity and jealousy conveyed by his eyes and reined-in strength. When fury finally erupts, he rends the handkerchief with his teeth and even foams at the mouth. Calm returns after Desdemona's murder, as he and Cassio stand with foreheads pressed together, sharing a deeply moving moment of regret and forgiveness.

The decade separating this film from James Keane's *Richard III* (1912, p. 193) feels like a quantum leap for silent Shakespeare, the more sophisticated blending of words and pictures most apparent in the intertitles. Keane's film had no speech titles; Buchowetzki's has more than 250 lines' worth, in addition to extensive scene-setting and character description. The titles quote verbatim, paraphrase or introduce powerful new pleas and retorts. Emilia, for instance, takes a more active and vocal role than in the play. Roughly the same age as Desdemona, she finds Iago's brutish embraces strangely irresistible, lies to Othello on her husband's orders and then asserts Desdemona's innocence *before* the murder: 'If any wretch have put this jealousy in your head, [Othello], let heaven requite it with the serpent's curse!'

Unlike Keane, Buchowetzki rarely relies on interior tableaux and masters several complex sequences, playing with Scenes i, ii and iii of Act I to cross-cut between Roderigo and Iago rousing Brabantio, Desdemona and Othello's church wedding, and the Senators in emergency session. The film is paced exactly as *Othello* should be, its urgent first and last Acts book-ending the central section's more gradual development of plot and character. The grand, expensive sets (built at studios in Berlin) include a canal and bridge for Venice and the high-ceilinged chambers and wide courtyards of the Cyprus garrison, which are like something out of Piranesi; all are photographed with astonishing depth of focus.

Buchowetzki uses dozens of extras like a Verdi chorus (see *Otello*, p. 176), so that a cheering crowd greets Desdemona and Othello as they emerge from his Senate 'trial', perhaps 100 soldiers fill the Cyrpus quayside for his arrival and Cassio announces his death to an expectant crowd. At every opportunity, Othello's private tragedy is presented as a very public affair.

Dir: Dimitri Buchowetzki; **Prod:** Wörner-Filmgesellschaft; **Scr:** Dimitri Buchowetzki, Carl Hagen; **DOPs:** Karl Hasselmann, Friedrich Paulmann; **Main Cast:** Emil Jannings (Othello), Werner Krauss (Iago), Ica von Lenkeffy (Desdemona), Lya de Putti (Emilia), Ferdinand von Alten (Roderigo), Theodor Loos (Cassio), Friedrich Kühne (Brabantio).

A Double Life
US, 1947 – 105 mins (B&W)
George Cukor

Carnival (1923) and *Men Are Not Gods* (1936) also feature stage actors playing the Moor and becoming murderously involved with their Desdemonas, as Ronald Colman's Tony John does in *A Double Life*. Thanks to its undeserved success at the Academy Awards, however, this remains the best known of several films to have turned *Othello* into backstage melodrama.

A leading light of post-war Broadway, famed for immersing himself in every part, Tony is persuaded by producer Max Lasker to play Othello opposite ex-wife Brita (Signe Hasso) as Desdemona. During a one-night stand with a lonely waitress, Pat (Shelley Winters, in a sexy, breakthrough performance), Tony starts 'becoming' the Moor, imagining himself in blackface while an inner voice denounces Desdemona. A montage charts the *Othello* rehearsals as Colman's breathless voiceover insists actors endure hell before confronting that 'terrifying monster with a thousand heads' (better known as the audience). On opening night we watch the first of three enactments of Desdemona's murder, with stiff performances from Colman and Hasso; Cukor cuts to misty-eyed spectators to reassure us this is great acting.

Tony becomes convinced that Brita is having an affair with unscrupulous Broadway publicist Bill Friend (the perennially hardbitten Edmund O'Brien), the voice in his head keeps quoting *Othello* on jealousy, Cukor relentlessly deploys Miklós Rózsa's jarring score to amplify Tony's madness and at the play's 300th performance he almost strangles Brita for real; she improbably shrugs this off as 'overdoing it'.

The production has been running two years when Tony, certain that Brita is going to marry Friend, finally snaps. Incapable of venting his rage on Brita, he returns to the waitress Pat's shabby apartment and suffocates her. Though the cops pin the crime on a neighbour, Friend suspects Tony and, after he convinces a police captain to investigate further, the script rips off the 'Mousetrap' from *Hamlet*. Friend, now a cross between private dick and Prince of Denmark, hires an actress who vaguely resembles Pat and gives her a blonde wig and the dead woman's earrings. He brings Tony (now more Claudius than Othello) to a bar where the actress serves them and the captain (acting as Horatio) watches Tony react in guilty horror.

Before he can be arrested, however, Tony stabs himself in the *Othello* murder scene, and as he dies in Brita's arms, Othello's 'Speak of me as I am . . . one that loved not wisely, but too well' becomes Tony's 'Don't let them say I was a bad actor.'

Husband-and-wife writers Garson Kanin and Ruth Gordon have so undermined the play's two central relationships that one feels greater sympathy for the doomed Pat than Tony or Brita. Where Othello rages against betrayal by the adored and adoring new wife who defied prejudice to marry him, we have scant evidence that Tony and Brita were close even while married. Tony is his own worst enemy and Colman's Jekyll-and-Hyde histrionics are no substitute for the Iago–Othello relationship, and while the actor's good looks and smooth talking were ideal for light comedies, or adventures such as *The Prisoner of Zenda* (1937), the intensity demanded by Tony's double life is beyond him. This makes it all the more astonishing that Colman took the Best Actor Oscar, beating, among others, Gregory Peck for *Gentleman's Agreement* (Rózsa won Best Score), and leading the *Guardian* to suggest: 'The magic of the word "Shakespeare" must simply have made the judges swoon away.'

Dir: George Cukor; **Prod:** Michael Kanin; **Scr:** Ruth Gordon, Garson Kanin; **DOP:** Milton Krasner; **Editor:** Robert Parrish; **Score:** Miklós Rózsa; **Main Cast:** Ronald Colman (Tony John/Othello), Signe Hasso (Brita Kaurin/Desdemona), Edmund O'Brien (Bill Friend), Shelley Winters (Pat Kroll), Philip Loeb (Max Lasker).

Othello
Morocco, 1952 – 91 mins (B&W)
Orson Welles

The making of *Othello* stretched across three troubled years, as cast and crew shuttled uncertainly between locations in Italy and Morocco. Somehow, a masterpiece emerged.

Filming began in Mogador, Morocco, in June 1949, funded out of Welles's own pocket, and over the next eighteen months a haphazard

'Give me a living reason she's disloyal.': the Moor (Orson Welles), left, demands further proof of Desdemona's infidelity from Iago (Micheál MacLiammóir) in Welles's *Othello*

pattern emerged. Welles starts filming; after four or five weeks he runs out of money, suspends production and disappears to appear in another movie, then uses his acting fee to resume the Shakespeare.

When a scene in *Othello* does not look as smooth as it should (many do not), one actor's contribution was probably shot in Italy in 1949, the other's in Morocco in 1950, and the footage spliced together in 1951. An equally erratic dubbing schedule means voices seldom emerge in anything close to perfect sync. Micheál MacLiammóir, the film's Iago (and partner of Hilton Edwards, its blustering Brabantio), catalogued every chaotic development in his hilarious production diary, *Put Money in Thy Purse* (named after Iago's Act I advice to Roderigo).

The miracle is that despite all the technical inconsistencies, *Othello* grips from the moment that heavy, repetitive piano chords, timpani and a wailing chorus begin the unforgettable, wordless pre-credits sequence showing Othello and Desdemona's funeral processions along battlements. A chained figure is thrown into a cage and winched aloft: Iago. Then we fade to Venice and *Othello*'s plot unfolds with a speed unimaginable in screen versions that do not decimate the text as Welles does (his film lasts ninety minutes; Trevor Nunn's magnificent 1990 television production lasts almost three-and-a-half hours). He forsakes long conversations and the 'Will he? Won't he?' tension of full-length *Othello*s and once the Moor has sworn to kill Desdemona it takes only twenty minutes to reach the climax.

As in *Citizen Kane*, Welles shows his genius for evoking moods through stark black-and-white photography and unconventional perspectives. Early on, he places the characters in bright, windswept exteriors; once Iago takes control, darkness spreads into almost every frame, amplified by discordant piano. Figures hurry down flooded passageways, or eavesdrop from behind pillars. The camera looks down from a great height, then suddenly someone towers above us; Welles wants our perspective to become as disoriented as Othello's view of Desdemona. Othello's features are often partially concealed by shadow and at his death we see only a black face surrounded by darkness as the image fades back into the double funeral.

The pronounced visual contrasts match the physical and vocal gulf between Welles and MacLiammóir. Othello is an exceptionally imposing figure, who gives full vent to his magnificent bass voice and looms over Iago, a hunched weasel of a man with lank hair, who dispenses malicious advice in a whining Irish accent. MacLiammóir and Welles had decided the key to unlocking Iago was that he was impotent ('That's why he hates life so much,' wrote MacLiammóir), and the Iago–Othello relationship is clearly the only one that fascinated Welles, at the expense of the other principals.

The Desdemona of Suzanne Cloutier (Welles's third choice) is a saintly, sacrificial victim, of great beauty and scant personality (though her murder generates intense horror, as Cloutier's features strain against a sheet like a tormented ghost). Emilia becomes a middle-aged ballbreaker, Cassio a brainless hunk and Robert Coote's aristocratic Roderigo (spectacularly stabbed through the floorboards of a Cyprus steam bath) is purest caricature, his simpering, aristocratic voice dubbed by Welles.

Hugely in debt, Welles finally completed *Othello* in time for the Cannes Film Festival in 1952, where it shared the Palme d'Or with *Two Cents Worth of Hope* by Renato Castellani (whose next film was *Romeo and Juliet*, p. 213). It then languished unreleased until September 1955, when a critical drubbing drove it from New York cinemas after only a week, and in the UK in February 1956 most of the reviewers who had recently showered superlatives on Olivier's *Richard III* launched venomous attacks; two were headlined 'Mr Welles Murders Shakespeare in the Dark' and 'The Boor of Venice'.

The Times's critic who greeted one of cinema's 'most intellectually stimulating, visually beautiful and emotionally exciting' tales was in a minority until 1992, seven years after Welles's death, when a restored print was reissued in Britain and America and *Othello* was justly rediscovered as a classic, the *Independent on Sunday* calling it 'the most intense, invigorating, mobile and heart-stabbing Shakespeare film of all time'.

Welles remained very proud of the film, which is not to say he thought it perfect. In 1951, he had directed himself as the Moor on stage in London and judged his performance 'much better' than his screen portrayal, and in *Filming Othello*, a 1978 television documentary, he sits watching his film and mutters about all the improvements he wishes he could make.

Dir/Prod/Scr: Orson Welles; **DOPs:** Anchise Brizzi, G. R. Aldo, George Fanto; **Editors:** Jenö Csepreghy, Renzo Lucidi, William Morton, Jean Sacha; **Score:** Francesco Lavagnino, Alberto Barberis; **Main Cast:** Orson Welles (Othello), Micheál MacLiammóir (Iago), Suzanne Cloutier (Desdemona), Fay Compton (Emilia), Robert Coote (Roderigo), Michael Lawrence (Cassio), Hilton Edwards (Brabantio).

Othello
USSR, 1955 – 106 mins
Sergei Yutkevich

Othello has never received more spectacular screen treatment than in this Russian epic. Before a word is uttered, Yutkevich translates the Moor's account to the Senate of the tales that won Brabantio's daughter into a pre-credits action sequence, as imagined by Desdemona: Sergei Bondarchuk's majestic Othello leads a seaborne assault, is whipped and chained as a galley slave, miraculously escapes a shipwreck and is finally restored to his flagship. This typifies Yutkevich's achievement (rewarded with Best Director at Cannes) in cutting away *Othello*'s theatrical roots even more decisively than Orson Welles had done. Action, spectacle and Aram Khachaturian's yearning strings and emphatic organ blasts take precedence over language, as the cast speak a heavily edited version of Pasternak's *Othello* translation (the English subtitles use Shakespeare).

Rather than confine the intimate Othello–Iago and Othello–Desdemona scenes within the Cyprus citadel, here represented by a vast medieval fortress, Yutkevich places the principals against breathtakingly photographed, sunny locations – vineyards, mountains, golden beaches – and this holiday brochure beauty is superbly contrasted against the darkening plot; the operatic performances are less effective.

Bondarchuk's bombastic technique builds on the heroic prologue to set Othello up as a figure of mythic, godlike love and hate. Andrei Popov, resembling a Russian Vincent Price, provides an oddly roguish, rather than malevolent Iago, and the Desdemona of Irina Skobtseva (plucked straight from drama school in Moscow) is a one-dimensional victim. When a crazed Othello bears down on her like Frankenstein's monster, bathed in demonic red light, Yutkevich crosses the sometimes thin line between horrifying tragedy and melodramatic horror – an over-the-top moment in keeping with an adaptation whose consistently broad effects impress, without ever moving you as *Othello* should.

Dir/Scr: Sergei Yutkevich; **Prod:** Mosfilm; **DOP:** Evgeny Andrikanis; **Editors:** Klavdiya Aleyeva, Grigori Mariamov; **Score:** Aram Khachaturian; **Main Cast:** Sergei Bondarchuk (Othello), Andrei Popov (Iago), Irina Skobtseva (Desdemona), Antonina Maximova (Emilia), Yevgeny Vesnik (Roderigo), Vladimir Soshalsky (Cassio), Yevgeny Teterin (Brabantio).

All Night Long
UK, 1961 – 91 mins (B&W)
Basil Dearden

Othello allows directors to make the Moor's jealousy appear to simmer
for days or weeks; *All Night Long*'s gripping London tale of sex, lies and
audiotape unfolds almost in real time. It is close to midnight when the
Roderigo figure, Bentley-driving aristocrat the Hon. Rod Hamilton
(Richard Attenborough at his most genteel), arrives at his converted
Thames-side warehouse to host a first wedding anniversary bash for
black jazz pianist and band leader Aurelius Rex (the tall, dignified Paul
Harris) and white singer Delia Lane (Marti Stevens).

Othello vs. Iago: Aurelius Rex (Paul Harris), left, confronts Johnny Cousin (Patrick
McGoohan) in Basil Dearden's *All Night Long*

Rod's performance lounge fills up with caterers, sundry guests, jazz stars, including Charles Mingus, Johnny Dankworth and Dave Brubeck (all appearing as themselves), and the remaining *Othello* substitutes, all Americans like Rex and Delia: sax player and band manager Cass Michaels (a laidback Keith Michell) and his adoring black girlfriend, Benny (the feisty Maria Velasco), a twitchy Patrick McGoohan as drummer Johnny Cousin, and Betsy Blair as his mousy, neglected wife, Emily, a former groupie, now Delia's bosom pal.

In a phone call to promoter Lou Berger (Bernard Braden; part-Doge, part-Montano), Johnny reveals that with cash from Rod (who carries a torch for Delia) he plans to form a breakaway band fronted by Delia, who gave up singing at Rex's insistence when they married, but has been secretly rehearsing a new style with Cass. When Delia tells Johnny she cannot join his group because she would lose Rex, and rejects the drummer's sudden declaration of love, he instantly starts emulating Iago, telling Rod that Cass and Delia are lovers and swiping her gold cigarette case, a gift from Rex.

In a nice twist on Cassio's 'unhappy brains for drinking', Cass is seeing a shrink for his dormant dope habit and Johnny dupes him into sharing a joint. His stoned taunting of the newly arrived Berger (with Rod as peacemaker rather than, as in the play, provocateur) leads Rex to fire him, because 'I'm not going to have any hophead run my business.'

Johnny gives Rex 'audible proof' of Delia's infidelity by splicing together his covert recordings of Cass talking about Benny and being affectionately consoled by Delia. Cue melodramatic thunder and lightning as the tape ends.

Though the musicians' self-consciously hip slang has dated, one is still drawn in by the claustrophobic, though never theatrical, atmosphere Dearden creates on Pinewood Studios sets allowing frequent movement between downstairs lounge, library and fire escape and an upstairs bedroom. The staccato dialogue is interrupted by regular musical interludes, including Brubeck on piano, Mingus on bass, McGoohan drumming convincingly and Stevens singing 'All Night Long', during which Dearden replaces *Othello*'s soliloquies and several of its duologues with lingering close-ups of characters alone with troubled thoughts.

The loudest number coincides with Rex's furious outburst. He half-strangles Delia, socks Cass and sends him tumbling over a balcony. Emily and Benny expose Johnny's plot and Delia stops Rex from strangling him. Husband and wife are reconciled, the concussed Cass forgives Rex ('Don't worry, man, everything's cool') and as dawn breaks the self-loathing Johnny rejects Emily and launches into a maniacal drum 'soliloquy'.

The jazz milieu has neatly accommodated *Othello*'s themes. Although Johnny displays insidious racism ('I belong to that new minority group: white American jazz musicians'), black performers' general prominence and the presence of Velasco and Mingus make Rex less of an outsider than Othello, and interracial marriage is less important to the story than the question of Rex's 'right' to suppress Delia's artistry, and whether she can forsake her career for love.

Dir: Basil Dearden; **Prod:** Michael Relph; **Scr:** Neil King, Peter Achilles; **DOP:** Ted Scaife; **Editor:** John D. Guthridge; **Score:** Philip Green; **Main Cast:** Paul Harris (Aurelius Rex), Patrick McGoohan (Johnny Cousin), Marti Stevens (Delia Lane), Betsy Blair (Emily), Richard Attenborough (Rod Hamilton), Keith Michell (Cass Michaels), Maria Velasco (Benny), Lou Berger (Bernard Braden).

Othello
UK, 1965 – 166 mins
Stuart Burge

Laurence Olivier said Othello demanded the 'enormously big' acting for which theatregoers had queued for hours when he played the Moor at London's Old Vic in 1964, and he did nothing to tone down what the *Spectator* called his 'outsize, elaborate, overwhelming' performance when the acclaimed National Theatre production, directed by John Dexter, was filmed the following year.

His gym-enhanced physique coated in thick black make-up, Olivier strides around barefoot, cradling a scimitar, and his voice, deepened a full octave by six months of exercises, sometimes gives the poetry a haunting West Indian lilt. When jealousy takes hold he roars and howls like a wild animal. This is a uniquely uninhibited portrayal of male hysteria, which many who saw it at the Old Vic recall as one of their greatest theatrical experiences – even though to many contemporary viewers it now seems laughably over-the-top. Indeed, Olivier's Othello would be horribly out of place in a screen adaptation that attempted to be cinematic, whereas Burge's must be judged as filmed theatre, made in a studio in just three weeks, with Venice and Cyprus represented by simple façades. The static camerawork obliges the cast to move in and out of view as they would on stage and there is nothing to distract us from impeccably spoken verse and fine acting.

Frank Finlay's Iago is excessively restrained, an unassuming chap whose matter-of-fact tone suggests destroying Othello is a bit of a chore. Joyce Redman's Emilia is affectingly desperate to win back his affections and Maggie Smith brings great spontaneity to Desdemona, perfectly capturing her wisdom and bewilderment. All four won Oscar nominations and helped *Othello* take a remarkable $1.2m in its first weekend on release in America, while the *Sunday Times*'s great critic Dilys Powell concluded: 'It is difficult not to feel that Shakespeare diminishes everything else on screen.'

Dir: Stuart Burge; **Prods:** Anthony Havelock-Allan, John Brabourne; **DOP:** Geoffrey Unsworth; **Editor:** Richard Marden; **Score:** Richard Hampton; **Main Cast:** Laurence Olivier (Othello), Frank Finlay (Iago), Maggie Smith (Desdemona), Joyce Redman (Emilia), Robert Lang (Roderigo), Derek Jacobi (Cassio), Anthony Nicholls (Brabantio).

Otello
Italy, 1986 – 119 mins
Franco Zeffirelli

This Franco Zeffirelli extravaganza enables illuminating comparison between *Othello* and Verdi's 1887 masterpiece *Otello*, the greatest Shakespearean opera. As adapters, Verdi and his librettist Arrigo Boito were acolytes and iconoclasts. Their plotting stays close to Shakespeare's, they sometimes transpose verse into song almost verbatim and Plácido Domingo's imperious Otello shares the pride and passion of Shakespeare's Moor.

Yet they dispense entirely with Act I, plunging straight into Otello's storm-tossed arrival on Cyprus. Their Iago and Desdemona are less complex than Shakespeare's and Zeffirelli simplifies them even further. Justino Díaz's dark, bearded Ensign, often framed in shadow or half-light, gives no hint of racism or sexual jealousy, and when he tells Roderigo of his fury at Cassio's promotion this motivation merely covers a deeper existential malice, a Satanic misanthropy linked to Boito's allegorical poem, 'Re Orso' (1864), and expressed in Iago's astonishing Act I 'Credo': 'I'm evil because I am a man and I feel within me the primeval slime.'

As counterweight to Iago's pure evil, the play's preternaturally wise Desdemona becomes the opera's angelic innocent, cleared of filial deception by the loss of the Venice scenes. Zeffirelli's soft-focus caressing of Italian soprano Katia Ricciarelli's blonde beauty suits this characterisation, especially in the Act I love duet that brilliantly assimilates Otello's speech to the Senate and outdoes Shakespeare in conjuring the romantic Eden that Iago will destroy. Here, however, Zeffirelli is as reluctant to rely solely on music and lyrics as he is to trust Shakespeare's language in his original-text films, inserting distracting 'show-and-sing' flashbacks (Otello captivating Brabantio, the boy Otello snatched into slavery). He also embellishes Iago's account of Cassio's whispered passion for Desdemona with soft-porn shots of bare-chested blond Urbano

Barberini (whose singing is dubbed by Ezio Di Cesare), and couples most religious references with cutaways to images of Christ or the Virgin Mary.

Dramatically, the need to have great singers perform to playback is such a handicap that in close-up the disjuncture between mouthing and soundtrack makes *Otello* seem dubbed from another language *into* Italian. This is not a problem with wide shots of the choruses, which emphasise Verdi's genius for giving voice to a community with a power never matched when Shakespeare inserts brief exclamations from, say, shocked servants or citizens. The Cypriot men's cries of 'Long live Otello!' as Domingo is carried ashore become supremely ironic when repeated after he denounces Desdemona; the women serenade her with a folk song in counterpoint to her husband's burgeoning jealousy. The loss of the chorus's Act I celebration of love is regrettable, worse still is the cutting of Desdemona's 'Willow Song' from the final scene, which thins her already slight relationship with Emilia. These cuts cannot be justified, as they might be with *Othello* films, by the need to cut a three-hour-plus play for the screen; an unexpurgated *Otello* lasts only ten minutes longer than this film.

Zeffirelli also gratuitously rewrites *Otello*'s climax, which spares Emilia and allows Iago to flee. He emulates Shakespeare by having Iago murder Emilia, but Otello kills his nemesis with a well-aimed spear – terminal punishment that makes a mockery of Boito's bleak vision. To forestall howls from the purists, the film's opening and closing credits carry an advertisement that is really a disclaimer: 'The complete recording of the original opera *Otello* is available on EMI.'

Dir: Franco Zeffirelli; **Prods:** Menahem Golan, Yoram Globus; **Scr:** Libretto by Arrigo Boito, adapted by Franco Zeffirelli and Masolino D'Amico; **DOP:** Ennio Guarnieri; **Editors:** Franca Silvi, Peter Taylor; **Score:** Giuseppe Verdi; **Main Cast:** Plácido Domingo (Otello), Justino Díaz (Iago), Katia Ricciarelli (Desdemona), Petra Malakova (Emilia), Sergio Nicolai (Roderigo), Urbano Barberini (Cassio).

Othello
US/UK, 1995 – 124 mins
Oliver Parker

Othello looks good for its $11m budget, with locations in Venice and the Cyprus citadel (in fact Bracciano Castle, north of Rome) decked out in fine, 1570s' style by Tim Harvey, Kenneth Branagh's regular production designer, and lushly photographed by David Johnson. First-time feature director Oliver Parker, who had played Iago on stage in 1989, trims about 50% of the text, delivering an audience-friendly two-hour running time without muddling the play's clear plotting. When the dialogue is at its most intense, however, he relies too much on close-ups of talking heads, raising the spectre of staid, television Shakespeare.

Parker's 'big idea' was to go further than previous versions in portraying the intense physical bond between Othello and Desdemona, telling interviewers that the play was 'an erotic thriller', and insisting that previous screen adaptations had lacked passion. He shows Irène Jacob's Desdemona and Laurence Fishburne's Othello making love after the latter's arrival in Cyprus and, later, twice presents Othello's crazed hallucinations of his wife in bed with Cassio. All three scenes are brief, more discreet than Zeffirelli's vulgar take on Cassio's supposed erotic reverie in *Otello* (p. 176) and partially justified by verse that dwells at explicit length on physical betrayal.

His script severely restricts the dialogue entrusted to Desdemona, which is both a blessing, since Swiss-born Jacob struggles with verse in what was for her a foreign language, and a shame, because the cuts leave the actress little time to build a Desdemona whose guiltless plight can really move us.

Language also handicaps Fishburne. He exudes hearty sexual swagger and adopts a rich, almost Caribbean accent, but pentameters are alien to an actor more at home in the expletive-ridden worlds of 1990s' thrillers like *King of New York* and he sometimes rushes lines as though trying to spit out something unpalatable. Crucially, he misses

Othello's despairing grief in the final scenes, and one wonders what Morgan Freeman, slipping back into his Moor's costume from *Robin Hood: Prince of Thieves* (1991), might have made of the part. A Freeman Othello would certainly have restored the intended age gap between husband and wife (the Moor laments being 'declined/Into the vale of years'; Fishburne is only five years older than Jacob) and been more of a match for Kenneth Branagh's robust, leather-jacketed Iago. Relishing his first shot at screen villainy, Branagh delivers most of his soliloquies directly to camera, and his brazen running commentary is a model lesson in manipulative evil. He has a convincing rapport with Nathaniel Parker (the director's brother) as a bright Cassio, and Michael Maloney, who makes Roderigo a more plausible victim than is usually the case. Branagh features in *Othello*'s best scene (Iago and Othello swearing their blood oath on a turret roof), its most derivative shot (Cassio and Desdemona reflected in the blade of Iago's knife, an image shamelessly stolen from Yutkevich's 1955 *Othello*) and its crudest moment: he ends a soliloquy by grasping a smouldering log and wincing slightly at the pain, like a slasher-movie psycho.

While *The Times* called this 'a fair stab at turning the Bard into a decent night at the multiplex', other critics were scathing, and neither Parker's 'erotic thriller' hype nor an attempt to generate topical spin by linking the 'black husband murders white wife' storyline to 1995's sensational O. J. Simpson trial could turn *Othello* into a hit. It grossed only $2.8m in America and about $900,000 in the UK.

Dir: Oliver Parker; **Prods**: Luc Roeg, David Barron; **Scr**: Oliver Parker; **DOP**: David Johnson; **Editor**: Tony Lawson; **Score**: Charlie Mole; **Main Cast**: Laurence Fishburne (Othello), Kenneth Branagh (Iago), Irène Jacob (Desdemona), Anna Patrick (Emilia), Michael Maloney (Roderigo), Nathaniel Parker (Cassio), Pierre Vaneck (Brabantio).

O
US, 2000 – 93 mins
Tim Blake Nelson

Brad Kaaya was the only black student at his American high school and
so is Odin 'O' James, hero of Kaaya's *O* screenplay. At Palmetto Grove,
an elite co-ed boarding school in Charleston, South Carolina, scholarship
boy and 'Most Valuable Player' Odin (Mekhi Phifer) is leading the
Palmetto Hawks towards the state basketball championship finals,
alongside teammates Mike Cass and reliable Hugo (Josh Hartnett), whose
father, 'Duke', is their passionate, exacting coach: sporting brothers
instead of *Othello*'s military comrades. Odin is deeply involved with Desi
(Julia Stiles), the Dean's daughter. Hugo goes out with Desi's roommate,
Emily; Mike's girlfriend is Brandy (Bianca); Hugo's overweight, friendless
roommate, Roger (Roderigo), is hopelessly in love with Desi.

   The leads and supporting players are all convincing, with Phifer nobly
passionate and Stiles mixing steel and vulnerability, and Kaaya
compensates intelligently for their youth. Hugo is a neglected son
motivated by desperate envy for the affection and pride his father shows
towards Odin. Duke's presence also circumvents the problem of Odin
lacking Othello's authority over Iago and Cassio; the coach suspends
Mike for his drunken fight with Roger, and Desi tries to persuade Odin to
have Duke reinstate him.

   In following the play, Kaaya thoughtfully tweaks specific incidents
and adds noir-ish complexity to the climax, which, outlined in flash-
forward, is meant to see Roger shoot Mike, making it look like Mike
committed suicide after strangling Desi. The plan goes horribly awry.
Roger wounds Mike; Hugo shoots Roger dead; Odin strangles Desi; Hugo
shoots Emily for denouncing him; Odin shoots himself and the cops drive
the handcuffed Hugo away as we hear again the opening scene's 'Ave
Maria' (from Verdi's *Otello*) and Hugo's voiceover: he wanted to be a
hawk, like Odin, and 'soar over everything and everyone' – an awkwardly
pretentious flash of poetry in an otherwise relentlessly prosaic script

('Reputation is an idle and most false/Imposition' becomes 'Who gives a fuck about reputation?').

In appropriating Shakespeare, *O* powerfully connects with contemporary American society and film genres. Duke's locker-room rhetoric, Hugo's injury-battling steroid abuse and ten minutes of on-court action fit Hollywood's basketball template (see *Hoosiers*, *Coach Carter*, *Glory Road*). Odin and Desi's affair taps interracial anxieties previously explored from *Guess Who's Coming to Dinner* (1967) to *Jungle Fever* (1991) and, as Tim Blake Nelson observed, setting *Othello* amid Charleston's pre-Civil War architecture, with Odin studying alongside 'the scions of former slave-owning families', gives the racial theme 'immeasurable rhetorical value'. Hugo's suggestion that Mike and Desi call Odin 'nigger' wounds him deeply, and he dies distancing himself from the curse of black-on-black violence: 'I wasn't no gang-banger.' Rap and hip-hop songs accompany the basketball, party and dorm-room scenes, and the white boys incessantly call each other 'man', 'bro', 'dawg' and 'player' – like so many wealthy, suburban white kids, Palmetto's pupils adopt black 'ghetto' music and slang – and Odin.

Above all, *O* is a high-school movie. A world away from the breezy comedy of *10 Things I Hate about You* or *She's the Man* (pp. 241 and 278), darker even than *Heathers* (1989), its ending reflected and became embroiled in real-life tragedies. Blake Nelson had shown news footage of recent school shootings to his cast and had been editing for two weeks when, on 20 April 1999, the Columbine Massacre occurred. Overnight, *O*'s potent realism became too provocative for US distributors Miramax, who postponed its release and eventually sold it to Lionsgate Films. *O* finally opened in the US in August 2001, entering the box-office Top Ten alongside its teen antithesis, *American Pie 2*.

Dir: Tim Blake Nelson; **Prods:** Eric Gitter, Daniel L. Fried, Anthony Rhulen; **Scr:** Brad Kaaya; **DOP:** Russell Lee Fine; **Editor:** Kate Sanford; **Score:** Jeff Danna; **Main Cast:** Mekhi Phifer (Odin James), Josh Hartnett (Hugo Goulding), Julia Stiles (Desi Brable), Rain Phoenix (Emily), Elden Henson (Roger), Andrew Keegan (Mike Cass), John Heard (Dean Brable), Martin Sheen (Coach 'Duke' Goulding), Rachel Schumate (Brandy).

Othello
UK/US, 2000 – 98 mins (TVM)
Geoffrey Sax

In 1999, the MacPherson Report into the Metropolitan Police's failure to convict the killers of black London teenager Stephen Lawrence branded the force 'institutionally racist'. A year later, Andrew Davies, British television's king of literary adaptation, used the racial theme and military-political hierarchy of Shakespeare's *Othello* to hold a mirror up to the Met.

A *Sun* newspaper hack exposes the closet racism of Met Commissioner Carver (Bill Paterson) just after he promises to promote black officers. Carver is forced to resign and political correctness determines that a Tony Blair-like PM and his Home Secretary (standing in for Doge and Senators) replace him not with white Assistant Commissioner Ben Jago (Christopher Eccleston), but the officer whom Jago has mentored, John Othello (Eamonn Walker). He becomes the force's first black leader on the day that he marries journalist Dessie Brabant (Keeley Hawes), three months after she interviewed him (with Desdemona as mature career woman, a possessive father is easily omitted, as also happens in *All Night Long* and *Souli*, pp. 171 and 184).

Having made intense professional resentment his Iago's sole motivation, Davies replaces Shakespeare's romantic subplot with MacPherson-inspired police procedural. Othello launches an internal investigation into the fatal beating of a black drugs suspect by white officers, shown in the opening sequence, and Roderigo becomes Alan Roderick, the vulnerable rookie constable who witnessed the assault without participating. Jago's interrogation persuades Roderick to testify against three guilty colleagues, but their manslaughter trial collapses when Jago has Roderick killed (making it look like suicide), destroying Othello's hopes of a PR coup and leaving the film's second half largely clear for the jealousy plot.

The unmarried Jago has an affair with Dessie's best friend, Lulu, and twists her pillow-talk to insinuate to Othello that his wife was a promiscuous teenager and is now cosying up to Othello's trusted, supposedly womanising Superintendent, Michael Cass (the laidback, charming Richard Coyle), assigned to protect Dessie at the couple's luxury canalside apartment (a nod to Venice?) after she was threatened by racist thugs.

The fact that husband and wife scarcely know each other helps Davies emphasise their first-flush sex life and explain why Othello has less trust in this 'rich man's daughter' from a racially, socially and professionally alien background, than in Jago, his fellow working-class officer; absolute honour between cops instead of Shakespeare's soldiers.

Jago seals Dessie's doom by faking a DNA test 'proving' that Othello's dressing gown (this version's 'handkerchief') contains 'sexual secretions' from Cass, whom Jago has encouraged to come on to Dessie (she rejects him) with the credibility-straining 'revelation' that Othello is impotent. Othello ransacks Dessie's home-office, cracks up on a television discussion programme and beats up Cass. At the apartment, he smothers Dessie and shoots himself. Though Lulu survives, Davies's ending is grimmer than Shakespeare's: PM and Home Secretary replace Othello with 'a safe pair of hands'; cut to Jago in Commissioner's dress uniform.

Though Geoffrey Sax overdoes the doom-laden solo vocals and bell chimes, *Othello* is constantly gripping, its greatest assets Walker's hauteur and Eccleston's 1,000-yard stare and assured delivery of Jago's many asides and sometimes ranting soliloquies, mostly to camera. These were clearly influenced by the Shakespearean solos that Davies had written for scheming politician Francis Urquhart (Ian Richardson), Richard III-like anti-hero of television series *House of Cards* (1990).

Dir: Geoffrey Sax; **Prods:** Anne Pivcenic, Julie Gardner; **Scr:** Andrew Davies; **DOP:** Daf Hobson; **Editor:** Nick Arthurs; **Score:** Debbie Wiseman; **Main Cast:** Eamonn Walker (John Othello), Christopher Eccleston (Ben Jago), Keeley Hawes (Dessie Brabant), Rachael Stirling (Lulu), Richard Coyle (Supt. Michael Cass), Del Synnott (PC Alan Roderick), Bill Paterson (Sinclair Carver).

Souli
France/UK, 2004 – 93 mins
Alexander Abela

Alexander Abela followed *Makibefo* (2000, p. 114) with this absorbing present-day *Othello*. In Amboula, Madagascar, a fishing village of wooden huts, Souli (Makena Diop), a celebrated Senegalese poet in his forties, has taken refuge from literary fame and found love with a beautiful, idealistic young Frenchwoman, Mona (Jeanne Antebi), ex-partner of Amboula's other white inhabitant, a brutish French trader, Yann (Aurélien Recoing, an actor of intimidating bulk and hangdog gaze).

These are Abela's Othello, Desdemona and Iago, and his modified Shakespearean quintet is completed by Emilia and Cassio: Yann's young Madagascan girlfriend, Abi (the statuesque Fatou N'Diaye), desperate for their promised escape to a better life in France, and Carlos (Eduardo Noriega, handsome villain of *The Devil's Backbone*), a French-speaking Spaniard intent on interviewing Souli for his PhD thesis.

Yann sets out to destroy Mona not only because she left him for Souli and he still desires her (giving him aspects of Roderigo's motivation), but because they are professional adversaries. She runs the women's co-operative that makes straw giraffes for the tourist trade, and her improvised ice machine threatens the monopoly that helps Yann exploit the fishermen, Souli included, because only he can keep their catch fresh enough to reach market. Yann and Mona's fatal confrontation is thus a metaphor for France's post-colonial relationship to Africa: he is the oppressive throwback, she the progressive liberal who wants the villagers to be self-sufficient; less obviously, Abi symbolises young Africans' fascination with the West.

The characters reveal themselves mostly through touch or glances, and it is typical of Abela's minimalist French dialogue that Yann only need utter a single Iago-esque remark ('Beware of her. She's deceived more than one') to arouse Souli's jealousy. Yann finds a pliable, willing accomplice in Abi (a more ambiguous figure than Emilia), who views Mona as a sexual threat and independently steals her silver bracelet and gives it to Yann. After Yann beats Abi, she tearfully helps him frame the drunken Carlos for the assault, then gives the student the bracelet. Souli sees Carlos wearing it, smothers Mona and runs suicidally onto Yann's knife. Carlos and Yann both flee, and we recall Souli telling Yann that in Africa his breed of exploiter will always win.

While it might have been pat to broaden the political metaphor by suggesting that Souli's poetic voice resembled Wole Soyinka's (battling for Africans with pen rather than Othello's sword), Abela instead gives him an unconvincing mythic burden. Souli is the last surviving guardian of the ancient 'Thiossane tale', and Carlos hopes to find academic glory by persuading him to transcribe it. Souli demurs, because 'fate will tell me when the right man has come', and the film ends as the dying poet holds Abi's hand, their silent communion hinting that the tale is passing to the chosen one.

Abela re-edited *Souli* in late 2006, adding a night-time opening that shows Souli among cactuses, 'dancing the passage' between life and death. Souli speaks in voiceover to an African musician (Ali Wagué) on a windswept jetty and frequent cutaways to Wagué trilling his *Peule* flute punctuate the new cut. It replaces Deborah Mollison's original score with music by Wagué and David Aubaile. Although Abela's revisions were designed to clarify the mystical elements, the Thiossane storyline still feels underdeveloped, never gelling with the more powerfully realised politics and emotion of the romantic tragedy.

Dir/Scr: Alexander Abela; **Prods:** Albertino Abela, Farida Fdani, Christophe Duthoit, Alexander Abela; **DOP:** Joseph Areddy; **Editor:** Christel Dewynter; **Score:** Deborah Mollison; **Main Cast:** Makena Diop (Souli), Aurélien Recoing (Yann), Jeanne Antebi (Mona), Fatou N'Diaye (Abi), Eduargo Noriega (Carlos).

(*Next page*) Emilia and Othello in Madagascar: Abi (Fatou N'Diaye) and Souli (Makena Diop) at the climax of Alexander Abela's *Souli*

Omkara
India, 2006 – 152 mins
Vishal Bhardwaj

Vishal Bhardwaj's compelling adaptation of *Othello*, released theatrically in the US and UK in summer 2006, sticks more closely to Shakespeare than his *Maqbool* (2003, p. 123) followed *Macbeth*, yet still makes several inspired changes, the first in its opening scene. On a parched hillside in Uttar Pradesh, Bhardwaj's Iago, Langda, tells a dim, wimpish bridegroom, Raju (Roderigo), that Langda's boss Omkara is abducting his bride. His lavish wedding to Dolly (Desdemona) is abandoned, and in his subsequent role as Langda's accomplice, he is not the play's hapless suitor, but a justified avenger, pursuing the man who destroyed his future with a beautiful bride.

Next, Raghunath, Dolly's father, blames Omkara's 'seduction' of his high-born daughter on his being a half-caste, so status largely replaces *Othello*'s racial strand (although several characters remark on Dolly's comparatively fair skin). He only spares Omkara's life on the orders of their boss, Bhaisaab (the formidable Naseeruddin Shah as a shaven-headed Doge), head of the Brahmin youth party, who needs Omkara, his General, and Raghunath, his lawyer, to secure his release from jail so that he can win a parliamentary seat against his rival, Indore Singh.

As Bhardwaj shuttles between Omkara's fort-like family home in a hillside village and various city locations, constant political violence replaces the Turks' short-lived threat to Cyprus and enables the director to reflect the bloody world of contemporary politics in Uttar Pradesh by engineering a *Macbeth*-like cycle of attacks.

First, Langda's marksmanship saves Omkara and his handsome young lieutenant, Kesu (Cassio), from Singh's agents, one of whom, Kichlu, later tries to assassinate Bhaisaab. This incites reprisals against Kichlu and, finally, a rain-swept night-time assault on a train, in which Omkara and Langda kill Singh and his bodyguards. All this spectacularly overcomes the problem, for genre film-makers rather than stage

Brahmin youth party leader Bhaisaab (Naseeruddin Shah), left, and Omkara (Ajay Devgan) prepare to anoint their new lieutenant in this pivotal scene from *Omkara*

directors, of *Othello*'s dearth of incident between the drunken brawl and the climactic murders, which here take place, with terrible irony, on Dolly and Omkara's wedding night.

The rousing title song has proclaimed Omkara 'the greatest warrior of all' and links him to Uttar Pradesh folklore about a legendary band of brothers. Compared to Othello's heroic exploits, however, the ruthless political killings make Ajay Devgan's muscular, brooding Omkara a considerably less sympathetic figure than the Moor.

The open-air shootouts and arid widescreen landscapes sometimes give *Omkara* a Western tang, and Saif Ali Khan's Langda has the tough, mischievous presence of Eli Wallach in *The Good, the Bad and the Ugly* (1966). His customised conspiracy, involving Dolly's incriminating, jewel-encrusted cummerbund, and mobile-phone eavesdropping, is unambiguously attributed to the exhilarating early scene in which, following Bhaisaab's election, the newly promoted Omkara must appoint his successor. In a religious ceremony at the top of a high temple overlooking riverbanks filled with hundreds of expectant followers, Omkara anoints Kesu, dashing Langda's expectations and initiating his revenge. This simplified motivation works in tandem with Bhardwaj's most radical change: Emilia becomes Indu, Omkara's sister, and she and Langda have a young son, Golu, whose ninth birthday party is wrecked by Kesu's drunken punch-up with Raju.

Langda thus betrays bonds of family as well as professional loyalty and, compared to the isolated Moor, Omkara's close relationship with Indu and some amusing moments featuring their ancient grandmother, added to the loss of the interracial element, make him a far less isolated (as well as less admirable) hero than Othello. Konkona Sen Sharma's wisecracking Indu and Kareena Kapoor's saintly, vulnerable Dolly have a sisterly, rather than mistress–servant relationship, and Indu's horror at realising that Langda has caused Dolly's death motivates one final twist. After smothering Dolly, Omkara spares Langda (why take revenge, he asks, when 'our souls are forever damned'?), only for Indu to kill her husband with a single machete blow. Shakespeare's tragic love story is thus incorporated into a three-generation family tragedy of a kind very popular with Bollywood audiences (echoing Bhardwaj's domestication of *Macbeth* in *Maqbool*).

Bollywood convention explains the three love ballads on the soundtrack, including the syrupy duet played under a flashback as Dolly recalls falling in love when she nursed an injured Omkara. Song-and-dance numbers are also obligatory, although Bhardwaj (who doubles impressively as *Omkara*'s composer) roots them in the story by turning Bianca into Kesu's stunningly beautiful girlfriend, Billo (Bipasha Basu), a nautch girl who performs two dubbed, raunchy uptempo songs, the first at Golu's party and the second at a police club, just before Langda and Omkara turn up to kill Kichlu. This forced transition from jollity to chaotic gunplay is one of Bhardwaj's few missteps. One would also not miss the scene of Kesu teaching Dolly to sing Stevie Wonder's 'I Just Called to Say I Love You' in English (pure kitsch). The family relationships could have been made clearer at an earlier stage, and we do not know whether Langda or Kesu kills Raju.

These are minor flaws in a story of great power and occasional flashes of poetry. Dolly recalls falling in love 'like a blind bird plunging down an empty well', and, sitting on a jetty, Langa nods ruefully to Raju: 'Both of us are damned to lead donkeys' lives.'

Dir: Vishal Bhardwaj; **Prod:** Kumar Mangat; **Scr:** Vishal Bhardwaj, Robin Ghatt, Abhishek Chaubhey; **Lyrics:** Gulzar; **DOP:** Tassaduq Hussain; **Editor:** Meghna Manchanda; **Score:** Vishal Bhardwaj; **Main Cast:** Ajay Devgan (Omkara), Saif Ali Khan (Langda), Kareena Kapoor (Dolly Mishra), Konkona Sen Sharma (Indu), Deepak Dobriyal (Raju), Viveik Oberoi (Kesu), Kamal Tiwari (Raghunath Mishra), Naseeruddin Shah (Bhaisaab), Bipasha Basu (Billo).

Richard III (play synopsis)

Richard, hunchbacked Duke of Gloucester, has murdered King Henry VI and his son, the Prince of Wales. He sets out to seize the throne newly occupied by his ailing older brother, King Edward IV, and marries Lady Anne, widow of the Prince of Wales. He dupes Edward into believing that their other brother, Clarence, is plotting against him. Clarence is imprisoned in the Tower of London and Richard conspires to have him killed, despite the King having granted him a pardon. On hearing this news, Edward expires.

Richard quickly has his opponents, Lords Grey, Dorset, Rivers and Hastings executed. Aided by the Duke of Buckingham and Sir William Catesby, he has Edward's two young sons, the rightful heirs to the throne, wrongfully declared bastards and imprisoned in the Tower.

Anne joins Queen Elizabeth, Edward's widow, and Queen Margaret, Henry VI's widow, in cursing Richard, but they cannot prevent him from being crowned King Richard III. He immediately has the two princes murdered by Sir James Tyrell.

He then has Queen Anne killed and resolves to marry Princess Elizabeth, his niece and Edward's daughter. When Buckingham is refused the dukedom Richard promised him for loyal service, he joins the rebel forces led by Henry, Earl of Richmond, who has returned from France to fight for the throne. Buckingham is captured and Richard has him executed. On the night before the climactic Battle of Bosworth Field, the ghosts of Richard's victims, including Anne and Buckingham, torment the sleeping King and reassure the sleeping Richmond that they and God are on his side. In the battle, Richmond leads the rebels to victory and kills Richard. He is crowned King Henry VII and prepares to marry Princess Elizabeth.

The Life and Death of King Richard III
US, 1912 – 53 mins (B&W)
James Keane

James Keane's *The Life and Death of Richard III*, the first Shakespeare feature film, was believed lost for decades. When collector and former projectionist William Buffum, of Portland, Oregon, donated his lovingly preserved print to the American Film Institute in 1996 and it turned out to be America's earliest surviving feature, the discovery made headline news.

The AFI's beautiful restoration, accompanied throughout by a new score from Ennio Morricone that is among his most sombre, reveals a production of epic, non-stop confrontation.

Politics and psychology are inevitable casualties and Margaret, Hastings and Rivers among the notable absentees, as more than 3,000 lines of Shakespeare are boiled down to four text inserts (including Clarence's arrest and death warrants) and twenty-seven sparely factual intertitles, for example: 'Gloster [sic] incites the quarrel between the King and Clarence.' Menace abounds, however, thanks to Oxfordshire-born Frederick Warde, sixty-one, an enormously popular stage actor billed as 'America's Greatest Tragedian'. He is a permanently scowling villain whose ghostly complexion and black wig anticipate Olivier's Richard, though Warde does not limp and has a scarcely discernible hump. He murders Henry VI in his prison cell, stabbing the motionless corpse twice more for pleasure (Keane, like Richard Loncraine in 1995, begins with Henry and Edward's deaths). Once Richard's faked piety has served its purpose, Warde tosses away his Bible and later, in one of several scenes using a nocturnal blue filter, lurks by the ailing Anne's bedside instructing a doctor to add poison to her medicine. He collapses histrionically after an effective process shot brings the ghosts into his tent.

Keane directs entirely in medium and long shots and places Richard at the heart of numerous interior tableaux (his ascent to the throne resembles Jacques Louis David's 'Coronation of Napoleon'). Palace chambers, battlements and Tower of London cells are represented by flimsy stage flats placed over the walls of a ruined house on City Island, New York, and the Expressionistic artificiality of the sets alternates with realistic location work shot in Westchester County and City Island, where Keane lavished much of his huge, $30,000 budget on processions that reportedly used 200 horses and 1,000 extras playing clergymen, ladies-in-waiting, infantry and standard-bearing lancers, all elaborately costumed. We see Richmond's crowded flagship weigh anchor and at Bosworth the director himself plays England's saviour like a Dumas musketeer, making light work of half-a-dozen of Richard's men and then the tyrant himself.

Keane had a keen eye for casting (Richard, Edward and Clarence look more like brothers than in many other productions) and knew how to embellish Shakespeare without rewriting him. For instance, before the little princes' first scheduled appearance in the text, we see them (one portrayed by a girl) playing together by their father's throne and sickbed, then riding into London on ponies. This extra screen time helps compensate for the absence of the chilling exchange between uncle and nephews in Act III, Scene i ('So wise so young, they say, do never live long'), building an emotional connection to the princes that makes their eventual demise all the more shocking: smothered while they sleep and dropped into a dungeon by Clarence's killers.

Keane felt no need to explore motivation with actors giving necessarily mimetic performances (hands clasped to chest to indicate grief, or rubbed together in malicious glee). As Warde noted in the *Brooklyn Eagle* in 1912, the director told the other actors 'when to look glad or sorry, when to shout and when to fight, without telling them why they did any of these things.'

Before the first and after the last scenes, Warde, in three-piece suit, stands bowing, acknowledging audience applause, and reminding present-day viewers that he often accompanied *Richard III* to cinemas to recite extracts from the play and provide interpretive commentary between, and sometimes during, the film's five reels, delivering what the

News and Courier, Charleston, in January 1913 called 'the best combination moving picture entertainment yet brought to this city . . . truly wonderful.'

Dir: James Keane; **Prod**: M. B. Dudley; **Score**: Ennio Morricone [for AFI restoration]; **Main Cast:** Frederick Warde (Richard), Violet Stuart (Anne), Carrie Lee (Queen Elizabeth), Miss De Felice (Princess Elizabeth), Robert Gemp (Edward IV), James Keane (Richmond).

Richard III
UK, 1955 – 157 mins
Laurence Olivier

When he watched Laurence Olivier on stage as Richard III in 1944, Noël Coward described it in his diary as 'the greatest male performance' he had ever witnessed. Ten years after that Old Vic production, Olivier transferred his portrayal to film in what *Variety* greeted as 'one of the major classics of the screen'.

Stressing the darkness in Richard's soul, Olivier is repeatedly shown as a humped shadow, limping across the floor. He is hypnotically ugly, his shiny black wig and witch's nose based, said Olivier, on 'loathsome' American theatre director Jed Harris. Even while outlining his machinations to camera in conspiratorial soliloquy, Olivier can retreat into the background knowing that his extraordinary voice will still command the screen. He over-emphasises odd syllables, often close to shrieking pitch, suddenly accelerates through the end of a sentence and follows stillness with abrupt surges. Such bravura techniques earned him a Best Actor Academy Award nomination and made this one of cinema's most parodied performances, yet he does not steal every scene. Norman Wooland makes a smooth, menacing Catesby and Ralph Richardson's habitual benevolence makes Buckingham's power-hungry malice singularly unnerving. John Gielgud gives great dignity to the imprisoned Clarence, and his murder – skull bashed in before being drowned in a barrel of wine – is as horrific as a fleeting glimpse of the bloody axe that beheads Hastings (Alec Clunes, combining politician's vanity with patriotic woe).

Claire Bloom, tearful and saintly as Lady Anne, seals the wooing scene with a disarmingly passionate kiss. Pamela Brown's is the most intriguing performance. As Jane Shore, mistress to Hastings and King Edward, she hovers on the fringe of several scenes and, without saying a word, makes her hold over both men a major thread in the story; it is the most significant screen appearance by a Shakespearean character not seen on stage.

For two hours, the action stays firmly within Roger Furse's spacious sets, as Richard, his allies and his victims plot or plead in palace throne room, corridors and courtyards, or at the Tower, dressed in Carmen Dillon's dark, velvet-rich costumes. Olivier allows static scenes to run for as much as ten minutes without a cut, rightly confident that the brilliance of script and cast will rivet his audience.

Only in the finale does his direction disappoint. Despite another rousing William Walton score and Richard's spectacular death (twenty soldiers swoop down on him, then retreat to watch his death agonies), the Battle of Bosworth Field is a generally muddled affair, especially given the precedent of *Henry V*'s Agincourt sequence (1944, p. 60). There are deflating cuts between long and medium shots filmed on the sun-bleached earth of a bull farm outside Madrid, and close-ups of the mounted duel between Richard and Richmond, all too obviously staged on the artificial grass of a Shepperton soundstage.

Richard III took the BAFTA for Best British Film and did excellent business in UK cinemas. On the day of its US theatrical release in March 1956 an unprecedented $500,000 deal with NBC saw it transmitted in black and white in forty-five states and some 25 million tune in – almost certainly a larger audience than had watched *Richard III* in its 350-year stage history. Despite this popularity, in the years to come Olivier failed to raise the money to star in and direct his planned film of *Macbeth*.

Dir/Prod: Laurence Olivier; Scr: Laurence Olivier, Alan Dent; DOP: Otto Heller; Editor: Helga Cranston; Score: William Walton; Main Cast: Laurence Olivier (Richard), Claire Bloom (Lady Anne), Ralph Richardson (Buckingham), John Gielgud (Clarence), Mary Kerridge (Queen Elizabeth), Alec Clunes (Hastings), Stanley Baker (Richmond), Norman Wooland (Catesby), Pamela Brown (Jane Shore).

Richard III
UK, 1995 – 104 mins
Richard Loncraine

A tank smashes through the wall of an army base. A soldier wearing a gas-mask climbs from the turret and shoots dead a handsome young officer and his elderly father, then peels off his mask and a sneering Ian McKellen is revealed as gunshots blast letters onto the screen: RICHARD III.

Richard Loncraine said this stunning opening (showing the murders of the Prince of Wales and King Henry from *Henry VI, Part III*) was designed to hook sceptical cinemagoers, 'people going "Oh, yeah, bloody Shakespeare, what time's it finish?"' It set the tone for an intelligent adaptation driven forward with the pace and economy you would expect from the director of 400 commercials, and greeted by the *Independent on Sunday* as 'a powerful contender' for the title of most entertaining Shakespeare film ever.

It had been developed from 1990's acclaimed National Theatre production, starring McKellen and directed by Richard Eyre, which relocated the action from the 1480s to the 1930s, linking Richard's reign of terror to Mussolini and Hitler. McKellen and Loncraine's BAFTA-nominated screenplay (worth seeking out in print for McKellen's fascinating thirty-page Introduction and copious notes) retains this setting and tinkers with the characters' status to clarify the plot's complex York vs. Lancaster rivalries. Out go all those earls, dukes and knights (so hard to differentiate when all wearing fifteenth-century attire), and in come more recognisable and resonant factions: a military dictatorship (Richard, Buckingham, Catesby, Tyrell and Ratcliffe), opposed by Prime Minister (Hastings), air force chief (Stanley) and naval commander (Richmond).

(*Opposite page*) 'I am in so far in blood, that sin will pluck on sin.': Richard (Ian McKellen) reflects on the murder of the young princes in Richard Loncraine's *Richard III*

Shuna Harwood's costumes and Tony Burrough's production design won BAFTA awards and Academy Award nominations for filling the screen with quasi-Fascist imagery and making brilliant use of locations (St Pancras station for the Princes' arrival in the capital; London's disused Bankside Power Station as the Tower). Though they turn Richard's coronation rally into a miniature Nuremberg, McKellen does not play him as some ranting Führer. His BAFTA-nominated portrayal has authority, mischief and malice to spare. Pale and sickly (prosthetics made the left side of his face appear to sag), with a pencil moustache above chain-smoking lips, his deformity is less pronounced than Olivier's Richard, and so is his acting technique. Like his famous predecessor, he delights in speaking directly to camera (even concluding his opening soliloquy while urinating), but in softer, less mannered tones, and creates a more human, occasionally vulnerable anti-hero.

Around him, Annette Bening hits the right, despairing notes as Queen Elizabeth (her casting a historical nod to Edward VIII's scandalous 1937 marriage to American divorcee Wallis Simpson) and Kristin Scott Thomas's Anne consumes assorted narcotics to blot out the horror of sharing Richard's bed. Jim Broadbent is ambitiously oily as Buckingham and Adrian Dunbar plays Richard's bloodthirsty hitman, Tyrell, a role greatly expanded from the play. Robert Downey Jr, as Elizabeth's brash brother, Rivers, is the only actor unable to make the verse seem like his character's natural mode of speech, before being stabbed while in bed with an air hostess – the most spectacular death in a movie overflowing with horrors that Shakespeare kept off stage. In addition to the opening carnage, Richard's victims are hung, strangled and suffocated. Tyrell slices open the throat of Nigel Hawthorne's pitiful Clarence, whom McKellen re-imagines as a bachelor not a family man, because 'too many other children . . . distract from the young princes and their fate'. Richard even blows away one of his own men in the explosive Bosworth sequence when his jeep stalls ('My kingdom for a horse!'). The ending is marred slightly by the film's overblown final shot: Richard's slow-motion tumble from a high girder into a hellish inferno, as Al Jolson croons 'I'm

Sitting on Top of the World', in homage to James Cagney's fiery demise at the end of *White Heat* (1949).

On a budget of $10m, grosses of $2.7m in America and about $1.5m in the UK were smaller than the film deserved, perhaps bearing out the prediction of the Hollywood studio producer Sam Goldwyn Jr, who read the unfilmed screenplay and warned McKellen that *Richard III* was 'too dark: the public only wants Pollyanna Shakespeare'.

Dir: Richard Loncraine; **Prods:** Lisa Katselas Paré, Stephen Bayly; **Scr:** Ian McKellen, Richard Loncraine; **DOP:** Peter Biziou; **Editor:** Paul Green; **Score:** Trevor Jones; **Main Cast:** Ian McKellen (Richard), Kristin Scott Thomas (Lady Anne), Jim Broadbent (Buckingham), Nigel Hawthorne (Clarence), Annette Bening (Queen Elizabeth), Jim Carter (Hastings), Dominic West (Richmond), Adrian Dunbar (Tyrell), Robert Downey Jr (Rivers).

Looking for Richard
US, 1996 – 112 mins
Al Pacino

It is hard to label *Looking for Richard*. One moment it is gripping, original-text Shakespeare, the next a *Making of . . .* documentary. You could also call it a practical guide to Shakespearean acting. Best to throw away genre tags and celebrate a glorious one-off, greeted by universally admiring reviews.

At the start of his enthusiastic narration, Pacino tells us: 'It has always been a dream of mine to communicate how I feel about Shakespeare to other people.' To do so, he returned to Richard III, a role he had played in Boston and on Broadway. He considered filming the whole play 'straight'; prohibitive cost and the shadow of Olivier deterred him. Instead, he and his chief collaborator, writer and actor Frederic Kimball, accumulated eighty hours of documentary footage in a labour of love funded by Pacino himself over a three-year period during which he rejoined Kimball between acting appearances in other films.

With the aid of no fewer than four editors, they created a freewheeling, unpretentious patchwork. They make a pilgrimage to Shakespeare's birthplace and do vox pops, asking New Yorkers what they think about the playwright and his work. American and British actors, including Kevin Kline, Kenneth Branagh and Vanessa Redgrave, offer intelligent sound bites about iambic pentameters, or US actors' reputation for struggling with Shakespeare. Peter Brook, director of *King Lear* (1971, p. 79), and two unidentified English academics make equally pithy contributions.

The interviews are intercut with footage of Pacino and Kimball scouting locations for filmed scenes from the play and rehearsing their cast in a high-rise office. Their occasional disagreements and Pacino's frustration at the complexity of *Richard III*'s language and plot are hugely endearing. After failing to explain a particularly intricate scene to co-producer Michael Hadge, Pacino says: 'It's very confusing. I don't know why we even bother doing this at all.'

Even more enjoyable are the sparely designed extracts. Despite the omission of numerous characters and incidents, Pacino's sportscast commentary ('Richard's in pretty good shape'; 'Richard needs to move fast') means prior knowledge of the play is not required and ten decisive scenes propel the drama impressively towards its climax. Clarence pleads for his life with the two murderers, giving Alec Baldwin the chance to show a subtlety rarely evident in his Hollywood roles, and Winona Ryder does the same as Lady Anne in the grotesque seduction scene. We also watch the disintegration of the alliance between Richard and Buckingham (Kevin Spacey at his sly, intelligent best), before Pacino meets a bloody end at Bosworth, pinned down by Aidan Quinn's Richmond. A string of experienced if unfamiliar faces fill other roles superbly.

To his credit, Pacino the director does not over-indulge Pacino the star. His accent sometimes hovers between England and New York, but his trademarks (surges in volume on unexpected points in a speech, the frequent 'Hah!'s) are kept in check to give us quietly irresistible villainy, not so far removed from his *Godfather* role as Michael Corleone (another attractive tyrant who has his own brother executed) and he is more comfortable here than as Shylock (p. 134). He calls *Looking for Richard* a 'docu-drama type thing', and it leaves you longing to watch him and his cast perform *Richard III* in full.

Dir: Al Pacino; **Prods:** Michael Hadge, Al Pacino; **DOP:** Robert Leacock; **Editors:** William A. Anderson, Ned Bastille, Pasquale Buba, Andre Ross Betz; **Score:** Howard Shore; **Main Cast:** Al Pacino (Narrator/Richard III), Winona Ryder (Lady Anne), Kevin Spacey (Buckingham), Alec Baldwin (Clarence), Penelope Allen (Queen Elizabeth), Kevin Conway (Hastings), Aidan Quinn (Richmond), Frederic Kimball (Bishop of Ely).

King Rikki (aka *The Street King*, US video title)
US, 2002 – 91 mins
James Gavin Bedford

King Rikki is no better than any number of anonymously cast, straight-to-video urban gang thrillers, and its simplistic criminalisation of *Richard III* feels more contrived than *Joe Macbeth*'s gangster treatment of the Scottish play (p. 100). Yet it merits attention for handling Richard's soliloquies and asides with such flair.

James Gavin Bedford immediately thanks his source with speeded-up shots of a graffiti artist spraying sunglasses and red bandana onto a garage-door painting of the famous Martin Droeshout portrait of Shakespeare. A flashback narrated by Los Angeles-born Rikki Ortega (the slightly built, charismatic Jon Seda) reveals that at seven he was given away to relatives in Fresno by his poverty-stricken mother; so childhood trauma, not deformity, explains our handsome anti-hero's malice.

Rikki's explanation of a California Latino rivalry between red Norteños and blue La Eme (those living, respectively, north and south of Bakersfield) misleadingly hints at state-wide civil war to match *Richard III*'s conflict between Red Lancaster and White York; the budget only covers a turf war over the local crystal meth trade, which pits the Ortegas, whom Rikki rejoined on his return to East LA, against the Rojas and Gavilans.

In the first of more than twenty brief addresses to camera, Rikki introduces his brothers, Eduardo and Jorge (equivalents to King Edward and Clarence), Eduardo's brother-in-law, Rios (literally, Rivers), and various henchmen. All are one-dimensional macho dolts, while the women are all vain, fickle or both, so *Richard III*'s ensemble-backed virtuosity becomes Rikki's one-man show.

He gets straight into the action, killing Alejandro Rojas, a former childhood friend (equivalent to the Prince of Wales), and swiftly beds Alejandro's sultry girlfriend, Anita (the story's Lady Anne). Helped by three gang members (vague replacements for Buckingham, Catesby and

Tyrell), but mostly acting alone, he tricks Eduardo into having Jorge murdered in prison, kills Eduardo in hospital after poisoning him, then runs over Rios. He tries and fails to kill Eduardo's teenage son, Rafa, and is gunned down by Juan Vallejo (the wooden Mario López), another former barrio playmate-turned-corrupt detective.

Bedford's direction is leaden, and he cannot afford even run-of-the-mill action scenes (we see Rikki putting a grenade in a BMW's petrol tank, not the resulting explosion). He leans too heavily on Alec Costandinos's score (lots of 1980s' guitar, synth and drums in the style of television's *Miami Vice*) and his mostly third-rate cast speak boilerplate hoodlum ('This is shit we don't need!' etc.), with snatches of subtitled Spanish ('Hijo de puta!').

Yet the film is redeemed by Seda's vigorous charm and the comparative wit of Rikki's soliloquies and asides. He is mostly alone when speaking to camera, though Bedford is bold enough to retain the theatrical convention that allows Rikki to confide in us while in company, without other characters noticing – not even Anita as they have sex, or his mother at Eduardo's graveside. There's also more direct engagement with the audience than in Shakespeare; Rikki calls us ''mano', short for 'hermano' (brother), and even suggests we are on his evil wavelength: 'We're going to get along, 'cos I can talk to you. It's good to have someone who thinks the way I do.'

Dir/Editor: James Gavin Bedford; **Prod:** John D. Vaughan; **Scr:** Jesse Graham; **DOP:** Rob Sweeney; **Score:** Alec Costandinos; **Main Cast:** Jon Seda (Rikki Ortega), Tonantzin Carmelo (Anita), Timothy Paul Perrez (Eduardo Ortega), David Labiosa (Rios), Manny Perez (Jorge Ortega), Mario López (Juan Vallejo).

Romeo and Juliet (play synopsis)

Verona. A bloody streetfight between members of the feuding Montague and Capulet clans forces Verona's Prince to threaten Lords Montague and Capulet with death if the violence resumes.

That night, Montague's son, Romeo, joins his cynical friend, Mercutio, and cousin, Benvolio, at a masked party at Capulet's house. There, Romeo and Juliet, Capulet's thirteen-year-old daughter, fall instantly in love and immediately decide to get married.

The next morning, Romeo tells Juliet's garrulous, devoted Nurse to send her to his confessor, Friar Laurence, who weds the lovers in secret, hoping their union may reconcile their families.

Immediately afterwards, Juliet's hot-headed cousin, Tybalt, insulted by Romeo's uninvited appearance at the party, challenges him. When Romeo refuses to fight, Mercutio takes his place and is fatally wounded by Tybalt as Romeo tries to part their swords. In revenge, Romeo kills Tybalt and flees the scene. The Prince banishes him for life. After spending the night with Juliet, he leaves for Mantua.

Juliet's parents order her to marry Paris, a young count, in two days' time, and the Nurse advises her to forget Romeo. In suicidal despair, she goes to Friar Laurence, who gives her a sleeping potion, to be taken the night before the wedding. It will make her appear dead for forty-two hours, after which time Laurence will have summoned Romeo to meet her inside the Capulet tomb.

The potion works, and Juliet's shocked and grieving parents lay her in the tomb. But Friar John, who carries Laurence's explanatory letter to Romeo, cannot reach Mantua. Believing Juliet is really dead, Romeo buys poison and returns to Verona to die beside his wife. Paris tries to stop Romeo entering the tomb, they fight and Paris is killed. Once inside, Romeo kisses Juliet goodbye and swallows the poison. Juliet awakes, sees Romeo and, ignoring the Friar's pleas for her to leave, stabs herself. The lovers' deaths convince Montague, whose wife has died of grief at Romeo's banishment, and Capulet to make peace.

Romeo and Juliet
US, 1936 – 123 mins (B&W)
George Cukor

MGM's *Romeo and Juliet* was Hollywood's first feature-length adaptation of a Shakespeare tragedy. Irving G. Thalberg pronounced it 'a cultural undertaking of importance' and ensured that his studio pulled out all the stops. In the quest for 'authenticity', months of research went into the vast sets designed by Cedric Gibbons, Frederic Hope and Edwin B. Willis, and the 1,200 costumes designed by Oliver Messel and Adrian. William Strunk Jr, Professor of English at Cornell University, was hired as literary adviser to ensure, he said, 'that no injustice was done' to Shakespeare. It all cost $2m (more than $80m today); if only the finished product had matched the stupendous effort that created it.

Casting was its fatal flaw. Juliet, Romeo, Tybalt and Mercutio were portrayed by Norma Shearer (Thalberg's wife), aged thirty-five, Leslie Howard, forty-three, Basil Rathbone, forty-four, and John Barrymore, fifty. Once they were chosen, the film unquestionably had star power; it could never hope to capture the tragic spirit of a play about impetuous, *young* lives cut short.

Howard and Shearer move in a spectacular world of romantic luxury, with Herbert Stothart's original compositions and arrangement of Tchaikovsky's *Romeo and Juliet* Overture as appropriately grand accompaniment. The ballet during the Capulet ball is a breathtaking highlight: Romeo watches Juliet rejecting a dozen masked suitors before dancing with Ralph Forbes's muscular Paris. Once mute admiration turns to conversation, however, Howard and Shearer seem overwhelmed by an obligation to deliver Shakespeare's verse with more reverence than feeling. Cukor and his stars forget that however ornate the language of the balcony or wedding night scenes, the words come to life only in the mouths of engaging characters.

Howard had suggested in a tie-in book that making Romeo interesting was 'a task to frighten any actor', and it proves beyond him.

Perhaps inevitably, given his age, this self-absorbed Romeo would be more at home playing Hamlet.

Only when Romeo has been banished can Shearer lift Juliet clear of a chaste, Snow White persona (she is first seen feeding deer in the Capulet garden), and her Best Actress Oscar nomination owed much to her agonised soliloquy before taking the potion and the scenes in which she silently renounces Edna May Oliver's shrill Nurse and defies her father (the towering C. Aubrey Smith, as gruffly authoritarian here as when playing umpteen generals and colonels).

Barrymore's scenery chewing as Mercutio at least brings fleeting *joie de vivre* to Cukor's Verona until he dies cursing Capulets and Montagues with absurd politeness, the characteristic that deadens the film. By the time the lovers have died prettily, the energy of the opening sequence's massed swordfight, broken up by the Prince and his cavalry, seems a distant memory.

Critical opinion generally rated the production values above the performances, the *New York Times* declaring that MGM had 'gloriously released the play from the limitations of the stage.' The *New York Sun* mourned the absence of tragedy: 'It does not wring the heart, nor stir tears of sweet sympathy or bitter resentment.' Having nurtured the project for ten years, Thalberg lived just long enough to absorb the critical response, but not his Best Picture Oscar nomination; he died of pneumonia three weeks after *Romeo and Juliet*'s premiere, aged thirty-seven. It eventually grossed almost $2m, yet the huge print and marketing costs left the studio with a loss of $900,000 that contributed to Hollywood's refusal to tackle Shakespeare for more than a decade, until MGM re-entered the arena with *Julius Caesar* (p. 73). Looking back in 1971, Cukor himself conceded that his lovers had been 'too stodgy . . . It's one picture that if I had to do over again, I'd know how. I'd get the garlic and the Mediterranean into it.'

(*Opposite page*) Leslie Howard and Norma Shearer as the star-crossed lovers in George Cukor's *Romeo and Juliet*

Dir: George Cukor; **Prod:** Irving G. Thalberg; **Scr:** Talbot Jennings; **DOP:** William Daniels; **Editor:** Margaret Booth; **Score:** Herbert Stothart; **Main Cast:** Leslie Howard (Romeo), Norma Shearer (Juliet), John Barrymore (Mercutio), Basil Rathbone (Tybalt), Edna May Oliver (Nurse), Henry Kolker (Friar Laurence), Reginald Denny (Benvolio), C. Aubrey Smith (Capulet), Violet Kemble (Lady Capulet), Ralph Forbes (Paris), Basil Rathbone (Tybalt).

The Lovers of Verona (*Les Amants de Vérone*)
France, 1949 – 105 mins (B&W)
André Cayatte

Transplanting *Romeo and Juliet* to post-war Venice, André Cayatte
replaces two households 'both alike in dignity' with one family in decline.
The Maglias (Capulets) live in impoverished splendour in a canal-side
palazzo. Pompous Ettore is a former fascist attorney-general finding relief
from his joyless marriage to Luccia in the arms of housekeeper Laetitia
(the Nurse), who looks after Ettore's cousin, Amedeo, a crazed army
veteran. Ettore has promised his 'fresh, beautiful and innocent' daughter,
Georgia (slender, red-headed Anouk Aimée), to white-suited tour guide
Raffaele (Pierre Brasseur) – the story's Paris (as unloved fiancé), but also
its chief villain, blackmailing Ettore over his wartime use of the death
sentence.

When he introduces Bettina Verdi (Martine Carol), star of a *Romeo
and Juliet* film shooting in Venice, to the Maglias she offers Georgia
work as a studio extra. As Verdi's stand-in for a camera rehearsal of the
balcony scene, Georgia meets her Romeo, Angelo (Serge Reggiani), a
handsome young glassblower from working-class Murano Island. It is
cross-class love at first sight, and the first of several moments when
fateful timing exerts as strong a pull as in the play. A stand-in for Romeo
is required just as Angelo bluffs his way on set; Raffaele happens to steer
his vaporetto past the lovers kissing in a gondola; he drives up as Angelo
climbs away from Georgia's Verona hotel bedroom when the film goes
on location. The pair's idyllic twenty-four hours in Verona – working
together, visiting Juliet's tomb, skinny-dipping and evading Laetitia's
chaperoning to spend the night together – is the heart of the story. The
lovers' intense passion is conveyed by Aimée and Reggiani's vivacious,
unaffected performances and astonishing beauty. They scarcely speak,
and the only poetry is the sonorous male voiceover quoting Juliet's 'It
was the nightingale . . .' as they part. Cayatte can devote proportionately
more time than Shakespeare to the romance by excluding counterparts

for Benvolio, Mercutio, Friar Laurence, the Prince or Montague, and giving brief appearances to Angelo's widowed mother and ex-girlfriend Clio, a young flower-seller whom he has impregnated (though she insists the baby is not his).

The lovers are frequently upstaged by the broad-brush portrayals of the Maglias, and Brasseur veers towards caricature, spitting out lines like 'Decay is the motto of the house of Maglia', trying to have Angelo killed and denouncing Georgia as a whore (Ettore's subsequent tirade resembles Capulet's in Act III).

When Georgia takes the ferry to Murano Island she fails to see Angelo on the lower deck, and arrives at his house seconds after he leaves for work. She entrusts to Clio a letter, which she does not pass on, telling Angelo her plan for them to elope. Instead, Laetitia lures Angelo to an ambush at the Maglias'. As Angelo flees, Amedeo shoots dead Raffaele and mortally wounds Angelo, who dies in Georgia's arms on the set of Juliet's tomb, where they first kissed. She slits her wrists, the Chorus repeats 'Now Romeo is beloved and loves again' (as after their first embrace), and the orchestra surges one last time.

Though not a profound work, *The Lovers* interestingly embraces different types of Shakespearean adaptation. Essentially a melodramatic genre reworking of *Romeo*, it features the production of an original-text film of the play, evidently in the grand, reverential style of Cukor or Castellani (pp. 207 and 213). Although Georgia and Angelo are not professionals, Cayatte also upholds the cardinal rule of showbiz melodrama (see *A Double Life*, 1947, p. 163): an actor playing a Shakespeare character must behave like them.

Dir: André Cayatte; Prod: Raymond Borderie; Scr: André Cayatte, Jacques Prévert; DOP: Henri Alekan; Editor: Christian Gaudin; Score: Joseph Kosma; Main Cast: Serge Reggiani (Angelo), Anouk Aimée (Georgia Maglia), Pierre Brasseur (Raffaele), Marianne Oswald (Laetitia), Louis Salou (Ettore Maglia), Solange Sicard (Luccia Maglia), Marcel Dalio (Amedeo Maglia).

Romeo and Juliet
Italy/UK, 1954 – 138 mins
Renato Castellani

Renato Castellani had already filmed stories featuring young people struggling against a hostile society, such as *Two Cents Worth of Hope* (1951), so it was no surprise that when he turned to Shakespeare he chose *Romeo and Juliet*.

Following the Italian neo-realist fashion for location filming, Castellani led a seven-month shoot in Siena, Venice, Verona and Montagana and Robert Krasker, who shot Olivier's *Henry V* (1944, p. 60), captured sunlit stone walls, scarlet canopies on market stalls and cloudless blue skies. In interior scenes, figures appear in neat, portrait poses, the costumes and set decoration influenced by Renaissance artists like Raphael and Bellini. Some acknowledged Castellani's attempt to match the play's verbal lyricism with visual lyricism, but it palls quickly; there is much to enjoy by way of travelogue and art history – and almost no drama.

Posters promised that Laurence Harvey, then twenty-five and a rising star with the Royal Shakespeare Company, would bring 'new fire and excitement to Romeo', yet he appears to love himself, his poetry and his poses, with Juliet in fourth place. His velvety voice over-emphasises every rhyme, and the 'fire-eyed fury' that drives Romeo to kill Tybalt and Paris comes across as mild irritation.

Susan Shentall's Juliet, looking like a prim Grace Kelly, has the lighter, unaffected touch you would expect from an eighteen-year-old Derbyshire girl making her acting début after being plucked from secretarial college. Opposite such an unresponsive Romeo, she has little opportunity to suggest teenage ardour (the pair hardly even kiss), but makes the most of her scenes with a furious father (the blusteringly operatic Sebastian Cabot). She married soon after shooting ended and never returned to screen acting.

The flat love story might be tolerable if only the supporting characters were livelier. Yet Castellani trims the Nurse's part to the bone, makes Friar Laurence an irritating ditherer, and, unforgivably, reduces Mercutio to the tiniest of cameos, losing all sense of the deep friendship between Romeo and Mercutio, so that Tybalt might just as well have killed a total stranger.

Although the plot's major incidents survive the cuts that allow Castellani to dwell so long on pretty images, so much of the finest dialogue is absent that characters' behaviour sometimes seems confusingly unmotivated. The *New Statesman* reviewer felt that no other screen adaptation had left Shakespeare's text 'so hacked, patched and insensitively thrown away.'

The drama is weakened further by Castellani's neo-realist use of non-professional Italians. Aldo Zollo (Mercutio) was a Veronese architect, Giulio Garbinetto (Montague) was a Venetian gondolier and Giovanni Rota (the Prince) wrote novels; though they might have been at home with Italian-speaking parts in a contemporary, realist tale like *Two Cents Worth of Hope*, they inevitably struggle with the rarefied demands of Elizabethan tragedy in a foreign language.

Remarkably, the Jury at the 1954 Venice Film Festival gave *Romeo and Juliet* its Grand Prix, ahead of *On the Waterfront*, among other competitors. British couples likely to have gone home from the film disappointed could at least relax with exclusive accessories, perhaps sitting back on a couch covered in the 'Romeo and Juliet Fabric', while the woman rested her tired feet in a pair of 'Juliet Slippers', available in black, red or emerald suede for thirty-nine shillings a pair.

Dir/Scr: Renato Castellani; **Prod:** Sandro Ghenzi; **DOP:** Robert Krasker; **Editor:** Sidney Hayers; **Score:** Roman Vlad; **Main Cast:** Laurence Harvey (Romeo), Susan Shentall (Juliet), Bill Travers (Benvolio), Aldo Zollo (Mercutio), Enzo Fiermonte (Tybalt), Flora Robson (Nurse), Mervyn Johns (Friar Laurence), Sebastian Cabot (Capulet), Lydia Sherwood (Lady Capulet), Norman Wooland (Paris), Giovanni Rota (Prince of Verona), Guilio Gardinetti (Montague).

West Side Story
US, 1961 – 153 mins
Robert Wise, Jerome Robbins

West Side Story magically transmutes *Romeo and Juliet*'s dramatic momentum and rich verse into the wit and longing of Stephen Sondheim's lyrics, Leonard Bernstein's pulsating music and the poetry in motion of Jerome Robbins's choreography.

   As in the stage musical triumphantly directed by Robbins on Broadway in 1957, gangs of white American Jets (Montagues) take on Puerto Rican Sharks (Capulets) on the streets of New York. Romeo becomes Tony, who works in the soda shop run by the elderly Doc (the Friar Laurence figure), leaving Jets co-founder Riff (Mercutio) to run the

'I like to be in America!': Anita (Rita Moreno), front right, leads the Sharks' rooftop dance in Robert Wise and Jerome Robbins's *West Side Story*

gang alone. Maria (Juliet) works in a bridal shop after being brought over from Puerto Rico by her volatile brother, Bernardo (Tybalt and Capulet combined). Bernardo runs the Sharks, dates Anita, who replaces the Nurse as Maria's confidante, and wants his sister to marry Chino (Paris). Two cops, racist Lieutenant Schrank and ineffectual Officer Krupke, assume the Prince's judicial role at the end of a dazzling opening 'fight', in which the gangs trade dance-steps instead of blows.

Romeo and Juliet's love poetry is matched by the duets and solos for handsome, anodyne Richard Beymer (dubbed by Jimmy Bryant) and radiant Natalie Wood (dubbed by Marni Nixon), who gives a devastating portrayal of innocence betrayed. Their songs include the tingling anticipation of Maria's 'I Feel Pretty', the dazed joy of Tony's 'Maria' and the shared hope of 'Tonight' in their fire-escape 'balcony' scene. Their hesitant intimacy is played off against the overwhelming vitality of the Jets' delinquent's lament, 'Gee, Officer Krupke', and the Sharks girls' equally ironic view of immigrant life, 'America', an incomparable rooftop stomp led by Moreno's fiery Anita and Chakiris's brooding Bernardo.

These arm-thrusting, pelvis-tilting ensembles are a delight and, crucially, make you care about *all* the singers, from the smouldering Anita/Bernardo relationship, down to the most junior Jet. Where Shakespeare alternates between children, parents and surrogate parents (Friar and Nurse), here the focus on youth never wavers (Doc, Schrank and Krupke make a handful of appearances; Maria's parents remain off screen), and the racial prejudice dividing the kids is a more convincing plot motor than the motiveless 'ancient grudge' pitting Capulets against Montagues.

Granted, nobody in 1961 thought the choreographed 'violence' or the Jets' expletive-free street slang reflected contemporary gang culture. The singing and dancing take us several steps from reality and Robert Wise (who took sole charge after MGM sacked Robbins as co-director mid-shoot) pushes us further, occasionally surrounding Tony and Maria with dreamlike optical effects. Yet you believe in the story totally, and the ending shocks without recourse to sleeping potions or fateful bad timing.

After the 'rumble' in which Bernardo kills Riff and Tony kills Bernardo, Anita is almost raped by the Jets as she tries to deliver Maria's message to Tony. Enraged, she tells the Jets that Chino has killed Maria. Tony goes looking for Chino, who shoots him, and he dies in Maria's arms. As he is carried away by Jets and Sharks nobody says, or sings, a word and the silence provides a stunning conclusion to a masterpiece that grossed more than eight times its lavish $5m budget in the US, and won ten Oscars – just reward for the greatest film musical ever made.

Dirs: Robert Wise, Jerome Robbins; **Prod:** Robert Wise; **Scr:** Ernest Lehman; **Book:** Arthur Laurents; **Lyrics:** Stephen Sondheim; **DOP:** Daniel L. Fapp; **Editor:** Thomas Stanford; **Score:** Leonard Bernstein; **Main Cast:** Richard Beymer (Tony), Natalie Wood (Maria), Russ Tamblyn (Riff), George Chakiris (Bernardo), Rita Moreno (Anita), Ned Glass (Doc), Jose De Vega (Chino), Simon Oakland (Lt Schrank), William Bramley (Officer Krupke).

Romeo and Juliet
Italy/UK, 1968 – 152 mins
Franco Zeffirelli

Franco Zeffirelli sowed the seeds of this box-office triumph in 1960, when the Italian director–designer made his Shakespeare stage début with *Romeo and Juliet* at London's Old Vic. He cast John Stride, then twenty-three, and Judi Dench, twenty-five, as probably the youngest star-crossed lovers ever seen in the West End, and the production was a huge hit. In 1967, he set out to replicate that Old Vic passion on film, immediately after his success with *The Taming of the Shrew* (1967, p. 239). Despite that film's popularity, most studios reckoned Shakespeare remained a poor commercial bet. Paramount eventually put up $800,000, much less than Zeffirelli wanted. He was confident of attracting a large international audience and, believing that 'the kids in the story are like teenagers today', took a gamble by casting actors almost as young as their characters: Leonard Whiting was seventeen, Olivia Hussey, chosen ahead of 350 other hopefuls, just fifteen.

Emulating Renato Castellani's 1954 precedent (p. 213), Zeffirelli spent much of the three-month shoot at Italian locations: small towns in Tuscany and Umbria, with some interiors recreated at Cinecittà studios in Rome. Shakespeare's action unfolds in medieval churches, sun-drenched piazzas and shady side streets filled with handsome, athletic boys in colour-coded tights and codpieces (garish red and yellow for Capulets, discreet blue for Montagues).

From the opening, frenzied brawl to the final procession of Capulet and Montague mourners, the whole film, as Richard Burton said to Zeffirelli after seeing some early footage, 'looks sensational'. Yet Burton also cautioned: 'You've got problems with the verse' and Whiting and Hussey were the chief culprits.

Their youth makes the lovers' infatuation more credible than in

(*Opposite page*) 'A plague o' both your houses': the dying Mercutio (John McEnery), right, with Romeo (Leonard Whiting) in Franco Zeffirelli's *Romeo and Juliet*

Cukor; their beauty is beyond question (the nudity in the wedding night scene caused a minor stir), and every intimate moment is underscored by Nino Rota's soaring love theme (later to become a hit record). Yet their struggle to convey the meaning of the language is painful to behold, even though Zeffirelli had cut more than half the text. Hussey fares marginally better of the two, her face conveying memorable dread as the story spirals towards her suicide. Whiting's London-accented Romeo remains more love-struck wimp than desperate, fate-driven hero, an impression reinforced because Zeffirelli (unlike Cukor and Castellani) does not jeopardise audience sympathy by showing Romeo killing Paris.

Among the strong supporting cast, Michael York overdoes the blazing-eyed fury as Tybalt, Pat Heywood's Nurse chatters with splendid vulgarity and Robert Stephens makes an imperious Prince. Best of all, John McEnery's Mercutio is a cynical livewire whose death, as it should, leaves a mournful void in the second half.

As Benvolio, Bruce Robinson (later to direct cult comedy *Withnail and I*) is among several British actors whose performances suffer from poorly post-synched dialogue. Zeffirelli's idol, Laurence Olivier, delivers the Prologue.

The film opened to mixed reviews in the UK and US: the *New Statesman* felt Zeffirelli 'might just as well have jettisoned the Bard altogether'; *Time* hailed 'one of the handful of classic Shakespeare films.' The visual splendour brought Academy Awards for cinematographer Pasqualino De Santis and costume designer Danilo Donati, with unsuccessful nominations for Best Picture and Best Director (*Oliver!* won both). At box offices Zeffirelli's casting gamble and populist instincts paid off spectacularly; a worldwide gross of $48m made this the biggest Shakespeare hit of all time.

Dir: Franco Zeffirelli; **Prods:** Anthony Havelock-Allan, John Brabourne; **Scr:** Franco Brusati, Masolino D'Amico; **DOP:** Pasqualino De Santis; **Editor:** Reginald Mills; **Score:** Nino Rota; **Main Cast:** Leonard Whiting (Romeo), Olivia Hussey (Juliet), John McEnery (Mercutio), Michael York (Tybalt), Pat Heywood (Nurse), Milo O'Shea (Friar Laurence), Bruce Robinson (Benvolio), Paul Harwick (Capulet), Natasha Parry (Lady Capulet), Roberto Bisacco (Paris), Robert Stephens (Prince of Verona).

Tromeo and Juliet
USA, 1996 – 107 mins
Lloyd Kaufman

Tromeo and Juliet takes every major character (Lady Montague apart) and incident from *Romeo and Juliet* and systematically drains them of humanity in a tedious, appallingly acted feast of mutilation and softcore sex. As Chorus, Lemmy (of heavy metal group Motorhead), narrates the contemporary, Manhattan-set rivalry between the delinquent followers of black Monty Que, an obese alcoholic, and white Cappy Capulet, who stole Monty's white wife Ingrid and his share of their porn film business.

Cappy's daughter Juliet (slender, blonde Jane Jensen) has repellent erotic nightmares, enjoys lesbian clinches with the tattooed family cook, Ness (the Nurse), and is sexually abused by her dad in a plexi-glass cage. Monty's son, Will Keenan's dumb, horny Tromeo, falls for Juliet at the Capulet costume party. 'Parting is such sweet sorrow,' she says. 'It totally sucks,' he replies (the lovers periodically quote or paraphrase the play; the rest of the dialogue is expletive-laced trash-talk).

Father Lawrence is a child-abuser, Tyrone (Tybalt) and Tromeo's friend Murray (Mercutio) are killed in exceptionally sadistic fights and a surfeit of grotesque make-up sees Juliet put off her twittering fiancé, meatpacking heir London Arbuckle (Paris), by drinking a potion that briefly turns her into a mutant. The film's one inventive addition has Juliet visited by the ghosts of her love affair's 'victims', including Tyrone and Merrie, like Richard III before Bosworth.

After a police detective (the Prince) pardons the lovers for killing Cappy in self-defence, Ingrid reveals that Capy was Tromeo's real father. Undeterred by being brother and sister, an epilogue shows them playing with incestuously deformed twin daughters. Despite this being the nadir of screen Shakespeare, Troma Pictures, specialists in brainless, low-budget splatter movies, have enough fans for *Tromeo* to have merited a tenth anniversary, two-disc DVD reissue in 2006, as though it were a modern classic.

Dir: Lloyd Kaufman; **Prods:** Michael Herz, Lloyd Kaufman; **Scr:** James Gunn, Lloyd Kaufman; **DOP:** Brendan Flynt; **Editor:** Frank Reynolds; **Score:** Willie Wisely; **Main Cast:** Will Keenan (Tromeo), Jane Jensen (Juliet), Valentine Miele (Murray Martini), Patrick Connor (Tyrone), Debbie Rochon (Ness), Flip Brown (Father Lawrence), Stephen Blackehart (Benny), Maximillian Shaun (Cappy Capulet), Wendy Adams (Ingrid Capulet), Steve Gibbons (London Arbuckle).

William Shakespeare's Romeo + Juliet
US, 1996 – 115 mins
Baz Luhrmann

In the stunningly inventive world of *William Shakespeare's Romeo + Juliet*, rapiers are a brand of automatic pistol, Juliet's father behaves like the Godfather, Mercutio sports a sequined bikini top and the 'balcony' scene moves to a swimming pool.

Many critics argued that this was really *Baz Luhrmann's Romeo + Juliet*, burying Shakespeare beneath an avalanche of gaudy tricks, car chases, gunplay and pop songs, all edited at MTV pace. Others recognised that these elements made the play's love story leap off the screen with unprecedented energy and immediacy, while neglecting its mature characters. Luhrmann defended his approach by noting that the playwright had employed disparate techniques and styles without ever losing narrative control, leaving Shakespearean film-makers free to be 'as outrageous and mad as you like, as long as there's clarity'; *Romeo + Juliet* is outrageous *and* clear, leaving audiences dazed, but not confused.

It turns sixteenth-century Verona into 1990s' Verona Beach, a Miami-like city. A TV anchorwoman reads the Prologue, and news footage illustrates the feud between property tycoons Ted Montague (a weary-looking Brian Dennehy) and Fulgencio Capulet, played by Paul Sorvino as a volatile Mafia chieftain, married to Diane Venora's fading Southern belle. The opening brawl becomes a gun battle at a petrol station, as Jesse Bradford's mumbling Benvolio and John Leguizamo's sneering Tybalt blast away in a slow-motion cross between John Woo and Sergio Leone, with pastiche Ennio Morricone on the soundtrack. Leonardo DiCaprio's idle, rich-kid Romeo hangs out at a ruined beachside theatre, writing poetry, and shoots pool with Benvolio. Capulet and 'Bachelor of the Year' Paris (the blandly likeable Paul Rudd) talk weddings while relaxing in a sauna.

This frantic half-hour of short scenes gives a wonderfully clear sense of the characters' lives and styles, and every aspect of the production design is geared towards making the language more digestible for teenagers, without actually changing the words. When Harold Perrineau's black, transvestite Mercutio (probably gay, and definitely in love with Romeo) denounces idle dreams in the 'Queen Mab' speech he is hymning the hallucinatory pill he gives Romeo to get him in the mood for the Capulets' fancy-dress ball, where Mercutio struts to disco anthem 'Young Hearts Run Free' (Luhrmann's deft use of songs by Radiohead, the Cardigans and others spawned two hit soundtrack albums). Then, magically, everything calms down, as Romeo, in knight's armour, and Juliet, sporting angel's wings, glimpse each other through a tropical fish tank. Time stands still, and cinematic love at first sight has never seemed more convincing. They embrace in Juliet's pool, then enlist the help of Pete Postlethwaite's Father Laurence, a mystic with a Celtic Cross tattoo, and Miriam Margolyes's plump, Hispanic Nurse (forever crying 'Hooliet, Hooliet!').

Claire Danes, just sixteen when the film was made, displays that elusive 'wiser-than-her-years' quality the part demands, and emerges as the first big-screen Juliet whose speeches sound spontaneous, which is why, among Luhrmann's heavy textual cuts, his butchering of the heroine's potion soliloquy is perhaps the unkindest: forty-five lines of hope, terror, trust and love reduced to 'Romeo, I drink to thee.' We also lose most of the relationship with her mother and father, as Luhrmann's fixation on youth reduces both sets of parents to cameos and Laurence and the Nurse to servants of the plot rather than complex characters in their own right.

Compared to Danes, DiCaprio's throwaway, sometimes inaudible delivery is, for those not inclined to swoon uncritically at his beauty, the movie's weakest link. He comes into his own only after Mercutio's operatically filmed death on the beach, screaming with rage and frustration as he blows Tybalt away and the victim tumbles into a fountain; his blood stains the water – and the pure love symbolised earlier by the clear water of the fish tank and pool.

Laurence's letter explaining Juliet's faked death goes undelivered because Romeo misses the 'Post Haste' courier who calls at his Mantua trailer park and he shoots his way into the Capulets' church as the cops close in (Luhrmann, like Franco Zeffirelli, cuts the killing of Paris, with cowardly Hollywood reluctance to show his hero in a negative light). As Romeo makes his way down an aisle lined with neon crosses, to the altar where Juliet lies surrounded by hundreds of candles, Don McAlpine's camerawork is at its shimmering best. With a sentimental trick first used on stage in England in the seventeenth century, Juliet wakes moments *before* Romeo swallows the poison, too dopey to stop him. He dies aware that she lives. She shoots herself, and the TV newsreader delivers the Epilogue.

The church scene is the culmination of the catholic imagery that has filled Verona Beach (actually Mexico City and Vera Cruz), and designer Catherine Martin also decorates the streets with fleeting nods to Shakespeare (the Shylock Bank, a billboard for Prospero Whiskey), giving us a sense that the story is unfolding in what Luhrmann called 'a created world', where you have to let the director write his own dramatic rules, as in, say, a science-fiction film. If you stop to wonder why the teenagers openly carry guns, or why Captain Prince (Vondie Curtis-Hall), the black police chief, does not remand Romeo in custody for Tybalt's murder instead of banishing him, Luhrmann's spell is broken.

It is necessary to acknowledge his creative debts as well as praise his originality. Like Zeffirelli, he cast very young lead actors. From *West Side Story* he borrowed the notion of a modern urban setting, with cars, guns and pop songs. Nor was he the first to place original-text Shakespeare in a recognisable present-day setting, Christine Edzard having done so, albeit disastrously, with her London-set *As You Like It* (p. 8) in 1992.

Launched by Twentieth Century-Fox with blanket advertising on MTV, *Romeo + Juliet* took $144m worldwide – more than any other Shakespeare film; more, even, than a lowest-common-denominator action blockbuster such as *Volcano*. The figures confirmed that Luhrmann's most remarkable achievement was to have made millions feel like the Californian girl who wrote of seeing the film aged twelve: 'I did not even notice the Shakespeare language, because I was so drawn in by the characters and the modern inventions. It felt like a regular teen movie.' No other director, before or since, has managed to erase young cinemagoers' resistance to Shakespeare's language so effectively, by producing a movie that sounds like original-text Shakespeare but looks and feels like a genre adaptation – and succeeds as both.

Dir: Baz Luhrmann; **Prods:** Gabriella Martinelli, Baz Luhrmann; **Scr:** Craig Pearce, Baz Luhrmann; **DOP:** Donald M. McAlpine; **Editor:** Jill Bilcock; **Score:** Nellee Hooper; **Main Cast:** Leonardo DiCaprio (Romeo), Claire Danes (Juliet), Harold Perrineau (Mercutio), John Leguizamo (Tybalt), Miriam Margolyes (Nurse), Pete Postlethwaite (Father Laurence), Jesse Bradford (Benvolio), Paul Sorvino (Fulgencio Capulet), Diane Venora (Gloria Capulet), Paul Rudd (Dave Paris), Brian Dennehy (Montague), Vondie Curtis-Hall (Captain Prince).

Shakespeare in Love
US, 1998 – 122 mins
John Madden

With one foot in the 1590s and the other in the 1990s, *Shakespeare in Love* offered comedy built from anachronism, wordplay, bedroom farce and knockabout; a passionate love story with a bittersweet ending; a tastefully squalid recreation of Elizabethan London for lovers of period drama. John Madden's panache, Stephen Warbeck's busy, romantic score and the cast's obvious enjoyment turned it into a phenomenon. Made for $25m, it grossed $290m and won seven Oscars, including Best Picture and Best Actress, reward for Gwyneth Paltrow's exemplary English accent and radiant, if ingratiating performance. Millions will always picture Shakespeare as Joseph Fiennes's wide-eyed, horny and not particularly bright Bard.

The screenplay, originally written by Marc Norman in 1993, then substantially doctored by Tom Stoppard, takes us to London, 1593, where young Will has promised his new comedy, *Romeo and Ethel, the Pirate's Daughter*, to Rose Theatre boss Philip Henslowe (a manic Geoffrey Rush), who needs a hit to pay off vicious loanshark Fennyman (Tom Wilkinson).

Will is hopelessly blocked until he receives plot hints from Christopher Marlowe (an effortless cameo from Rupert Everett) and falls for wealthy merchant's daughter Viola De Lesseps (Paltrow), unhappily betrothed to dastardly Lord Wessex (Colin Firth), who is about to take her to his Virginia tobacco plantation.

Since women are forbidden from acting, the stage-struck Viola dresses as a young man, 'Thomas Kent', and is cast as Romeo. Once Will has learned her true identity, they begin an affair and verse pours forth, turning the comic *Romeo and Ethel* into the tragic *Romeo and Juliet*. Viola's lasciviously helpful nurse (Imelda Staunton) inspires Juliet's nurse, while Tybalt and Paris are inspired by Wessex, whose villainy is underlined by the fact that he detests theatre, a terrible failing exploited by Judi

Dench's imperiously caustic Queen Elizabeth, who wagers him fifty pounds that a play 'can show us the very truth and nature of love'.

In the farcical rehearsals, Ben Affleck's swaggering Ned Alleyn and his colleagues display the same vanity and sentimentality as actors in twentieth-century backstage comedies. Monty Python-style anachronisms (Will visits a shrink and has a souvenir mug from Stratford-upon-Avon) rub shoulders with 'hindsight' jokes bearing the mischievously literate hallmark of Stoppard's *Rosencrantz & Guildenstern Are Dead* (1990, p. 43), especially gags about Marlowe's mysterious death and John Webster, a bloodthirsty boy who hangs around the Rose and will grow up to write gruesome Jacobean tragedies such as *The White Devil*.

When Webster reveals that 'Thomas' is a woman, the officious Master of the Revels (Simon Callow) closes the Rose, setting up a classic, eleventh-hour crisis. Richard Burbage (Martin Clunes) allows Henslowe to use his rival venue, the Curtain, and Will steps in as Romeo. When the adolescent playing Juliet finds his voice is breaking, Viola, who has slipped away after marrying Wessex, takes over. *Romeo and Juliet*, reduced to a wondrous ten minutes, is a sensation, and we realise that despite mocking Shakespeare the man, Madden and co.'s ultimate goal has been to celebrate his work.

The Queen, who has been watching in secret, claims her fifty pounds from Wessex, before insisting that Viola rejoin him, and Madden ends on a dreamy shot of Paltrow after a shipwreck, striding along a vast American shore as Will begins a comedy with a cross-dressing heroine called Viola, *Twelfth Night*.

Dir: John Madden; **Prods:** David Parfitt, Donna Gigliotti, Harvey Weinstein, Edward Zwick, Marc Norman; **Scr:** Marc Norman, Tom Stoppard; **DOP:** Richard Greatrex; **Editor:** David Gamble; **Score:** Stephen Warbeck; **Main Cast:** Joseph Fiennes (William Shakespeare), Gwyneth Paltrow (Viola De Lesseps), Colin Firth (Lord Wessex), Imelda Staunton (Nurse), Judi Dench (Queen Elizabeth), Ben Affleck (Ned Alleyn), Geoffrey Rush (Philip Henslowe), Tom Wilkinson (Fennyman), Simon Callow (Sir Edmund Tilney), Martin Clunes (Richard Burbage).

Chicken Rice War (*Jiyuan qiaohe*)
Singapore, 2000 – 98 mins
CheeK (Cheah Chee-kong)

First-time feature director Cheah Chee-kong's (known as CheeK) recipe
for turning classic romantic tragedy into lowbrow romantic comedy is to
take parts of Luhrmann's *William Shakespeare's Romeo + Juliet* (1996),
add a variation on *The Lovers of Verona*'s life-imitating-performance
scenario (1949, p 211) and stir in Singaporean ingredients.

The debt to Luhrmann includes freeze-frame character introductions
and a young male TV reporter announcing 'in fair Ang Mo Kio, where
we lay our scene . . . a pair of star-crossed lovers choose their chicken
rice.' The Hawker Centres Authority of Singapore has accidentally given
adjacent berths to the rice stalls of the film's Capulet, Vincent Chan, and
Montagues, milquetoast Wong Terr and fiery matriarch Wong Ku, whose
twenty-year grudge began when Chan's dad suspected that his wife had
been seduced by Wong's father. Now they and their respective
'henchmen', Muscle Mike (a quasi-Tybalt) and Chan Tick, and adolescent
offspring, jovial Sydney Wong and tomboyish Penelope Chan, trade
insults ('Your brain is in your butt!') and plant cockroaches or rats in each
other's kitchens when health inspectors call.

The older offspring assume dual *Romeo and Juliet* roles. Mild-
mannered, stuttering Fenson (Singapore heart-throb Pierre Png) is
besotted with the aloof Audrey (willowy local supermodel Lum May Yee)
and longs to replace her latest dumb squeeze (and Paris substitute), Nick,
as Romeo to Audrey's Juliet in their university's experimental production,
directed by camp, pony-tailed Mr Pillay.

On the advice of best friend and Benvolio/Friar Laurence surrogate
Leon, Fenson blows his savings on a Tiffany pendant, hoping it will get
him into Audrey's twenty-first birthday party (the Capulet ball) and her
affections. After barring him from the party, the love poem wrapped
around the gift wins her over. She dumps Nick (only cast as Romeo
'because he looks like Leonardo DiCaprio'), passes him on to her clingy

confidante Cheryl (standing in for the Nurse) and professes undying love for Fenson, though it's hard to see why he adores this shallow, spoiled princess, the film's least sympathetic character.

The pair wow Mr Pillay with their passionate acting but when their families ruin the *Romeo and Juliet* performance (bizarrely staged in a car park) they resolve to end the feud by revealing each stall's secret ingredient at the climactic Hungry Ghost Festival. However, their parents end up accidentally giving away the secrets when they turn furiously on their poultry wholesaler, Hugo A Go Goh, whose supplies have caused mass food poisoning at the festival.

CheeK does his best to inject some energy by playing a 'zoom' effect over scene transitions and packing in cheerful songs by local pop star Tanya Chua. There's some humour to be drawn from the sleazy Hugo, and two jobless friends, one Malay, one Indian, who hang around delivering a choric running commentary and are supposed to emphasise the multiracial nature of Singapore society in a cast dominated by Chinese actors (the characters speak mostly in Singlish dialect; Wong Ku speaks only Cantonese).

Though *Chicken Rice War* took a respectable SG$400,000 in domestic cinemas (half its budget) and won the Discovery Award at the Toronto International Film Festival in 2001, its incidental pleasures cannot compensate for slack pacing, and the broad, stilted acting typical of mainstream Singapore film comedy. When the youngsters sit gossiping in fast-food joints or argue with their siblings or parents we are much closer to a Singapore version of *Neighbours* (1985–) than to Shakespeare.

Dir/Scr: CheeK; **Prods:** David Leong, CheeK; **DOP:** Daniel Low; **Editor:** Lawrence Ang; **Music producer:** Lim Sek; **Main Cast:** Pierre Png (Fenson Wong), Lum May Yee (Audrey Chan), Catherine Sng (Wong Ku), Gary Yuen (Vincent Chan), Kevin Murphy (Leon Deli), Wui Seng Cheong (Wong Terr), Gary Loh (Muscle Mike), Kelvin Ng (Sydney Wong), Su Ching Teh (Penelope Chan), Edmund L. Smith (Mr Pillay).

The Taming of the Shrew (play synopsis)

In an Induction, a drunken tinker, Christopher Sly, is persuaded that he is really a nobleman and consents to watch a play. In Padua, wealthy nobleman Baptista Minola reminds Gremio and Hortensio, rivals for his beautiful younger daughter Bianca's hand, that she cannot marry until Katharina, his shrewish elder child, also finds a husband.

Hortensio convinces his friend Petruchio, a wild-tempered bachelor in search of a wealthy wife, to woo Katharina, and bets that he will never marry her. Meanwhile, Lucentio, a young bachelor, has fallen instantly in love with Bianca. Aided by his servants, Tranio and Biondello, he disguises himself as a Latin tutor, 'Cambio', and secretly woos Bianca, who falls for him, ignoring Hortensio, who has disguised himself as a music teacher. Tranio also woos Bianca on his master's behalf, disguised as 'Lucentio'.

Despite Katharina's fury at her first meeting with Petruchio, Baptista consents to their marriage. After a wild wedding ceremony, which Petruchio attends dressed in rags, he insists on skipping the celebratory feast and immediately takes Katharina back to his country home, where he tames her by depriving her of food and sleep for days and insisting that she accept his will in all matters, even if it means agreeing that the sun is the moon.

In Padua, Baptista agrees to let Bianca marry 'Lucentio', so long as he can guarantee that he will inherit his old, wealthy father Vincentio's fortune. Vincentio promptly arrives to find himself being impersonated by a stranger hired by Lucentio, who marries Bianca in secret. All the various deceptions are swiftly revealed and forgiven and at a celebratory banquet, Petruchio wagers Lucentio and Hortensio (who has married a rich widow) that Katharina will prove the most dutiful of the three new brides. He wins when Katharina declares that wives must show unquestioning obedience to their husbands.

Once Upon a Time (*Der var engang*)
Denmark, 1922 – 75 mins (DVD version; original length unknown)
(B&W)
Carl Theodor Dreyer

Carl Theodor Dreyer's witty, affecting version of Holger Drachmann's 1883 'fairytale in five acts' combines Hans Christian Andersen's *The Swineherd* with a loose, simplified reworking of *The Taming of the Shrew* and allusions to several other Shakespeare plays.

Believed lost until the 1960s, it was restored by the Danish Film Institute in 2003 with some sixty minutes of original footage, and missing scenes explained by fifteen minutes' worth of stills and explanatory intertitles, accompanied by Neil Brand's sensitive new piano score.

We begin in the Versailles-like palace of Illyria, where the bullying hauteur and blue-blooded admirers of Princess Katherine (Clara Wieth) make her a cross between the *Shrew*'s Kate, Portia in *The Merchant of Venice* and the Emperor's daughter in the Andersen tale. As she receives a Prince of Morocco-like suitor, the ancient, bespectacled King (Peter Jerndorff) says 'Take him! He looks rich' (the first of many disarmingly funny lines), but she sends the Prince to the pillory.

Enter the story's Petruchio, dashing Jørgen Prince of Denmark (Svend Methling), and his servant, Kasper Smokehat, who, though there is no Bianca/Lucentio subplot, is endowed with Tranio's irreverent resourcefulness. Rejected by Katherine, Jørgen returns home and has a *Macbeth*-like encounter with a strange-looking 'old peddler of fairy ancestry', whose magic kettle predicts that Jørgen will marry the Princess.

Now bearded and disguised as a humble potter, Jørgen returns to Illyria, persuades the Princess to kiss him and let him sleep in her chamber as payment for the tinker's kettle and wooden rattle (items used to similar effect by Andersen's prince, who promptly ends *The Swineherd* by rejecting the Princess's lightly won affections). Smokehat, disguised as a knight, informs the King that the Princess has a 'rogue' in her room and that for so insulting the Prince she must be exiled or Denmark will declare war. He complies.

The couple's exhausting journey to Denmark corresponds to Petruchio and Kate's trek to Verona; their exchange of courtly luxury for pastoral seclusion suggests *As You Like It*. At their hut in the forest she refuses to sweep the floor, Jørgen shouts 'My will is the law!' and his determined gaze makes you expect a title card with Petruchio's 'Thus have I politicly begun my reign.'

Her taming involves learning to apply handles to his clay pots, and appreciating 'values . . . worth more than jewellery and toys.' After being humiliated by armed foresters and saving him from arrest for poaching, in two tense sequences, she comes to love him as Kate loves Petruchio, in spite of herself.

Hardship sends her to the palace for food just as the Prince is supposedly about to marry a foreign princess whose illness calls for a stand-in bride. Smokehat, now engaged to a buxom scullery maid, catches Katherine in his Cinderella-search for a woman who will fit the wedding dress. The final, lost scene – Jørgen revealing himself by repeating Katherine's earlier declaration of love, as the King is reunited with her – evokes the climaxes of *As You Like It* and *The Winter's Tale*.

Dreyer later regretted not dramatising 'a stormy struggle between two people' (the dramatic heart of the *Shrew*), yet the film is immensely rewarding verbally (the King and Smokehat's dry wit) and visually (Illyria's manicured gardens; the play of light and shadow in the forest). Above all, the elements found in Andersen and Shakespeare – royal characters, exile, disguise, true love triumphant – remind one that fairytales and Shakespearean comedy have much in common.

Dir: Carl Theodor Dreyer; **Prod:** Sophus Madsen Film; **Scr:** Carl Theodor Dreyer, Palle Rosencrantz; **DOP:** George Schnéevoight; **Editors:** Carl Theodor Dreyer, Edla Hansen; **DVD Musical Accompaniment:** Neil Brand; **Main Cast:** Clara Wieth (Princess Katherine), Svend Methling (Jørgen), Peter Jerndorff (King), Hakon Ahnfeldt-Rønne (Kasper Smokehat).

The Taming of the Shrew
US, 1929 – 68 mins
Sam Taylor

Two years after *The Jazz Singer* ushered in the sound era, *The Taming of the Shrew* became the first 'all-talking' Shakespeare feature and brought together for the first and only time two of Hollywood's brightest stars: Mary Pickford, nicknamed 'America's Sweetheart' for her string of Cinderella roles, and husband Douglas Fairbanks, swashbuckling hero of *The Thief of Bagdad* (1924). Posters invited America to watch as 'a cave man woos and wins an Amazon' – and wonder if Kate and Petruchio's battle resembled the Pickford–Fairbanks rows hinted at by gossip columnists.

It cost $500,000 (at least $20m today) to pay the stars, fill the world's largest soundstage with enormous Padua sets and make 'a vastly extravagant burlesque' (*Variety*) that grossed an impressive $1.1m by inverting Shakespeare: here the shrew tames her husband.

It opens with Bianca already secretly in love with handsome young Hortensio, but apart from an early glimpse of their clandestine embrace and Hortensio's disguised appearance as a music teacher after he and the elderly Gremio have persuaded Petruchio to woo Katharina, nothing remains of the younger sister plot. Lucentio, Tranio, Biondello and Vincentio are absent and Clyde Cook's weary, Stan Laurel-voiced Grumio is the only other character allowed a brief share of the spotlight in the 'Doug'n'Mary Show'.

First seen as pots and chairs go flying and servants dive for cover, Pickford's Katharina is a five-foot firebrand dressed like a 1920s' flapper, with pearls and feather boa, long whip at her side. Glowering, she growls her lines; the piratical Fairbanks bawls his like a carnival barker and guffaws at every lash from her whip or tongue, as Taylor turns crash-bang-wallop comedy – plentiful in the play – into the film's be-all and end-all. Petruchio forces his bride to say 'I do' by stomping on her

(*Opposite page*) 'Myself am moved to woo thee for my wife.': Petruchio (Douglas Fairbanks) meets Katharina (Mary Pickford) in Sam Taylor's *The Taming of the Shrew*

foot during the lavishly staged wedding ceremony (ten bridesmaids, dozens of guests), which is only described on stage.

At Petruchio's house, Katharina overhears him tell his huge mastiff, Troilus, how he plans to subdue his bride and fights back when he tries to torment her in their bedroom. After some tit-for-tat mayhem, peace breaks out after Katharina brains him with a well-aimed stool. Cradling her wounded boy, she flings her whip into the fire and pledges to swear the moon is the sun, though we know that he is now the weaker vessel. We cut abruptly to Padua, where Kate politely tells her fellow diners how wives must honour their husbands, only to aim a knowing wink at Bianca that says 'Don't think I believe this baloney!' and ensures America's womenfolk were not *too* offended by this one remaining trace of Elizabethan chauvinism.

Taylor earned an 'additional dialogue' credit for some pseudo-Shakespearean lines (Baptista to Priest before the wedding: 'What say you to this shame of ours?') and some absurdly modern ones (Priest to bride and groom: 'You are about to enter into . . . a relationship so close and so intimate that it will profoundly influence your whole life'). This led to an American newspaper cartoon showing a bust of the director ousting Shakespeare's from the Library of Congress, yet with so little of the original text surviving, and three-minute stretches without any dialogue, the film could – and did – screen as a silent, with title cards distributed to many theatres.

Dir/Scr: Sam Taylor; **Prod:** Pickford Corporation/Elton Corporation; **DOP:** Karl Struss; **Editor:** Allen McNeil; **Main Cast:** Mary Pickford (Katharina), Douglas Fairbanks (Petruchio), Dorothy Jordan (Bianca), Edwin Maxwell (Baptista), Geoffrey Wardwell (Hortensio), Joseph Cawthorn (Gremio), Clyde Cook (Grumio).

Kiss Me Kate
US, 1953 – 106 mins
George Sidney

Produced in garishly coloured 3-D, five years after the original stage musical became a Broadway smash, George Sidney's *Kiss Me Kate* combines Cole Porter's songwriting genius with energetic backstage comedy. It opens as Porter (played by Ron Randell) helps blazered actor–director Fred Graham (Howard Keel) persuade his fearsome ex-wife, Lilli Vanessi (Kathryn Grayson), to star in their new show, *Kiss Me Kate*, as 'a perfect shrew' opposite the Bianca of Lois Lane (the leggy Ann Miller), Fred's current squeeze.

We cut to opening night, with time before the curtain rises to leave several plot strands dangling. Bill Calhoun (Tommy Rall), Lois's on-off boyfriend and the show's Lucentio, has lost $2,000 to a gangster, Hogan, in a craps game, and signed his IOU in Fred's name. Hogan's henchmen, the dapper Lippy (Keenan Wynn) and numb-skulled Slug (James Whitmore), turn up in Fred's dressing room demanding payment, or else. Lilli is all set to wed her cattle baron fiancé, Tex, but suspects Fred wants her back.

The four principals launch into their musical *Shrew* as 'Shakespearean portrayers', a play-within-a-play device that acknowledges Shakespeare's Induction, and Sam and Bella Spewack use small chunks of his dialogue to bridge the gaps between musical numbers. Bianca's 'Tom, Dick or Harry' disposes briefly of the younger sister subplot and showcases Miller's supercharged dancing. Porter channels Katharina's violent temper into 'I Hate Men', a wittily damning inventory of twentieth-century male failings, vigorously delivered by Grayson. Keel shows off his emphatic baritone, strapping physique and uncomplicated charm as one of Petruchio's most famous lines, 'I've Come to Wive It Wealthily in Padua', becomes the title of an appropriately rousing number, and the new husband's rueful question, 'Where Is the Life That Late I Led?', becomes his cue to sing the praises of 'Momo from Milano' and many other ex-girlfriends. Compared to these showstoppers, the off-stage numbers are mostly fine, if conventional, love duets, presenting Fred/Lilli and Bill/Lois as the 'Can't live with or without you' couples beloved of vintage Hollywood comedies.

Shortly after 'I Hate Men', Lilli realises her pre-show bouquet from Fred was meant for Lois and assaults him and he gives her an unscripted, *Shrew*-like spanking. Lilli threatens to quit and Fred enlists Lippy and Slug to stop her, leading to splendid comedy with the hoodlums dressed as Katharina's 'maids of honour'.

After a perfunctory 'taming' scene in Petruchio's house (you would expect a musical to sugar the *Shrew*'s less palatable moments), it is time to tie up the backstage business. Lilli and Tex head for the airport. Lippy and Slug cancel Fred's IOU when they hear that Hogan has been murdered, then cheer him up by tapdancing down the alley and celebrating the Bard's value to pick-up artists: 'Brush up your Shakespeare, start quoting him now/Brush up your Shakespeare, and the women you will wow.' Lilli's inevitable return comes just in time for her abbreviated version of Katharina's closing speech, and she jumps into Fred's arms for the title song.

So concludes a vivacious crowd-pleaser whose use of the 3-D format explains why Grayson is forever flinging plates and tankards at the camera, and why Miller and the fabulously agile Rall try to leap off the screen. Although such moments lose their original impact on the small screen, the plastic glasses dished out in 1953 must have worked – one review was headlined: 'I don't mind a chorus girl landing in my lap.'

Dir: George Sidney; **Prod**: Jack Cummings; **Scr**: Dorothy Kingsley; **Book**: Sam and Bella Spewack; **DOP**: Charles Rosher; **Editor**: Ralph E. Winters; **Music and Lyrics**: Cole Porter; **Main Cast**: Howard Keel (Fred Graham/Petruchio), Kathryn Grayson (Lilli Vanessi/Katharina), Ann Miller (Lois Lane/Bianca), Tommy Rall (Bill Calhoun/Lucentio), Ron Randell (Cole Porter), Keenan Wynn (Lippy), James Whitmore (Slug).

The Taming of the Shrew
UK/Italy, 1967 – 122 mins
Franco Zeffirelli

The Taming of the Shrew deserved its Oscar nominations for the luxurious period costumes and the elaborately furnished, almost fairytale studio sets. What lingers, however, is the film's assault on your ears: Natasha Pyne's screams as Bianca, the shrieks of Elizabeth Taylor's Katharina, Richard Burton's Petruchio bellowing at Cyril Cusack's scruffy Grumio. Objects and people keep crashing to the ground, accompanied by Nino Rota's inexhaustibly exuberant orchestral score and extras greeting every pratfall or insult with explosive laughter. The *Guardian* reviewer's 'dearest wish was that everyone would stand still and shut up', but Franco Zeffirelli's début feature worked superbly at the box office, and Burton and Taylor profited from their $2m investment in the budget.

Like Fairbanks and Pickford in their 1929 *Shrew* (p. 234) they were the most celebrated husband and wife in showbiz, and had just appeared as a warring modern-day couple, George and Martha, in the film of Edward Albee's *Who's Afraid of Virginia Woolf?* – so the *Shrew* would again allow audiences to imagine they were peaking into the stars' famously tempestuous home life. While Mike Nichols had respected Albee's text, Zeffirelli and his two co-writers sliced away about 70% of Shakespeare's. They inserted many new lines (Petruchio becomes even more money-obsessed than in the play) and their screenplay credit is characteristically irreverent: 'With acknowledgements to William Shakespeare, without whom they would have been at a loss for words.'

Despite the cuts, the script devotes considerable attention to the Bianca subplot, and while Pyne does little with the thankless role of (mostly) saintly younger sister, Michael York, making his film debut, and Alfred Lynch, who is permitted the occasional aside to camera, provide a sprightly double act as Lucentio and Tranio. Michael Hordern, later to excel as Prospero and King Lear on television, splutters ineffectually at the mayhem that engulfs him.

Arriving in Padua, Lucentio and Tranio pass a caged drunkard (a fleeting homage to Christopher Sly), and are then caught up in a frantic parade of handsome university students, which begins the uproar that peaks when Burton and Taylor seize the limelight. Petruchio's wooing of Kate is a stop-start chase that ends when they fall through a tiled roof into a vast pile of wool. The 'mad wedding' receives such spectacular and over-extended treatment that preparations and ceremony take up a tenth of the running time, and each of Petruchio's outrages (snatching the Communion wine, punching the priest) is accompanied by gales of laughter from the congregation. Petruchio appears almost constantly drunk (imbued with the loutish spirit of Christopher Sly?), as Burton delivers a roaring, carousing turn seldom witnessed since Charles Laughton played Henry VIII in 1933. At least with Petruchio's finest speeches largely intact, Burton's powerful, precise voice can become the film's lone champion of verbal comedy.

Zeffirelli and Taylor do little to make Katharina convincing as resentful sister, shrew or wife, as she yelps, weeps and sighs in an assortment of dresses with plunging necklines. After her rain- and snow-swept journey on mule-back to Petruchio's house, the glamour queen turns somewhat bizarrely into a head-scarfed *Hausfrau* before giving up her cursory attempt to domesticate him, and complying with his demand for total obedience – if only for a bit of peace and quiet. Taylor infuses Katharina's closing declaration with great love, not the heavy irony Burton had expected, but suggests that Kate's 'inner shrew' still lives by sneaking away after he kisses her, leaving Petruchio to pursue her, and leading Kenneth Rothwell to speculate in his *History of Shakespeare on Screen* that 'the newlyweds are doomed to grow older and turn into George and Martha.'

Dir: Franco Zeffirelli; **Prods**: Richard Burton, Elizabeth Taylor; **Scr**: Suso Cecchi D'Amico, Paul Dehn, Franco Zeffirelli; **DOP**: Oswald Morris; **Editor**: Peter Taylor; **Score**: Nino Rota; **Main Cast**: Richard Burton (Petruchio), Elizabeth Taylor (Katharina), Michael Hordern (Baptista), Natasha Pyne (Bianca), Michael York (Lucentio), Cyril Cusack (Grumio), Alan Webb (Gremio), Victor Spinetti (Hortensio), Alfred Lynch (Tranio), Michael York (Lucentio).

10 Things I Hate About You
US, 1999 – 97 mins
Gil Junger

This high-school take on *The Taming of the Shrew* was one of the most enjoyable and intelligent teen comedies of the 1990s, thanks to fine ensemble acting and a good-natured script, which followed the *Shrew*'s plot as faithfully as Hollywood conventions and contemporary sexual politics would allow.

Joseph Gordon-Levitt (the teen alien in TV sitcom *Third Rock from the Sun*, 1996–2001), plays Cameron, the Lucentio figure who enrols at Padua High, Seattle, and instantly falls for Bianca (the cutesy Larisa Oleynik), a vapid sophomore. 'I burn, I pine, I perish,' Cameron exclaims, borrowing from the *Shrew*. The trouble is that Bianca's father is refusing to let her date until her older sister does, and since bookish, university-bound Kat (Julia Stiles) is 'a heinous bitch' with a reputation for assaulting boys, Cameron's chances appear slim.

Pat (Heath Ledger) and Kat (Julia Stiles) go to the Prom in Gil Junger's *10 Things I Hate About You*

Tranio's role is assumed by Cameron's nerdish new friend, Michael (David Krumholtz, a junior cross between Woody Allen and Billy Crystal), who dedicates himself to aiding his pursuit of Bianca, first suggesting that he help her with her French homework (mirroring Lucentio's disguise as a Latin tutor).

The plot moves into gear once a wealthy and impossibly vain pupil, Joey Donner (Andrew Keegan, as Hortensio and Gremio rolled into one), sets his sights on Bianca. Michael and Cameron convince Joey he can only reach her by hiring a boyfriend for Kat, and Pat Verona (Heath Ledger), the school's Australian-accented wildman, takes on the assignment, for which Joey will pay $100 per date.

Pat soon realises that his habitual macho tactics will not work this time, so the *Shrew* takes on a 'caring, sharing' 1990s' slant: to tame the shrew – or, rather, appeal to a discerning, spirited teenager – the hero must tame himself. Assisted by inside information from Bianca, he adapts to Kat's tastes. He quits smoking, pretends to admire Sylvia Plath and looks after Kat when she gets drunk at a wild house party – an obligatory component for a teen movie, even one with sixteenth-century roots (as is a Various Artists pop soundtrack, so there are fourteen strategically placed songs from the likes of the Cardigans and Semisonic). Kat is finally won over by the best of several silly set-pieces: Pat's sportsfield rendition of 'Can't Take My Eyes off You', accompanied by the school band. This being a Hollywood romantic comedy he, naturally, has genuinely fallen for her.

Accompanied by Bianca, who has rejected the obnoxious Joey in favour of Cameron, Kat hooks up with Pat at the Prom. But when she overhears Joey remonstrating with him over the cash-for-dating scam she rushes out, furious. Back at school the following Monday he convinces her he really cares and they are reconciled.

From start to finish, experienced sitcom director Gil Junger generates laughs without resorting to the *American Pie*-style 'gross-out' gags that might have boosted the film's worldwide takings of $63m (impressive nonetheless). There are some original touches courtesy of Padua High's eccentric teachers (including Miss Perky, played by *The West Wing*'s Allison Janney) and bizarre student cliques, although not every Shakespeare reference comes off (one of Kat's friends is lumbered with a deeply contrived obsession with the playwright). Ledger's abundant charm in his Hollywood début helps explain his subsequent success in many more American films, while Stiles's quick-witted performance immediately earned her two more Shakespearean roles: Ophelia in Michael Almereyda's *Hamlet* (p. 47) and Desdemona in *O* (p. 180), where Keegan rejoins her as Cassio.

Stiles excels during the scene in which Kat attributes her boy-hatred not to resentment at paternal favouritism towards the 'perfect' younger sister (a major factor in the *Shrew*, and one that would surely still have connected with the female portion of *10 Things*' target audience), but shame and regret at losing her virginity to the preening Joey three years earlier. In addition, because 1990s' audiences would never accept an American dad treating his girls like 'goods and chattels' to be sold to the highest bidder, Walter Stratford (a marvellous cameo from Larry Miller) acquires an equally moral motive for his 'no dating' rule: he is an obstetrician desperate for his daughters not to end up like the teen mothers whose unplanned babies he delivers every week. Thus a film financed by Disney, supreme upholder of family values, updates Shakespeare while poignantly and wittily condemning underage sex.

The significance of the title is finally revealed in the penultimate scene. A hip, black English teacher has instructed Kat's class to write a Shakespearean sonnet and her classroom recital replaces Katharina's 'honour thy husbands' speech, as she tearfully itemises Pat's flaws, ending on: 'I hate the way I don't hate you/Not even close, not even a little bit, not even at all.'

Dir: Gil Junger; Prod: Andrew Lazar; Scr: Karen McCullah Lutz, Kirsten Smith; DOP: Mark Irwin; Editor: O. Nicholas Brown; Score: Richard Gibbs; Main Cast: Julia Stiles (Katarina Stratford), Heath Ledger (Patrick Verona), Larry Miller (Walter Stratford), Larisa Oleynik (Bianca Stratford), Joseph Gordon-Levitt (Cameron James), David Krumholtz (Michael Eckman), Andrew Keegan (Joey Donner).

The Taming of the Shrew
UK, 2005 – 89 mins (TVM)
David Richards

Reflecting twenty-first-century sexual equality, Sally Wainwright's BBC
Shakespeare Retold screenplay turns the possessive Baptista into Mrs
Minola, wealthy mother to two career women. Supermodel Bianca
(hyper-confident brunette Jaime Murray) picks up a beautiful Italian
student, Lucentio, at Milan airport, and fires her besotted, long-serving
agent, Harry (hangdog Stephen Tompkinson as Hortensio/Gremio),
saying she will marry only when her sister does. Tory MP Katherine
(Shirley Henderson) is a thirty-eight-year-old virgin, dwarfed by the men
she terrorises in the Commons to *Jaws*-like music and suddenly needing
a husband to boost her wholly implausible campaign to become party
leader.

Still hoping to marry Bianca, Harry introduces Katherine to Petruchio
(the Byronic Rufus Sewell), a feckless Earl who needs 'to wive it wealthily'
to pay a huge tax bill. His almost psychotic rudeness, beautifully underplayed by Sewell, revolts and attracts Kate, and Wainwright gives them
fizzing dialogue, especially at the wedding (he turns up in drag) and
when he torments her on honeymoon at an Italian villa, where Harry
joins them. He tells Katherine that Petruchio is 'an unstable exhibitionist
who needs someone to think the world of him' and this unsubtle
prodding helps us view the couple as equally shrewish, perfectly matched
misfits. Like a Hollywood yuppy heroine, Katherine realises love matters
more than career, delivers a subservient-yet-feminist version of the 'lord
and master' speech *and*, in an end-credits epilogue, becomes PM, while
Petruchio looks after their triplets.

Sewell and Henderson so dominate the film that in comparison to
the *Shrew*'s, or indeed *10 Things I Hate About You*'s, rich ensembles, it
feels like barely half the play. Bianca's freedom renders Lucentio's
comical deceptions redundant, and Wainwright fails to generate
alternative humour in a perfunctory subplot, with pointless cameos for

Lucentio's brother, Tranio, and father, Vincentio, when his refusal to sign a pre-nuptial agreement leads to Bianca cancelling the wedding. There is, however, a neat, if telegraphed twist: the rich widow whom Harry marries is Mrs Minola.

Dir: David Richards; **Prod:** Diederick Santer; **Scr:** Sally Wainwright; **DOP:** Alan Almond; **Editor:** Catherine Creed; **Score:** Hal Lindes; **Main Cast:** Shirley Henderson (Katherine Minola), Rufus Sewell (Petruchio), Twiggy Lawson (Mrs Minola), Jaime Murray (Bianca), Stephen Tompkinson (Harry), Santiago Cabrera (Lucentio), Federico Zanni (Tranio), Alex Giannini (Vincentio).

The Tempest (play synopsis)

For twelve years, Prospero, deposed Duke of Milan, has lived on a remote, enchanted island with his daughter, Miranda, now a teenager, and his servants: Caliban, a monstrous savage who ruled the island until Prospero's arrival, and Ariel, a spirit whom Prospero rescued from imprisonment in an oak tree.

Through study, Prospero has acquired magical powers and he summons the storm that opens the play and wrecks the ship carrying Antonio, the evil brother who deposed him as Milan's rightful Duke. Antonio is cast ashore with Alonso, King of Naples, the King's brother, Sebastian, and Gonzalo, the counsellor who helped Prospero and the infant Miranda reach the island after the coup. Also washed up on other parts of the island are Alonso's son and heir, Ferdinand, Trinculo, a jester, and Stephano, a drunken butler.

Prospero sends Ariel to torment the Neapolitans and tell Alonso that Ferdinand has drowned. Ferdinand, who believes his father is dead, and Miranda fall in love at first sight, as Prospero intends. However, he then pretends that Ferdinand has come to usurp him and sets the Prince to log-carrying. Antonio and Sebastian resolve to kill Alonso. Caliban, bewitched by his first taste of wine, urges Stephano and Trinculo to kill Prospero so that Stephano can become king of the island and marry Miranda. Prospero foresees both plots and sends Ariel to foil them. Caliban and his two fellow conspirators are pursued by spirits disguised as dogs.

After blessing Miranda and Ferdinand's union with a supernatural Masque, Prospero rounds up his enemies. But at the last moment he chooses not to take revenge, forgives his brother and Caliban, and resolves to abandon magic. He sets Ariel free and prepares to set sail with the others, first to Naples for Miranda and Ferdinand's wedding, then home to Milan.

The Tempest
UK, 1908 – 8 mins (B&W)
Percy Stow

Of the many dozens of silent Shakespeare shorts produced in America, Britain and the rest of Europe, many are lost. Of those that survive, Percy Stow's *Tempest* is a fine example because it is representative of commonplace techniques and because, in tackling one of Shakespeare's shortest and fastest-moving plays, its incident-packed eight-minute précis feels far more satisfying than, for instance, a one-reel *King Lear*.

With cinema still rooted in the theatre, the story is set in a half-staged, half-real world: in a studio, the simplest of painted theatre flats represent a rocky island shore and Prospero's cell, while a sunlit English

Miranda, right, watches Prospero summon the winds in Percy Stow's *The Tempest*

wood is used for the open-air scenes that take up most of the running time.

Stow skilfully exploits the play's considerable flashback potential to begin with scenes set ten years before the main action. On board a ship, Gonzalo lowers the three-year-old Miranda, and a large book, into Prospero's hands as he stands in a dinghy. After arriving on the island, Prospero discovers and subdues Caliban, a bearded wildman in ragged clothes, then frees Ariel from a knotty tree; the spirit is played by a gambolling girl of no more than ten, and with no verse-speaking required her youth is perfect for Ariel's childish delight.

Rudimentary special effects, also evident in the earliest films of *A Midsummer Night's Dream*, beautifully enhance stage magic. For the tempest, footage of real waves is superimposed onto the stage flat, as Miranda and Prospero watch a flimsy model ship sinking in the background. Jump-cuts turn Ariel into a monkey, which scares the lustful Caliban away from Miranda, then make her vanish and reappear to amaze Ferdinand. The Prince kisses Miranda, a beautiful blonde in a diaphanous white dress, within ten seconds of their meeting.

Prospero, now with a God-like white beard, sets the Prince to log-carrying then blesses his and Miranda's union, which leaves no time at all for Stephano and Trinculo, and there is only the briefest of appearances for the other Neapolitans, all, like Ferdinand, wearing Elizabethan doublet and hose. They awake on the grass, are dumbfounded by Ariel's disappearing picnic, instantly bow down on Prospero's entrance and then everyone shakes hands. Ariel is set free, skipping off into the woods, and the characters board a ship, except for the pleading Caliban, who is roughly pushed away by the sailors.

As is often the case with silent shorts, Stow depends on audience familiarity with the play to fill in the blanks, most importantly the question of why Antonio and his party were Prospero's enemies, and the penultimate title card beautifully sums up the play's spirit of reconciliation: 'Friends once more.'

Dir: Percy Stow; **Prod:** Clarendon Film Company; **Scr:** Langford Reed.

Forbidden Planet
US, 1956 – 96 mins
Fred McLeod Wilcox

The headline over the *Evening Standard*'s review, 'Shakespeare takes a journey into space', neatly sums up this hugely enjoyable and influential picture, with critic Alan Brien praising Cyril Hume for writing 'the most rumbustiously enjoyable of all Hollywood planetary melodramas, apparently by dressing *The Tempest* in space suits.'

Shakespeare and Hume both drew on contemporary exploration. Just as the discovery of America and the wreck of several ships in the Bermudas in 1609 inspired Shakespeare, so the space race ignited the 1950s' sci-fi boom in which *Forbidden Planet* played a significant role. *The Tempest* snugly fits this genre mould, as play and film transport audiences to a remote island/planet, where mankind encounters strange and sometimes hostile creatures.

In AD 2257, a Universal Planets cruiser skippered by unflappable Commander J. J. Adams (Leslie Nielsen) lands on planet Altair-4 to search for survivors from the Beleraphon, a spaceship that lost contact with Earth twenty years earlier. Adams and his senior officers, Lt Farman and 'Doc' Ostrow, meet the Beleraphon's sole survivor (and the film's Prospero), the bearded, refined Dr Morbius (Walter Pidgeon). He lives happily with his beautiful daughter, Altaira (mini-skirted Anne Francis), who, like Miranda, has 'never known any human being except her father'. The pair's Ariel is Robby the Robot, an electronic Jeeves who speaks 187 languages and can manufacture everything from hors-d'oeuvres to emeralds ('It's the housewife's dream,' quips Adams).

Adams and Farman instantly follow Ferdinand's lead by falling for Altaira, who flirts innocently in crassly written exchanges. Back at the cruiser, the bourbon-swilling cook (Earl Hollimann) takes on Stephano and Trinculo's low-life comedy roles, dismissing Altair-4 as 'another one of them new worlds. No beer, no women, no pool parlours' and when Robby samples his Kentucky bourbon the robot fleetingly becomes Caliban.

Cheesy romance and humour are then pushed aside by the return of a 'terrible, incomprehensible force', which Morbius claims wiped out the Beleraphon's crew. A vast, invisible monster, immune to laser blasts, twice attacks the ship, killing Farman and three other crewmen. Morbius reluctantly shows Adams and Doc the vast machine created 500,000 years earlier by the planet's original inhabitants, the Krell, a race infinitely superior to man. Doc takes a Krell 'brain boost', realises the invisible foe is a 'monster from the Id', then dies, leaving Adams to convince Morbius that the monstrous creature was the product of his own subconscious, and is now attacking again – an inventive variation on Prospero's motivation, albeit wrapped up in sci-fi psycho-hokum. The exiled Duke wants to punish the men who drove him from Naples to the island; Morbius killed off his Beleraphon shipmates when they tried to return from Altair-4 to Earth. Prospero tells Miranda: 'I to my state grew stranger, being transported and rapt in secret studies.' When Morbius had been on the planet for some time with his wife, he felt 'a boundless longing to make a home here, far from the scurry and strife of human kind.' His Id took over to such an extent that he was prepared to kill to fulfil that longing, but now, as the monster bashes its way into the Krell lab to attack Adams and Altaira, Morbius – like Prospero – renounces vengeance, killing off his 'evil self' at the cost of his own life. The film ends with Altair-4 blown to smithereens by a Krell chain reaction, as Adams, Altaira and Robby fly back to Earth.

Forbidden Planet's $1m-plus budget made it, at the time, the most expensive sci-fi movie ever made, and MGM were not going to jeopardise that investment by allowing dusty old Shakespeare's name to feature in its marketing or the credits. That million dollars paid for Louis and Bebe Barron's 'electronic tonalities', which provide an atmospheric undercurrent of beeping, whirring and screeching, standing in for the

(*Opposite page*) Altaira (Anne Francis), left, and Robby the Robot watch Commander Adams (Leslie Nielsen) cradle the dying Doc (Warren Stevens) in Fred McLeod Wilcox's *Forbidden Planet*

'sounds and sweet airs' of Prospero's island. The matte-painted planetary backdrops and Oscar-nominated special effects now look primitive; the expansive sets still impress (the cavernous Krell lab anticipates the vertiginous footbridges of the Death Star in *Star Wars*).

There are disappointingly flat performances by Pidgeon, Baxter and, especially, Nielsen, whose unvarying, deadpan style points the way to his appearances in the *Naked Gun* films. Robby remains a terrific creation. Built like a steel Michelin Man, with the staid voice of a 1950s' radio announcer, he was the first movie robot to become a hero in his own right, appearing again in *The Invisible Boy* in 1957. It is fascinating to think of Ariel inspiring Robby, and Robby becoming godfather to C-3PO and Robocop, and to consider how Farman's dalliance with Altaira pointed the way for Captain Kirk's numerous *Star Trek* romances with conveniently humanoid alien women. These are fascinating, Shakespearean connections: *The Tempest* influences *Forbidden Planet*, which then exerts its own lasting influence on the science-fiction genre.

Dir: Fred McLeod Wilcox; **Prod:** Nicholas Nayfack; **Scr:** Cyril Hume; **DOP:** George Folsey; **Editor:** Ferris Webster; **Score:** Louis and Bebe Barron; **Main Cast:** Walter Pidgeon (Dr Morbius), Anne Francis (Altaira), Leslie Nielsen (Commander Adams), Warren Stevens (Lt 'Doc' Ostrow), Jack Kelly (Lt Farman), Earl Hollimann (Cook), Robby the Robot.

The Tempest
UK, 1979 – 96 mins
Derek Jarman

In 1978, Derek Jarman had directed the outlandish *Jubilee*, in which
Queen Elizabeth I is transported from 1578 to the heyday of punk, along
with a magician and his assistant, called Ariel. It was a short step from
here to *The Tempest*, which, Jarman wrote, 'obsessed' him. After writing
a script that reorders scenes without altering the plot, he set out to make
'a dream film . . . [on] an island of the mind', with production design and
camerawork focused on characters' thoughts, not their environment.
While this intimate, low-budget (£150,000) vision might have worked
superbly on stage, on screen it feels monotonous and alienating.
Scathing reviews killed its commercial prospects in America, though it
fared better in Britain.

Prospero and Miranda live in the cold, high-ceilinged rooms of a
stately home (Stoneleigh Abbey on England's Suffolk coast) where faces
appear to be illuminated only by firelight or candles and the static
camera often watches characters speak from the middle distance. The
handful of exteriors, in which the shipwrecked Neapolitans walk along
sand dunes, are shot through a blue filter, suggesting perpetual dawn or
dusk, and the gloom is deepened by two performances fatally shorn of
feeling.

Heathcote Williams's waistcoated magician looks twenty years younger
than many stage Prosperos, and has a touch of the Romantic poet, shaggy
dark curls framing a stubbled face. He barely raises his voice above a
whisper, and contrasting emotions, especially pride in his magic and fury at
Antonio, are absent. Ariel shares his master's depressive tendencies. Wearing
white shoes, gloves and boiler-suit, Karl Johnson's pale face and drab speech
suggest a careworn ghost, not Shakespeare's 'gentle spirit', and you wait in
vain for sparks of tension or affection in this master–servant relationship.

Caliban, played by the hulking Jack Birkett (a bald, blind
performance artist also known as 'The Incredible Orlando'), is suitably

repellent, distinguished by his whining North of England accent, maniacal laugh and taste for raw eggs. His tattered overcoat and Miranda's ragged ball gown are typical of eclectic costumes drawing on 400 years of fashion, leaving the action dreamily out of time. Toyah Wilcox (who had made her screen début in *Jubilee*, alongside Johnson and Birkett), brings robust sexual energy to Miranda, whose sheltered innocence can seem vacuous on stage, but the heterosexual imagery of the scenes involving Miranda and Ferdinand (David Meyer, one of the twins from Celestino Coronado's *Hamlet* (1976, p. 36) is outweighed by a strain of camp that owes nothing to Shakespeare and everything to Jarman's homosexuality, a powerful force throughout his work.

Christopher Biggins plays Stephano as a hysterical queen, and when brightness symbolically floods the screen for the penultimate scene, Jarman brings in twenty pretty sailors from Alonso's ship, who pair up, dance a hornpipe and wolf-whistle the naked Trinculo. He is wiser to omit *The Tempest*'s masque (a supernatural celebration of fertility so firmly rooted in Elizabethan and Jacobean theatre and court practice that, as written, it seems unfilmable), and instead jazz diva Elisabeth Welch sings 'Stormy Weather' in punning tribute to the play's title.

This rousing finale cannot erase the preceding tedium of a movie that on all levels is weaker than Jarman's unconventional, riveting film of *Edward II* (1991), adapted from the play by Shakespeare's great contemporary, Christopher Marlowe, in which homosexuality (the eponymous King's doomed passion for Piers Gaveston) is integral to the story, not artificially imposed, as it is here.

Dir/Scr: Derek Jarman; **Prods:** Guy Ford, Mordecai Schreiber; **DOP:** Peter Middleton; **Editor:** Lesley Walker; **Score:** Brian Hodgson, John Lewis; **Main Cast:** Heathcote Williams (Prospero), Toyah Wilcox (Miranda), David Meyer (Ferdinand), Karl Johnson (Ariel), Jack Birkett (Caliban), Christopher Biggins (Stephano), Peter Turner (Trinculo), Neil Cunningham (Sebastian), Richard Warwick (Antonio), Peter Bull (Alonso), Ken Campbell (Gonzalo).

Tempest
US, 1982 – 134 mins
Paul Mazursky

Tempest devises easy-to-spot equivalents for Shakespeare's principal characters and plot, glossing *The Tempest* without ever revealing its soul.

An early morning scene establishes a Greek island setting and the four principals: the Prospero and Ariel figures, Phillip (John Cassavetes) and Aretha (Susan Sarandon), Phillip's petulant teenage daughter, Miranda (Molly Ringwald, three years away from Brat Pack fame), and Kalibanos, a sex-starved goatherd, energetically portrayed by Raul Julia as a lascivious caricature.

Leisurely flashbacks to New York, eighteen months earlier, reveal that Phillip is an architect in midlife crisis, sick of designing Atlantic City casinos for property magnate Alonzo. When he discovers that his actress wife, Antonia (Gena Rowlands, Cassavetes's wife), is sleeping with Alonzo, adultery replaces *The Tempest*'s coup, and Phillip goes into voluntary exile, fleeing with Miranda to Athens. There he begins an affair with Aretha, a twice-divorced American cabaret singer, and when Alonzo and Antonia track them down, he takes lover and daughter to the island and they meet Kalibanos.

Apart from Kalibanos emulating Caliban by attempting to take Miranda's virginity, the story to this point has less in common with Shakespeare than any number of American dramas about middle-aged professionals, and you wonder why Mazursky has restricted himself by inviting comparisons with *The Tempest*, when he could have written an original screenplay about a disenchanted, cuckolded architect.

Where Prospero is endearingly noble, Cassavetes (in a role originally offered to Paul Newman) makes Phillip selfish and inscrutable. Sarandon is as spirited and attractive as ever, despite Aretha's behaviour having to be awkwardly shoehorned into the Ariel mould, and Alonzo is improbably devoted to an elderly stand-up comedian, Trinc, purely to create an equivalent for Trinculo.

The only scene in which *Tempest* briefly matches the play comes when Phillip almost drowns Kalibanos, as punishment for assaulting Miranda, and the goatherd furiously retorts: 'I show you the olive and the fig and the sweet water!', echoing Act I, Scene ii, when Caliban angrily reminds Prospero how he showed him the island's 'fresh springs, brine-pits, barren place and fertile'. Kalibanos and Caliban both learn English from their 'colonial' masters, and their 'only profit' is that they know how to curse.

Only in the last forty minutes does the action begin directly to copy the play, as Alonzo's yacht cruises past the island, carrying Antonia, Alonzo, his staff and teenage son, Freddy. Freddy and Miranda 'meet cute' while swimming and are instantly smitten. Phillip spots Alonzo's party heading ashore and *seems* to conjure a violent thunderstorm that capsizes their speedboat; since Kalibanos has forecast bad weather, Mazursky shies away from giving Phillip explicitly magical powers. After the visitors escape drowning there is no attempt to make the island, as in Shakespeare, a testing ground for their true natures, and resolution follows swiftly. Aretha tells Phillip it is 'time to forgive' Antonia and Alonzo, so he does. The next day Phillip, Antonia and Miranda set off happily for New York – a pat conclusion compared to the audience satisfaction generated by *The Tempest* as the guilty are pardoned.

A *New York Times* review lambasting 'an overblown, fancified freak of a film' was typical of reactions that ensured *Tempest* flopped, leaving Mazursky 'devastated', and perhaps wishing his first idea for adapting Shakespeare had come off. He had approached Mick Jagger to play 'an androgynous Ariel' in a film that would have resembled a Marx Brothers musical.

Dir/Prod: Paul Mazursky; Scr: Paul Mazursky, Leon Capatanos; **DOP:** Donald McAlpine; Editor: Donn Cambern; Score: Stomu Yamashta; **Main Cast:** John Cassavetes (Phillip), Molly Ringwald (Miranda), Sam Robards (Freddy), Susan Sarandon (Aretha), Raul Julia (Kalibanos), Vittorio Gassman (Alonzo), Gena Rowlands (Antonia), Jackie Gayle (Trinc), Anthony Holland (Sebastian).

Prospero's Books
UK/Netherlands/France/Italy, 1991 – 120 mins
Peter Greenaway

As Peter Greenaway floods Shakespeare's text and John Gielgud's captivating Prospero with a torrent of live-action and animated imagery, *The Tempest*, as the *Financial Times* put it, 'becomes not so much a great, pure morality fable, as a blank cheque for Greenaway's imagination.' His inspiration was the magnificent speech (part of the longest scene in Shakespeare) in which Prospero tells Miranda how his exile was eased by Gonzalo: 'Knowing I loved my books, he furnish'd me/From mine own library with volumes that/I prize above my dukedom.'

The twenty-four books on science, mythology and other subjects, which Prospero has used to transform himself into a magician, are described by an uncredited patrician male voice. As each becomes relevant – the *Book of Water* when Prospero summons the storm, the *Book of Games* as Miranda and Ferdinand play chess – its pages come spectacularly to life through a vivid combination of computer animation (the then revolutionary Quantel Paintbox program) and high-definition video: text writes itself, diagrams rotate and bodily fluids splash onto the screen.

This conceit also expresses Greenaway's view that Prospero/Gielgud and Shakespeare 'are really one and the same', the director subscribing to the theory that the playwright was consciously saying goodbye to the stage through his hero's farewell to creative power. Gielgud provides all the characters' voices (airy tones for Ariel, a distorted growl for Caliban) and Prospero writes their lines in exquisite calligraphy. The 'Prospero is Shakespeare' concept is sealed in the concluding moments: Gielgud has been filling the last pages of Book 24: *Thirty-Six Plays* by William Shakespeare.

(*Next page*) Seated before *The Book of Water*, Prospero (John Gielgud) conjures the storm in Peter Greenaway's *Prospero's Books*

In addition to this dazzling, dramatically hollow visual trickery, Greenaway spent his four-month shoot filling the elaborate sets built in an Amsterdam studio with hundreds of mostly naked extras, representing Prospero's spirits and nymphs. A typically insistent and repetitive score from Michael Nyman, Greenaway's regular composer, accompanies agonisingly slow tracking shots of Gielgud alongside marching and dancing figures – young, old, male, female, thin, fat.

Somewhere, competing in vain for attention, is *The Tempest*, though even viewers familiar with the plot could be confused. There is no mistaking the naked Caliban, played with crab-like physicality by English dancer Michael Clark (also the film's choreographer), although it takes a while to adjust to an Ariel played by four different actors (aged about five to thirty-five). Greenaway's refusal to let the other actors use their own voices until the penultimate scene makes it difficult to know who is talking to whom, and impossible to talk about 'performances' from accomplished actors used as elaborately costumed pawns: Britain's Tom Bell, Kenneth Cranham and Mark Rylance, France's Isabelle Pasco and Michel Blanc, the great Erland Josephson from Sweden.

Greenaway called Gielgud 'the still, calm figure in the midst of all my pyrotechnical extravagance' and when, all too rarely, he lets us concentrate on the eighty-seven-year-old in full flow, Prospero's acute sense of mortality and tender concern for Miranda come movingly into focus. In his last major film appearance he shows total mastery of a role he had played four times on stage between 1931 and 1974 and longed to commit to film. Immensely proud of his performance, in 1997 he would tell *The Sunday Times* that Greenaway 'didn't know the point of the play.'

Greenaway suggested that *Prospero's Books*, which took a respectable $1.8m in America, 'needs to be seen several times' to be fully appreciated; certainly viewers with a solid grasp of art history or, better still, the illustrated *Prospero's Books* screenplay can spot references to da Messina (Prospero's study), Rembrandt (the Neapolitans' costumes), Botticelli and many others. Like the animation of the hero's library, these allusions from an art school-trained director with a passion for European painting mean that *Prospero's Books* should be judged not as narrative cinema but as a multimedia installation, in which Shakespeare's text is merely one subordinate element.

Dir/Scr: Peter Greenaway; **Prod:** Kees Kasander; **DOP:** Sacha Vierny; **Editor:** Marina Bodbijl; **Score:** Michael Nyman; **Main Cast:** John Gielgud (Prospero), Isabelle Pasco (Miranda), Mark Rylance (Ferdinand), Orpheo, Paul Russell, James Thierrée, Emil Wolk (Ariel), Michael Clark (Caliban), Michael Romeyn (Stephano), Jim Van De Woude (Trinculo), Kenneth Cranham (Sebastian), Tom Bell (Antonio), Michel Blanc (Alonso), Erland Josephson (Gonzalo).

The Tempest
US, 1998 – 88 mins (TVM)
Jack Bender

In Mississippi, 1851, benevolent widower Gideon Prosper (Peter Fonda) hands control of his plantation to his brother, Anthony, and studies black magic with one of his slaves, Azaleigh, 'a Mambo priestess' with a late-adolescent son, Ariel. Her magic saves Prosper from being lynched by Anthony, who murders her and wounds the fleeing Ariel. Prosper's bookkeeper, Gonzo, helps him escape with his daughter, Miranda, to a bayou island, which Prosper 'steals' from a feral hick, Gator Man (Caliban).

So ends an extended prologue spun from Prospero's account of Antonio's coup. We jump to 1863; the Civil War rages. While seeking a safe Mississippi crossing for General Grant's troops, Anthony, Gonzo and a handsome young Union captain, Frederick, are capsized by Prosper's conjured storm, after which Miranda and Frederick's romance and Anthony and Gator Man's murderous plotting stick close to Shakespeare.

The voodoo (accompanied by Terence Blanchard's tribal drums and chants) and Ariel's slave status are historically apt refractions of Prospero's magic and his enslavement of Caliban and Ariel (a theme seized upon by stage *Tempest*s with post-colonial settings). However, the Civil War subplot that, in effect, replaces the Stephano/Trinculo comedy and the conspiracy against Alonso is terribly misjudged. When Anthony tries to lead Union troops into a Confederate ambush, Prosper foils them with phantom bluecoats and the subsequent Confederate rout sees the Battle of Vicksburg (35,000 dead) played partly for laughs. Prosper then pardons Anthony, sanctions Miranda and Frederick's marriage and returns the island to Gator Man.

Impressive special effects (Ariel morphs into a bird and an old man) bring out the play's cinematic qualities and Jack Bender paces the story competently to meet the demands of the NBC network (a cliffhanger every eight minutes to prevent channel-hopping in ad breaks). The need to attract a mass audience also explains the patronising, picture-book simplicity of the dialogue and Fonda's ponderous voiceover narration.

Dir: Jack Bender; Prod: James Bigwood; Scr: James Henerson; DOP: Steven Shaw; Editor: Stephen Lovejoy; Score: Terence Blanchard; Main Cast: Peter Fonda (Gideon Prosper), Katherine Heigl (Miranda), Eddie Mills (Capt Frederick Allen), Harold Perrineau (Ariel), John Pyper-Ferguson (Gator Man), John Glover (Anthony Prosper), Dennis Redfield ('Willy' Gonzo).

Titus Andronicus (play synopsis)

Ancient Rome. Returning in triumph to Rome after defeating the Goths, General Titus Andronicus sacrifices Alarbus, eldest son of the Goth queen Tamora, to placate the ghosts of the many sons he has lost in battle. Saturninus and Bassianus are vying to succeed their late father as Emperor. Titus rejects the throne, which his brother Marcus has urged the people to offer him, and, on Titus's recommendation, Saturninus is elected instead. The new Emperor chooses Titus's daughter, Lavinia, as his bride, but she is already betrothed to Bassianus, who flees with her, aided by Titus's four surviving sons: Lucius (the eldest), Quintus, Marcus and Mutius. Titus pursues them and kills Mutius.

Saturninus rejects Lavinia and marries Tamora, who begins plotting her revenge, aided by Aaron the Moor, her slave and lover. On a hunting trip, Aaron instructs Tamora's savage sons, Chiron and Demetrius, to murder Bassianus, and successfully frames Quintus and Martius for the crime. Chiron and Demetrius rape Lavinia, cutting off her hands and tongue so that she cannot denounce them. After Lucius is sentenced to banishment from Rome for attempting to rescue his brothers, Aaron tricks Titus into cutting off a hand to secure Quintus and Martius's pardon; he receives only their severed heads and his hand. Titus sends Lucius to the Goths to raise an army.

Tamora has given birth to Aaron's bastard son. He flees Rome with the baby and is captured by Lucius and the Goths. After Lavinia has written the names of her rapists in the sand, Titus seizes Chiron and Demetrius when they come to his house with Tamora to torment him. He slits Chiron and Demetrius's throats and bakes their flesh into a pie, which he serves to their mother and the Emperor at a banquet. He stabs Lavinia to end her shame, then murders Tamora. Saturninus kills Titus and Lucius kills him. Elected Emperor, Lucius orders that Aaron be starved to death.

Titus
US/Italy, 1999 – 160 mins
Julie Taymor

Rape, murder, mutilation and cannibalism – *Titus Andronicus* contains so many atrocities that some critics have dismissed it as a juvenile gore-fest, unworthy of Shakespeare's name. Julie Taymor's *Titus* reveals that the play's horrors are matched only by its compassion.

Only the second major screen version of Shakespeare's bloodiest tragedy (following the BBC's 1985 production), Taymor's $25m feature-film début is utterly cinematic while demanding a theatrical suspension of belief, and shares the dazzling invention of her opera and theatre work (most famously the Disney stage musical *The Lion King*). It is closely based on her 1994 off-Broadway *Titus Andronicus*, and photographs illustrate that the film contains many images originally devised for the stage, notably the central, time-bending concept.

Titus opens with a young boy (Osheen Jones, from the 1996 *Dream* p. 144) violently transported from the 1950s'-style kitchen where he is bashing together ketchup-smeared action figures to the ruined Coliseum (in fact the Roman amphitheatre in Pula, Croatia), where he becomes Young Lucius and watches Anthony Hopkins's grizzled Titus lead the credits sequence's stylised victory parade. Horse-drawn chariots and clay-caked centurions, moving like automatons in time to Elliot Goldenthal's choral processional, are followed by motorbikes and armoured half-tracks, as Taymor establishes that a screenplay retaining Shakespeare's dialogue and structure will constantly straddle the fifth century and several parts of the twentieth.

Saturninus is headquartered in Mussolini's former government centre and guarded by Blackshirts; Chiron and Demetrius play pool and video games in a dungeon-like den, evoking the 'ultra-violence'-fixated thugs of Stanley Kubrick's *A Clockwork Orange* (1971); the Goth army wields pump-action shotguns, and when Titus turns chef, Hopkins repeats Hannibal Lecter's cannibalistic slurp from *The Silence of the Lambs*.

Dante Ferretti's sets and Milena Canonero's Academy Award-nominated costumes reference everything from ancient Rome to 1930s' Fascism, the jazz age and Grace Kelly glamour, and Goldenthal's magnificent score combines New York jazz, electro-metal (for Chiron and Demetrius) and varied orchestral themes.

The connection between the play's ancient horrors and more recent history or cinematic fiction is underlined by Taymor's expansion of Young Lucius's role. He is kept in regular view as a mostly silent witness to the horrors, simultaneously the inheritor of his father (Angus MacFadyen) and grandfather's brutal way of life and, as the Boy from the opening scene, an audience surrogate who views the story with our eyes (director Jane Howell used Young Lucius to comparable effect in the BBC production). All this, as Taymor wrote in her notes for *Titus: The Illustrated Screenplay* (2000), shows the play 'speaking directly to our times; a time whose audience feeds daily on tabloid sex scandals, teenage gang rape, high school gun sprees.'

She treats the most gruesome moments with a mixture of graphic verisimilitude (the slitting of Chiron and Demetrius's throats) and extreme stylisation. The mutilated Lavinia (the doe-eyed Laura Fraser) stands abandoned in a swamp, hands digitally replaced by bunched twigs, vomiting blood, in a scene of harrowing beauty, like some perverse designer perfume commercial. Her rape is later represented in one of four 'Penny Arcade Nightmares': brief visual effects shots that present a character's inner visions (Lavinia sees her assailants as leaping tigers; Titus pictures Mutius as a sacrificial lamb). This combination of realism and stylisation, like the melding of historical periods, takes us into a metaphorical realm where specific acts may stand for *all* violence and suffering.

Taymor also triumphantly meets the challenge of fusing horror with comedy, as when Aaron seals Titus's severed hand into a plastic

(*Opposite page*) 'Rome and the righteous heavens be my judge': Titus Andronicus (Anthony Hopkins) appeals to Saturninus in Julie Taymor's *Titus*

sandwich bag, or when the joyful bel canto song 'Vivere senza malincolia' ('Live without sadness') plays over a close-up of the steaming cannibal pies cooling on a windowsill.

In this final scene, Lavinia, Tamora, Titus and the Emperor are dispatched within two minutes, and as Lucius shoots Saturninus in the forehead, a digital freeze-frame and reverse-zoom transplant the diners into the Coliseum, now filled with spectators in 1990s' dress, their rapt attention a triple reminder: of ancient Rome's love of killing as spectator sport, the film's origins in live theatre and our contemporary consumption of gory movies, news items and video games. There is tentative consolation in the lingering final shot, accompanied by Goldenthal's symphonic 'Finale'. Young Lucius carries Aaron's bastard baby out of the killing field and into a spectacular dawn – Titus and Tamora's heirs united, entering a more hopeful future.

Despite the potentially incoherent blend of periods and techniques, not to mention accents (American, Scottish, Irish and Welsh among the principals), *Titus* is grounded by Taymor's separation of the opposing factions. The Goths and Saturninus live in orgiastic decadence that pays homage to the grotesque court of Trimalcione in Federico Fellini's *Satyricon* (1970). Cumming strikes camp, leering poses; Jessica Lange, clad in figure-hugging gold, is vampishly seductive; Jonathan Rhys Meyers and Matthew Rhys make her boys drug-addicted hysterics.

The Andronici live in a modestly furnished villa, and Hopkins, Feore and MacFadyen adopt a dignified acting style that would also suit an austere stage production of *Julius Caesar* or *Coriolanus*. Hopkins, surely drawing on his theatre experience of playing Lear and Marc Antony (Titus has aspects of both later characters), is unforgettable as the General shattered by the realisation that Rome, to which he was so blindly loyal, 'is but a wilderness of tigers'. He shows this man of violence to be filled with tenderness; when he tries to feed Lavinia and interprets her sign language, and when he snaps her neck, all are acts of equal care. The menacing Harry Lennix, the only survivor from Taymor's New York cast, moves effortlessly between the two camps, with a nice line in intellectually superior soliloquy to camera.

The comparatively small number of people who saw *Titus* on its initial theatrical release (despite strong reviews, it grossed just $1.7m in America) watched an achievement all the more remarkable because of what one might call *Titus Andronicus*'s 'difficulty tariff' within the Shakespeare canon. Taymor fashioned a masterpiece not from an inherently cinematic, fast-paced drama such as *Macbeth* or *Romeo and Juliet*, but a play that in the theatre may seem purely horrific or excessively comic, devoid of emotional or intellectual meaning.

There will always be new screen versions of *Hamlet* or *Macbeth*; *Titus* may well never be turned into another feature film, and Taymor has therefore ensured that, most probably via a superb two-disc American DVD, future generations will always have an opportunity to appreciate this still rarely staged work as a great, if rough-hewn, tragedy, and see it pointing the way to later, greater dramas: Aaron as the prototype for Iago and Richard III; Tamora as a forerunner of Lady Macbeth and Cleopatra. It is also a film that continues to move me more than any other, even after many viewings. For all these reasons I regard it as the greatest of all Shakespeare films.

Dir/Scr: Julie Taymor; **Prods:** Conchita Airoldi, Julie Taymor, Jody Patton; **DOP:** Luciano Tovoli; **Editor:** Françoise Bonnot; **Score:** Elliot Goldenthal; **Main Cast:** Anthony Hopkins (Titus), Jessica Lange (Tamora), Harry Lennix (Aaron), Alan Cumming (Saturninus), Jonathan Rhys Meyers (Chiron), Matthew Rhys (Demetrius), Angus Macfadyen (Lucius), Colm Feore (Marcus), Laura Fraser (Lavinia), James Frain (Bassianus).

Twelfth Night (play synopsis)

Viola of Messaline is washed up on the coast of Illyria after a shipwreck she believes drowned her identical twin, Sebastian. Disguised as a young man, 'Cesario', she is employed by Duke Orsino and acts as his go-between in wooing the Countess Olivia. In mourning for her brother, Olivia refuses to let Orsino court her in person, but falls instantly in love with 'Cesario', leaving Viola to lament the Countess's delusion and her own hopeless love for Orsino.

Malvolio, Olivia's pompous steward, reprimands her uncle, Sir Toby Belch, and his foolish companion, Sir Andrew Aguecheek, who hopes to marry Olivia, for their riotously drunken behaviour. Sir Andrew, Sir Toby, Olivia's servant Fabian, Feste the jester and Olivia's waiting gentlewoman, Maria (who loves Sir Toby), vow to take revenge. Maria forges a letter from the Countess, convincing Malvolio that she loves him and wishes him to smile constantly and wear yellow stockings and cross-garters. Following these instructions, his behaviour and dress so alarm Olivia that she has him locked up as a lunatic. He is further tormented by Feste, disguised as a priest, 'Sir Topas'.

Sebastian has arrived in Illyria, saved from drowning by a sea captain, Antonio, who risks arrest because he once fought against Illyria. He entrusts Sebastian with his purse and they arrange to meet later. Antonio comes to the aid of 'Cesario', whom he takes for Sebastian, as he and Sir Andrew reluctantly duel over Olivia's affections. Antonio is arrested and is horrified when 'Cesario' denies knowing him or receiving his purse.

Olivia mistakes the passing Sebastian for 'Cesario' and is overjoyed when he accepts her proposal that they instantly marry. Orsino and 'Cesario' arrive at Olivia's home and she is horrified when Cesario denies that they are husband and wife. When Sebastian emerges, having fought with and injured Sir Toby and Sir Andrew, the twins' true identities emerge. Olivia promises the freed Malvolio that he can judge his tricksters, but he exits vowing revenge. Fabian reports that Sir Toby has married Maria. Orsino prepares to marry Viola.

Twelfth Night (*Dvenadtsataya noch*)
USSR, 1955 – 90 mins
Yakov Fried

Yakov Fried presents *Twelfth Night* as a jolly, extravagant romp, full of laughter, music and song, never allowing Shakespeare's darker strains to be heard. He airbrushes the shadows much as Paul Czinner did in *As You Like It* (1936, p. 5) and as Viola/'Cesario', Klara Luchko remains as perky throughout as Elizabeth Bergner was as Rosalind/'Ganymede'. Resembling the young Claire Bloom, Luchko is first seen as Viola and Sebastian in impressive split-screen shots, as the twins reach out towards each other on the storm-tossed deck of a four-master. She later relishes her swordplay as a D'Artagnan-like Sebastian, and in the last scene the special effects convey the magic of the twins' reunion. As 'Cesario', however, she is merely a panto principal boy; there is no acknowledgment of grief at her brother's supposed death, nor doubt that her love for Orsino will have a happy outcome.

This softening extends to Olivia's mourning (lightly worn), Maria and Sir Toby's marriage (Fried's ending has them as the third pair of happy-ever-after newlyweds) and Malvolio's 'ordeal', which involves exasperation rather than torment, though Vasili Merkuriev's steward is the film's most memorable portrayal. It is amusing to hear puritanical reproaches from a figure of such Falstaffian stature that his cross-gartered calves resemble gift-wrapped Christmas hams, and he appears to escape imprisonment by ripping his cell door off its hinges.

The lavish costuming and production design blend Old Master portraiture and the court of Louis XIV: Toby is every inch the Laughing Cavalier, and the manicured gardens in which Vadim Medvedev's dashing young Orsino pens love poems suggest Versailles. Aleksei Zhivotov's music is liberally used, with Mussorgsky-like surges at romantic high points and Russian troubadour arrangements of Feste's songs. Fried takes the same approach to location shooting as Sergei Yutkevich in the same year's Russian *Othello* (p. 169), placing as many scenes as possible in beautiful open-air settings, with Olivia's fairytale castle perched on a hilltop overlooking the sea and a coastal mountain range.

Dir/Scr: Yakov Fried; **Prod:** Lenfilm; **DOP:** Yevgeni Shapiro; **Editor:** G. Schirkin; **Score:** Aleksei Zhivotov; **Main Cast:** Klara Luchko (Viola/Sebastian), Vadim Medvedev (Orsino), Alla Larionova (Olivia), Vasili Merkuriev (Malvolio), Bruno Friendlich (Feste), Anna Lisianskaya (Maria), Georgi Vitsin (Sir Andrew Aguecheek), Mikhail Yanshin (Sir Toby Belch).

Twelfth Night
UK, 1996 – 133 mins
Trevor Nunn

Trevor Nunn, arguably Britain's finest post-war director of stage
Shakespeare, regards *Twelfth Night* as a 'perfect work of art' and for his
big-screen Shakespeare début reworked the play to meet cinema's
demands only with great reluctance. He updated the story to the 1890s
and wrote a verse prologue to explain the attention-grabbing, ten-
minute opening sequence that precedes Orsino's 'If music be the food of
love' and places Act 1, Scene ii before i.

Viola and Sebastian are providing cross-dressed entertainment for
their fellow passengers when they are shipwrecked. Taking his cue from
Antonio's brave past service 'in a sea-fight' against Orsino, Nunn puts
Messaline at war with Illyria, forcing Viola and the other survivors to

Confusion envelops Olivia (Helena Bonham Carter), left, Viola (Imogen Stubbs), centre,
and Orsino (Toby Stephens) at the climax of Trevor Nunn's *Twelfth Night*

evade cavalry patrols, and making her disguise a means of avoiding arrest. The performance skills (and piano-playing) she demonstrated at sea prove indispensable in Orsino's all-male, *Prisoner of Zenda*-like military court (not unlike the Elsinore of Branagh's *Hamlet* (1996, p. 45) and Imogen Stubbs (Nunn's wife) makes her predicament suitably amusing and, given the state of war, far tenser than in most stage productions. She must fence, smoke cigars and play billiards – all activities that might blow her cover and expose her to the military justice that we see descend on Antonio.

Stubbs deftly captures Viola's hopeless love for the Duke, whom Toby Stephens makes appropriately self-pitying and vain, and the Orsino–'Cesario' strand is more gradually developed than on stage, as Nunn chops up their meetings to prevent Stephens disappearing for the whole of Acts III and IV and allow us to flit between simultaneous actions at his court and in Olivia's elegant country mansion. There, Ben Kingsley's depressive Feste accompanies himself on concertina accordion and has a touching relationship with Helena Bonham Carter, who expertly charts the Countess's disorienting awakening from grief to love – a change signified by her exchange of black dress for blue, and her progression from private chapel and curtained drawing room into fresh air and sunshine.

Nigel Hawthorne's fine Malvolio calls to mind his two most celebrated screen roles, combining the officious superiority of Sir Humphrey in the *Yes, Minister* (1980–4) sitcom and, once incarcerated, the torments of *The Madness of King George* (1994). Unfortunately, the considerable pleasure to be drawn from all these characters is diminished by Nunn allowing Richard E. Grant, as a blond, foppish Sir Andrew, and a bewhiskered Mel Smith as a Falstaffian Sir Toby, to give loud, hammy interpretations that belong in another, cruder film.

At the end, he emphasises that only the twins and their spouses seem likely to live happily ever after. Malvolio strides away from Olivia's house to plot his revenge; Sir Toby and Maria (the bustling Imelda Staunton) ride off to a marriage evidently founded for him more on convenience than love, though Staunton has shown how deeply Maria regrets not being able to make him change his ways. Feste wanders the cliffs in search of fresh employment, giving us a last glimpse of an Illyria whose autumnal mood has been created by autumnal Cornish locations, with several scenes in a picturesque, cobbled fishing village, St Michael's Mount doubling for Orsino's castle, and Olivia's house and gardens represented by the National Trust homes at Lanhydrock and Prideaux Place.

After reviews generally poorer than it deserved, Nunn's $5m adaptation grossed just $1m in the UK, not helped by a poster tagline that sought desperately to make Shakespeare hip by invoking three 1990s' film comedies about male drag artists: 'Before *Priscilla* crossed the desert, *Wong Foo* met Julie Newmar, and the *Birdcage* was unlocked, there was *Twelfth Night*.'

Dir/Scr: Trevor Nunn; **Prods:** Stephen Evans, David Parfitt; **DOP:** Clive Tickner; **Editor:** Peter Boyle; **Score:** Shaun Davey; **Main Cast:** Imogen Stubbs (Viola/'Cesario'), Toby Stephens (Orsino), Helena Bonham Carter (Olivia), Stephen McIntosh (Sebastian), Nigel Hawthorne (Malvolio), Ben Kingsley (Feste), Imelda Staunton (Maria), Richard E. Grant (Sir Andrew Aguecheek), Mel Smith (Sir Toby Belch).

Twelfth Night
UK, 2003 – 102 mins (TVM)
Tim Supple

Tim Supple's prologue makes Viola and Sebastian present-day Asian asylum seekers, fleeing their home in strife-torn Messaline as armed men arrest their mother (a photograph later reveals that their father, a high-ranking soldier, has been assassinated). The twins' flight and sea voyage are ironically intercut with Chiwetel Ejiofor's laid-back Orsino delivering 'If music be the food of love', and this opening sequence sets up a strikingly violent, sombre interpretation whose integrated casting imagines Illyria as a harmonious multicultural melting pot, in Supple's words 'contemporary London relocated to a small, hot island'. Orsino, his servant Valentine, and Olivia's servant and priest are of African or Afro-Caribbean descent; Olivia, Malvolio, Sir Toby, Sir Andrew, Maria, Fabian and Antonio are Caucasian; Feste, Viola and Sebastian are Asian, allowing Sebastian to converse in a mixture of English and Hindi with Antonio (portrayed as a professional mercenary, though Supple does not suggest, like Trevor Nunn, see p. 273, that Messaline and Illyria are at war). A beautiful final touch sees brother and sister confirm their identities ('My father had a mole upon his brow') in their subtitled native tongue.

Apart from Viola's arrival at a grey dockside and Sebastian and Antonio's meetings in a London greasy-spoon café and crowded street market, the action is confined to studio-shot interiors where design and performance reflect Supple's determination to emphasise the 'sadness and despair' in *Twelfth Night*, somewhat at the expense of its comedy.

David Troughton's flatulent Sir Toby and Richard Bremmer's tall, gaunt Sir Andrew drink themselves into despairing oblivion in Sir Toby's basement den (conveniently next door to Olivia's wine cellar) and join Feste in a drum'n'bass mix of 'Hold thy Peace' (Nitin Sawhney's eclectic arrangements also give Feste a Jeff Buckley-esque acoustic version of 'Oh Mistress Mine'). Claire Price's pale and introspective Olivia spends her days in high-Catholic mourning, her private chapel blacked out save for the candles burning in memory of the playboy brother she lost to a car crash, and she falls for Parminder Nagra's withdrawn 'Cesario' because they are kindred spirits, linked by grief. Orsino, aimless and friendless, lounges in a minimalist salon with sea-view and hot-tub, in which 'Cesario' awkwardly massages his shoulders (emulating an almost identical moment in Nunn's film). Michael Maloney drains the comic pomposity from Malvolio, turning him into an ascetic Home Office Private Secretary. When he reads the forged letter in Olivia's trellised garden, Supple adroitly side-steps the need for theatrical *sotto voce* by having the conspirators sit in Fabian the security guard's office, watching proceedings via a concealed video camera.

As the confusion builds, *Twelfth Night*'s violence can seldom have been pushed to such extremes. Instead of making Sir Andrew and 'Cesario' engage in the usual clumsy swordfight, Supple has them slash at each other with kitchen knives, and Andrew and Toby later emerge with nasty wounds inflicted by Sebastian. Malvolio is hooded and tied like a Beirut hostage and endures such torment that Sir Toby and Maureen Beattie's dour, Scottish Maria eventually weep at what they have done. These two do, at least, seem passionately devoted to one another, and the final embrace of the twins and their partners is joyful – though hesitantly so.

In his screen début, Supple, an accomplished director of stage Shakespeare, controls mood and pace impressively, and as one might expect from a production commissioned by Channel 4's educational arm, 4Learning, he and co-adapter Andrew Bannerman take few textual liberties. They have Feste perform for Orsino on CD rather than in person, relocate a couple of scenes and trim judiciously to hit the required running time for a two-hour slot on commercial television.

Dir: Tim Supple; **Prod:** Rachel Gesua; **Scr:** Andrew Bannerman, Tim Supple; **DOP:** Gavin Finney; **Editor:** Richard Milward; **Score:** Nitin Sawhney; **Main Cast:** Parminder Nagra (Viola), Chiwetel Ejiofor (Orsino), Claire Price (Olivia), Ronny Jhutti (Sebastian), Michael Maloney (Malvolio), Zubin Varla (Feste), Maureen Beattie (Maria), Richard Bremmer (Sir Andrew Aguecheek), David Troughton (Sir Toby Belch).

She's the Man
US, 2006 – 105 mins
Andy Fickman

When Karen McCullah Lutz and Kirsten Smith took *The Taming of the Shrew* to high school in *10 Things I Hate About You* (1999, p. 241), the use of a largely unknown cast meant no one performer had to dominate. When they put the same spin on *Twelfth Night* for *She's the Man*, the casting of twenty-year-old Amanda Bynes ensured that every scene must please the millions of 'tweenies' who adored her in *What a Girl Wants* (2003), and Shakespeare's most even-handed ensemble comedy was reluctantly converted into a solo vehicle.

Bynes's tomboyish Viola is denied the chance to try out for the boys' soccer team at Cornwall Prep, her private co-ed school, ahead of its big match with rivals Illyria, and dumps boyfriend Justin for not backing her. Her non-identical twin Sebastian bunks off from Illyria to join his rock band in England, because 'to chase your dreams sometimes you've got to break the rules', which is all the cheesy Hollywood inspiration Viola needs. She escapes her divorced Mom (ditzy Julie Hagerty) by pretending she's going to stay at her Dad's house, and sets out to play for Illyria (the writers never bother explaining why no one from Cornwall questions her absence).

Paul Antonio, Viola's camp hairdresser friend, provides wig, eyebrows and sideburns, Bynes drops her voice ('I'm a badass hunky dude!') and, as 'Sebastian', instantly falls for her Illyria roommate, gorgeous football captain Duke Orsino (Channing Tatum, a lifeless Josh Hartnett clone). She trains with the team, loudly coached by Vinnie Jones, and struggles to conceal the truth (to show her avoiding discovery in the showers once is fun, but *three* times?).

'Sebastian' bewitches school princess Olivia, who is adored by both Duke and pompous dormitory director, Malcolm, who has a pet tarantula called Malvolio. In the film's most amusing scene, at Cesario's Pizzeria, Viola has two girlfriends pretend to be Sebastian's drooling exes, convincing the watching Duke that 'Sebastian' is a stud not a girlish geek and infuriating Sebastian's high-maintenance girlfriend, Monique.

Duke snogs Viola at a carnival kissing booth and freaks out when 'Sebastian' suggests he pursue her, and there are entertaining shades of *As You Like It* when 'Sebastian' has Duke woo him as though he were Olivia. Olivia herself fakes a crush on Duke to make 'Sebastian' jealous, and ends up kissing the real Sebastian.

Monique and Malcolm rumble Viola's disguise and true identities are crudely revealed at the Illyria vs. Cornwall game. Sebastian drops his shorts to prove he's a he, Viola lifts her top and Illyria win. This feels like a natural climax. However, Bynes's fans, who propelled the film to a US/UK gross of $41m, cannot be denied their idol's Cinderella moment, so Viola and Duke pair up alongside Sebastian and Olivia at a débutantes' ball.

Andy Fickman's lacklustre animation of this pastel world of pretty faces is punctuated by third-gear montages (Viola's makeover; soccer training sessions), all set to perky pop songs, and Bynes's gurning, eye-rolling acting is mercilessly exposed in carrying a script that uses most of the *Twelfth Night*-derived characters as underwritten functionaries, there only to keep Bynes centre stage in a variety of 'wacky' scenarios. Malcolm is the flimsiest of comic villains, and her soccer teammates Andrew and Toby merely make inane choric remarks. *Twelfth Night* ultimately seems a less important source than *Shakespeare in Love* (1998, p. 227); the Violas of Gwyneth Paltrow and Bynes both cross-dress to perform in a male-only cast/team) and the girl-power soccer wish fulfilment of *Bend It Like Beckham* (2002).

Dir: Andy Fickman; **Prods:** Ewan Leslie, Jack Leslie, Lauren Shuler Donner; **Scr:** Ewan Leslie, Karen McCullah Lutz, Kirsten Smith; **DOP:** Greg Gardiner; **Editor:** Michael Jablow; **Score:** Nathan Wang; **Main Cast:** Amanda Bynes (Viola), Channing Tatum (Duke Orsino), Laura Ramsey (Olivia), James Kirk (Sebastian), James Snyder (Malcolm), Jonathan Sadowski (Paul Antonio), Vinnie Jones (Coach Dinklage).

Appendix 1

Shakespeare – The Animated Tales
UK/Russia, 1990–4 – 12 x 25 mins

Shakespeare – The Animated Tales was a remarkable co-production between S4C, the Cardiff-based Welsh arm of Channel 4, and Moscow-based animation studio Soyuzmultifilm, founded in 1935 and known as 'the Soviet Disney'. Adapter Leon Garfield scripted a dozen abridgements, which won three Emmy Awards and have screened in more than fifty countries. They merit collective rather than selective recognition among this book's 100 films, firstly because they provide an accessible introduction for young viewers to twelve plays, and, secondly, because they triumphantly demonstrated to viewers of all ages that a medium too often associated solely with children's stories could realise adult Shakespearean imagery and themes with as much imagination and poetry as live-action film.

The twenty-five-minute limit on each play made Garfield's task extraordinarily difficult, and almost every retained line of dialogue, he explained, had to 'carry the weight of narrative'. The scripts inevitably emphasise plot over character (*Romeo and Juliet* becomes almost absurdly frenetic), and use formal prose narration, delivered in voiceover, to set the scene and bridge gaps ('A fierce ambition burned in the heart of Richard,' announces Alec McCowen at the start of *Richard III*, and so on). They are admirably explicit with the more violent tales (Hastings's head is served on a platter in *Richard III*) and only a few of the omissions unnecessarily soften the mood (no imprisonment of Malvolio in *Twelfth Night*) or unbalance twinned storylines by neglecting a subplot (less than a minute of the *Shrew* is devoted to Bianca/Lucentio).

The animators worked from pre-recorded soundtracks superbly voiced by actors who have graced some of the best RSC or National Theatre productions, including Roger Allam (Orsino), Fiona Shaw (Viola), Brian Cox and Zoë Wanamaker (the Macbeths), Antony Sher (Richard III) and Timothy West (Prospero).

Production and costume designs place the action around Shakespeare's time, or the play's historical period, a tactic previously used by the BBC's complete television Shakespeare cycle (1978–85) and designed to give consistency and, with an eye on long-term educational and consumer video sales, prevent films from dating, as might happen with, say, *Romeo and Juliet* in a 1990s' city.

Conventional cel animation was used for *Julius Caesar* and *Othello* (both have the robust, chiselled heroes you might expect to find in an animated DC Comic), a rather bland *Romeo and Juliet*, a *Macbeth* as shadowy and brutal as an adult graphic novel, and a *Dream* whose garish colours made it the only *Tale* to feel like a children's television cartoon.

Three films – *Hamlet*, *Richard III* and *As You Like It* – saw every frame hand-painted onto glass suspended beneath the camera, photographed and then repainted, giving every characters' movement a blurred quality, which in the Doré-like *Hamlet* created an astonishing visual representation of the Prince's melancholy and Elsinore's shadowy *froideur*.

The Tempest, *Twelfth Night*, *The Taming of the Shrew* and *The Winter's Tale* used puppets made from metal skeletons, around six to ten inches high and animated by stop-motion filming. This gave us many memorable characterisations, including a translucent silver Ariel with angel's wings and ballerina's grace. It is not surprising that the magic of *The Tempest* and the *Dream* lent themselves to the visual freedom afforded by animation, but the more realistic *Tales* also contain dozens of arrestingly fluent effects that might seem laughable if placed beside flesh-and-blood actors but perfectly suit this more expressionistic form, as when the scroll thrown into Brutus's orchard morphs into a snake, or a stained glass window comes alive to depict the slaughter of Macduff's family.

Prod: Dave Edwards; **Scr:** Leon Garfield; *As You Like It* **Dir:** Alexei Karayev. *Hamlet* **Dir:** Natalia Orlova. *Julius Caesar* **Dir:** Yuri Kulakov. *Macbeth* **Dir:** Nikolai Serebriakov. *A Midsummer Night's Dream* **Dir:** Robert Saakiants. *Othello* **Dir:** Nikolai Serebriakov. *Richard III* **Dir:** Natalia Orlova. *Romeo and Juliet* **Dir:** Ephim Gambourg. *The Taming of the Shrew* **Dir:** Aida Ziablikova. *The Tempest* **Dir:** Stanislav Sokolov. *Twelfth Night* **Dir:** Maria Muat. *The Winter's Tale* **Dir:** Stanislav Sokolov. (Region 1 DVD: Ambrose Video; Region 2 DVD: Metrodome.)

Appendix 2 – Video and DVD Guide

Titles go in and out of print at regular and unpredictable intervals. However, online shopping has made it easier to track down new and second-hand copies of out-of-print titles. The most straightforward method is to locate a film's entry on the Internet Movie Database <www.imdb.com> and click on the constantly updated 'Shop' options in the top right-hand corner of the page. These links take you to Amazon's UK, US and other sites, where stock may be available from Amazon or its (generally reliable) Marketplace Sellers.

The best-stocked specialist online retailer for Shakespeare on video is the Ontario-based <www.bardcentral.com> (stocking mostly North American formats); other useful sites include <www.caiman.com>; <www.moviesunlimited.com>; <www.inetvideo.com>; <www.blackstar.co.uk> and Ebay. Google searches (e.g. 'Johnny Hamlet + DVD') can also yield results.

The information below (compiled in January 2007) lists titles available on Region 1 (R1) DVD and VHS NTSC (North America formats), and Region 2 (R2) DVD and VHS Pal (UK and Europe formats). R1 DVDs and NTSC videos require an NTSC-compatible television and a multiregion DVD player or NTSC-compatible VHS player. Films are listed alphabetically by title and, if relevant, year, followed by the format and distributor. [OP] indicates 'Out of Print', but worth hunting for online. Of the 100 films in this book, those not listed below appeared to be unavailable in any edition, in or out of print.

All Night Long – R2 DVD: Carlton.
Antony and Cleopatra – VHS NTSC: Embassy Home Entertainment [OP].
As You Like It (1936) – R1 DVD: Image Entertainment; VHS NTSC: United American Video Entertainment [OP]; R2 DVD: DD.V.
As You Like It (1992) – R2 DVD: Sands Films.

As You Like It (2006) – release pending.
Bad Sleep Well, The – R1 DVD: Criterion Collection; VHS NTSC: Home Vision Cinema; R2 DVD and VHS Pal: BFI.
Banquet, The – NTSC DVD (all regions): HanJi <www.hkdvdstore.com>.
Chicken Rice War – VCD NTSC: Mei Ah Entertainment <www.meiah.com>.

Children's Midsummer Night's Dream, The – R2 DVD: Sands Films.

Double Life, A – R1 DVD: Republic Pictures; VHS NTSC: Lionsgate.

Forbidden Planet – R1 and R2 DVD, VHS NTSC and Pal: MGM.

Hamlet (1948) – R1 DVD: Criterion Collection; R2 DVD and VHS Pal: Carlton.

Hamlet (1964) – R1 DVD: Facets Video.

Hamlet (1990) – R1 DVD and VHS NTSC: Warner; R2 DVD: Momentum.

Hamlet (1996) – VHS NTSC: Warner; VHS Pal: Columbia TriStar.

Hamlet (2000) – R1 DVD and VHS NTSC: Walt Disney Video; R2 DVD: Cinema Club.

Hamlet Goes Business (1987) – R2 DVD: Sandrew Metronome.

Henry V (1944) – R1 DVD: Criterion Collection; VHS NTSC: Hallmark Home Entertainment; R2 DVD and VHS Pal: ITV DVD.

Henry V (1989) – R1 DVD and VHS NTSC: MGM; R2 DVD: Universal; VHS Pal: 4 Front Video.

Johnny Hamlet – R2 DVD: Koch Media.

Julius Caesar (1950) – R1 DVD: VCI Entertainment.

Julius Caesar (1953) – R1 DVD and VHS NTSC: Warner; R2 DVD and VHS Pal: MGM.

Julius Caesar (1970) – R1 DVD: Paramount Home Video; VHS Pal: 4 Front Video.

King Lear (1970) – R1 DVD: Facets Video; VHS Pal: Tartan [OP].

King Lear (1970) – VHS NTSC: Warner; R2 DVD: 4 Front Video; VHS Pal: Cinema Club.

King of Texas – R1 DVD and VHS NTSC: Turner Home Entertainment.

King Rikki [sold as *The Street King*] – R1 DVD: Screen Media Films.

Kiss Me Kate – R1 and R2 DVD, VHS NTSC and Pal: Warner.

Looking for Richard – R1 and R2 DVD, VHS NTSC and Pal: 20th Century-Fox.

Love's Labour's Lost – R1 DVD and VHS NTSC: Walt Disney Video; R2 DVD and VHS Pal: Pathé.

Macbeth (1948) – VHS NTSC: Republic; VHS Pal: Second Sight.

Macbeth (1971) – R1 and R2 DVD, VHS NTSC and Pal: Columbia.

Macbeth (1997) – R2 DVD and VHS Pal: Cromwell Productions.

Macbeth (2006) – R2 DVD: Revolver Distribution (Autumn 2007).

Maori Merchant of Venice, The – R2 DVD & VHS Pal: He Taonga Films <www.homepages.ihug.co.nz/ ~hetonga/merchant>.

Maqbool – NTSC DVD (all regions): Eagle Home Video <www.eaglehomevideo.com>.

Men of Respect (1991) – R1 DVD and VHS Pal: Columbia.

Midsummer Night's Dream, A (1935) – VHS NTSC: Warner.

Midsummer Night's Dream, A (1969) –
  R1 DVD: Water Bearer Films; VHS
  NTSC: MGM.

Midsummer Night's Dream, A (1996) –
  R1 DVD and VHS NTSC: Walt Disney
  Video; VHS Pal: Cinema Club.

Midsummer Night's Dream, A (2005) in
  Shakespeare Retold – R2 DVD and
  VHS Pal: Acorn.

Midsummer Night – R2 DVD: Buena
  Vista Home Entertainment (original
  Spanish voice cast with English
  subtitles) <www.dvdenlared.com>.

Much Ado About Nothing (1993) – R1
  DVD and VHS NTSC: MGM; R2 DVD
  and VHS Pal: Entertainment in Video.

Much Ado About Nothing (2005) in
  Shakespeare Retold – R2 DVD and
  VHS Pal: Acorn.

My Kingdom – VHS Pal: Tartan Video.

My Own Private Idaho – R1 DVD:
  Criterion Collection; VHS Pal: 20th
  Century-Fox [OP].

O – R1 DVD: Lionsgate; VHS Pal:
  Metrodome.

Omkara – R1 and R2 DVD: Eros Intl.

Once Upon a Time – R2 DVD: Danish
  Film Institute <www.eshop.dfi.dk>

Otello – R1 and R2 DVD: MGM.

Othello (1922) – R1 DVD: Kino Video.

Othello (1952) – R1 DVD: Image
  Entertainment; VHS NTSC: Academy
  Home Entertainment; R2 DVD: Warner
  Home Video; VHS Pal: Second Sight.

Othello (1965) – R2 DVD and VHS Pal:
  British Home Entertainment.

Othello (1995) – R1 DVD and VHS
  NTSC: Turner Home Entertainment.

Othello (2000) – R1 DVD: Acorn.

Prospero's Books – VHS NTSC: Aae
  Films; VHS Pal: 4 Front Video.

Ran – R1 DVD: Criterion Collection; R2
  DVD: 20th Century-Fox.

Richard III (1912) – R1 DVD and VHS
  NTSC: Kino Video.

Richard III (1955) – R1 DVD: Criterion
  Collection; R2 DVD: Network; VHS
  Pal: DD Video.

Richard III (1995) – R1 DVD and VHS
  NTSC: MGM; R2 DVD: Pathé.

Romeo and Juliet (1936) – VHS NTSC:
  MGM.

Romeo and Juliet (1954) – R1 DVD and
  VHS NTSC: MGM; R2 DVD: DD.V.

Romeo and Juliet (1968) – R1 and R2
  DVD, VHS NTSC & Pal: Paramount.

Rosencrantz & Guildenstern Are Dead –
  R1 DVD: Image Entertainment; VHS
  Pal: Second Sight.

Scotland, PA – R1 DVD: Sundance
  Home Entertainment.

Shakespeare in Love – R1 and R2 DVD,
  VHS NTSC and Pal: Universal.

She's the Man – R1 DVD: Paramount;
  R2 DVD: Entertainment in Video.

Strange Illusion – R1 DVD: Alpha Video.

Taming of the Shrew, The (1929) – VHS
  NTSC: Jef Films Inc./Aikman Archive
  [OP].

Taming of the Shrew, The (1967) – R1
  and R2 DVD, VHS NTSC and Pal:
  Columbia.

Taming of the Shrew, The (2005) in
  Shakespeare Retold – R2 DVD and
  VHS Pal: Acorn.

Tempest, The (1908) in *Silent
  Shakespeare* – R2 DVD and VHS Pal:
  BFI.

Tempest, The (1979) – R1 DVD and VHS
  NTSC: Kino Video; R2 DVD: Second
  Sight.

Tempest (1982) – VHS NTSC: Columbia
  [OP].

Tempest, The (1998) – VHS NTSC:
  Trimark Home Video.

10 Things I Hate About You (1999) –
  R1 DVD and VHS NTSC: Walt Disney
  Video; R2 DVD and VHS Pal:
  Touchstone.

Thousand Acres, A – R1 DVD and VHS
  NTSC: Walt Disney Video; R2 DVD &
  VHS Pal: Universal.

Throne of Blood – R1 DVD: Criterion
  Collection; VHS NTSC: Public Media
  Home Vision; R2 DVD and VHS Pal:
  BFI.

Tromeo and Juliet – R1 DVD: Troma
  Team Video.

Titus – R1 DVD and VHS NTSC: 20th
  Century-Fox; R2 DVD: Buena Vista;
  VHS Pal: Hollywood Pictures.

Twelfth Night (1996) – R1 DVD: Image
  Entertainment; R2 DVD:
  Entertainment in Video.

Twelfth Night (2003) – R1 DVD: Home
  Vision Entertainment.

West Side Story – R1 and R2 DVD, VHS
  NTSC and Pal: MGM.

*William Shakespeare's The Merchant of
  Venice* (2004) – R1 DVD: Sony
  Pictures; R2 DVD: MGM.

*William Shakespare's A Midsummer
  Night's Dream* (1999) – R1 and R2
  DVD, VHS NTSC and Pal: 20th
  Century-Fox.

William Shakespeare's Romeo + Juliet
  (1996) – R1 and R2 DVD, VHS NTSC
  and Pal: 20th Century-Fox.

Appendix 3 – Further Reading

Autobiography, Biography and Production Diaries

Branagh, Kenneth, *Beginning* (London: Chatto & Windus, 1989).

Coleman, Terry, *Olivier* (London: Bloomsbury, 2005).

Heston, Charlton, *In the Arena* (London: HarperCollins, 1995).

Holden, Anthony, *Laurence Olivier: A Biography* (London: Weidenfeld & Nicolson, 1988).

Kozintsev, Grigori, *King Lear: The Space of Tragedy* (London: Heinemann, 1977).

Kurosawa, Akira, *Something Like an Autobiography* (New York: Random House, 1982).

MacLiammóir, Micheál, *Put Money in Thy Purse: The Diary of the Film of Othello* (London: Methuen, 1952).

Olivier, Laurence, *Confessions of an Actor* (London: Weidenfeld & Nicolson, 1982).

Thomson, David, *Rosebud: The Story of Orson Welles* (London: Little, Brown, 1996).

White, Mark, *Kenneth Branagh* (London: Faber and Faber, 2005).

Zeffirelli, Franco, *Zeffirelli: The Autobiography* (London: Weidenfeld & Nicolson, 1986).

Criticism and Reference

Ball, Robert Hamilton, *Shakespeare on Silent Fim* (London: Allen & Unwin, 1968).

Boose, Lynda and Richard Burt (eds), *Shakespeare the Movie II: Popularizing the Plays on Film, TV, Video and DVD* (London: Routledge, 2003).

Brode, Douglas, *Shakespeare in the Movies: From the Silent Era to Today* (New York: Berkely Blvd Books, 2001).

Crowl, Samuel, *Shakespeare at the Cineplex* (Athens: Ohio University Press, 2003; revised 2005).

— *The Films of Kenneth Branagh* (Westport, CT: Praeger, 2006).

Davies, Anthony and Stanley Wells (eds), *Shakespeare and the Moving Image* (Cambridge: Cambridge University Press, 1994).

French, Emma, *Selling Shakespeare to Hollywood* (Hatfield: University of Hertfordshire Press, 2006).

Henderson, Diana (ed.), *A Concise Companion to Shakespeare on Screen* (Oxford: Blackwell, 2005).

Jackson, Russell (ed.), *The Cambridge Companion to Shakespeare on Film* (Cambridge: Cambridge University Press, 2000).

Jorgens, Jack, *Shakespeare on Film* (Bloomington: Indiana University Press, 1977).

Manvell, Roger, *Shakespeare and the Film* (South Brunswick, NJ: A. S. Barnes, 1979).

McKernan, Luke and Olwen Terris (eds), *Walking Shadows – Shakespeare in the National Film and Television Archive* (London: BFI, 1994).

Richie, Donald, *The Films of Akira Kurosawa* (Berkeley: University of California Press, 1996).

Rosenbaum, Jonathan (ed.), *Orson Welles and Peter Bogdanovich: This Is Orson Welles* (London: HarperCollins, 1993).

Rothwell, Kenneth S., *A History of Shakespeare on Screen: A Century of Film and Television* (Cambridge: Cambridge University Press, 1999; revised 2004).

Rothwell, Kenneth S. and Annabelle Henkin Melzer (eds), *Shakespeare on Screen: An International Filmography and Videography* (New York: Neal-Schuman, 1990).

Screenplays

Almereyda, Michael, *Shakespeare's Hamlet* (London: Faber and Faber, 2000).

Branagh, Kenneth, *Henry V* (London: Chatto & Windus, 1989);

— *Much Ado About Nothing* (New York and London: W. W. Norton, 1993).

— *Hamlet* (London: Chatto & Windus, 1996).

Dent, Alan (ed.), *Hamlet: The Film and the Play* (London: World Film Publications Ltd, 1948).

Greenaway, Peter, *Prospero's Books* (London: Chatto & Windus, 1991).

Hoffman, Michael, *William Shakespeare's A Midsummer Night's Dream* (London: HarperCollins, 1999).

Kurosawa, Akira, *et al.*, *Throne of Blood*, in *Seven Samurai and Other Screenplays* (London: Faber and Faber, 1992).

McKellen, Ian and Richard Loncraine, *William Shakespeare's Richard III* (London: Doubleday/Transworld, 1996).

Norman, Marc and Tom Stoppard, *Shakespeare in Love* (New York: Hyperion, 1998).

Nunn, Trevor, *Twelfth Night* (London: Methuen, 1996).

Pearce, Craig and Baz Luhrmann, *William Shakespeare's Romeo + Juliet* (London: Hodder Children's Books, 1997).

Taymor, Julie, *Titus: The Illustrated Screenplay* (New York: Newmarket Press, 2000).

Van Sant, Gus, *My Own Private Idaho/Even Cowgirls Get the Blues* (London: Faber and Faber, 1993).

Welles, Orson, *Chimes at Midnight* (New York: Rutgers State University, 1998).

Index

Page numbers in *italics* denote illustrations

List of Illustrations

Whilst considerable effort has been made to correctly identify the copyright holders, this has not been possible in all cases. We apologise for any apparent negligence and any omissions or corrections brought to our attention will be remedied in any future editions.

As You Like It, Inter-Allied Film Producers; *Hamlet: The Drama of Vengeance*, Art Film; *Hamlet* (1948), Two Cities Films; *Hamlet* (1964), Lenfilm; *Hamlet Goes Business*, Villealfa Filmproductions Oy; *Hamlet* (2000), © Hamlet, Inc.; *Chimes at Midnight*, Internacional Films Española/Alpine Productions; *Henry V* (1944), Two Cities Films; *Henry V* (1989), Renaissance Films/BBC/Curzon Film Distributors; *Julius Caesar* (1950), Avon; *King Lear* (1970), Lenfilm; *Ran*, © Greenwich Film Production; *Joe Macbeth*, Film Locations Ltd/Columbia Pictures Corporation; *Throne of Blood*, Toho Co., Ltd; *Macbeth* (1971), © Playboy Productions/© Columbia Pictures Industries, Inc.; *Makibefo*, Blue Eye Films; *Bleeder*, Centro Nacional Autónomo de Cinematografía/Cinema Sur/Post Meridian Cinema; *William Shakespeare's The Merchant of Venice*, © Shylock Trading Limited/© UK Film Council/© DeLux Productions S.A./© Immagine e Cinema; *A Midsummer Night's Dream* (1935), © Warner Bros.; *Much Ado About Nothing* (1993), © Samuel Goldwyn Company/© Renaissance Films; *Othello* (1952), Mercury Productions; *All Night Long*, © Rank Organisation Film Productions; *Souli*, Blue Eye Films/Red Island; *Omkara*, Big Screen Entertainer; *Richard III* (1995), First Look Pictures/Mayfair Entertainment International/British Screen; *Romeo and Juliet* (1936), © MGM Corporation; *West Side Story*, © Beta Productions; *Romeo and Juliet* (1968), B.H.E. Productions, Ltd/Verona Produzione/Dino De Laurentiis Cinematografica; *The Taming of the Shrew* (1929), Pickford Corporation/Elton Corporation; *10 Things I Hate About You*, © Touchstone Pictures; *The Tempest* (1908), Clarendon Film Company; *Forbidden Planet*, © Loew's Incorporated; *Prospero's Books*, Allarts Enterprises/Cinéa/Caméra One/Penta Pictures; *Titus*, © Clear Blue Sky Productions; *Twelfth Night* (1996), Renaissance Films/Fine Line Productions.